The Ultimate Word On Sharing Sexual Pleasures

Masters and Johnson, the world's two leading experts on sexual behavior, have written the ultimate guidebook for loving couples — married, single, and soon-to-be-married. "They believe that promiscuity is boring ... and that if pleasure isn't shared it's no fun at all. It's a message that makes THE PLEASURE BOND indispensable to understanding The New Sexuality."—The Literary Guild.

"THERE'S AN OFF-HAND CHANCE THIS BOOK MAY TELL YOU A THING OR TWO YOU DIDN'T KNOW BEFORE."

"Unlike **Human Sexual Response** and **Human Sexual Inadequacy,** the new Masters and Johnson book is intended directly for the lay reader who should be told immediately that, amid the current clutter of books of sexual counsel, it stands somewhat like Pike's Peak. The book is in essence an analysis of the social and psychological aspects of sexual behavior, and is destined for reading and rereading. Some of the authors' material is drawn from seminars with newlyweds, twice-wed couples and group sexers. Nonjudgmental, clear, exceedingly well-written, the book examines the most delicate subjects with tact and common sense. As Masters and Johnson go to the heart of human sexuality they reveal sex not as technique, but as the deepest function of personality. It may well be the book that consolidates the gains of the sexual revolution."

—Publishers Weekly

THE
PLEASURE
BOND

---

*A New Look at Sexuality
and Commitment*

William H. Masters
and
Virginia E. Johnson

in association with
Robert J. Levin

BANTAM BOOKS
Toronto / New York / London

✔

THE PLEASURE BOND
A Bantam Book

PRINTING HISTORY

Little, Brown edition published January 1975
2nd printing ... January 1975   4th printing ..... March 1975
3rd printing ... February 1975   5th printing ...... April 1975
Psychology Today Book Club edition published March 1975
Literary Guild edition published April 1975
Playboy Book Club edition published May 1975
Woman Today Book Club edition published Summer 1975
*Exceprts from "The Pleasure Bond" have appeared in the follow-
ing magazines:* REDBOOK, MC CALL'S, READER'S DIGEST, BOOK DIGEST.
Bantam edition / February 1976

Contents

Preface

One problem that bothers many couples is how to keep alive the physical attraction that originally brought them together. Sooner or later—and for some husbands and wives it happens with dismaying swiftness—the magnetism of their bodies seems to lose much of its force. Neither partner may say anything about it but both are likely to be distressed by what appears to be the gradual decline of sexual excitement.

For a while they may struggle to revive the intense feelings that once dominated their lives. But if their efforts fail, the couple will probably accept their low-key sex life as an inevitable development, a natural consequence of marriage, and they may take what comfort they can from the belief that the same thing happens to everyone else.

It certainly seems true of most, if not all, of their friends. And how, they wonder, could it be otherwise? As they see it, a man and woman soon lose the thrill that comes from doing what is forbidden or from sexually exploring someone new and unfamiliar. Afterward—they believe—even fortunate couples cannot expect intercourse to be much more than a pleasing repetition of a familiar experience. For the less fortunate, it may become a stale and unrewarding routine.

The belief that with the loss of novelty sex must lose its power to arouse passion is a common assumption. Like all assumptions, it risks being turned into a self-fulfilling prophecy: what a person assumes to be true, he unknowingly proves to himself to be true. He interprets everything in the light of his preconceptions and acts accordingly. Consequently those actions produce the result he had anticipated, confirming his belief that it was all inevitable.

If, for example, a man believes that women generally have a limited enthusiasm for sex, especially after marriage, he is not going to be surprised to find that his wife's behavior fits the pattern. He may make some sporadic effort to change her outlook but, persuaded as he is that her disinterest is characteristic of the female sex, he believes the quest is hopeless and soon gives up. Once again a woman—this time, his wife—has proved that his assumptions about females and sex are correct.

He may be right, of course, about his wife. Her personality, her life history, her previous sexual experience —or lack of it—and her own beliefs and assumptions may have combined to create an individual with muted sexual feelings. On the other hand, her apparent lack of enthusiasm for sex may have an entirely different explanation. She may be reacting to cues that her husband is giving without knowing it, cues that indicate that he does not expect her to manifest any strong sexual urges and that in fact he may not be comfortable with an openly sexual female.

In adapting her behavior to his expectations, she may be genuinely trying to please him and to strengthen their marriage by being the kind of woman he seems to respect. Ironically, her husband will never realize that his sexual disappointment is largely of his own making.

In certain cases, one false assumption breeds another, as it did with a wife who had grown up believing that if a woman makes herself attractive and available, any man can automatically be counted on to make the most of the opportunity. This mistaken idea led her, on a number of occasions, to present herself seductively to her husband. Sometimes she succeeded; other times she did not. The failures upset her, however, because since she "knew" that men were always ready for sex, her husband's lack of interest at times surely had to mean that either she was unattractive to him, or that he lacked the usual male drive, or that he was interested in another woman.

By chance she met an old high school boyfriend

and, on impulse, she approached him in the same encouraging way that she did with her husband. This man reacted as she had expected. To her this proved that any man will want to go to bed with an attractive, available female—and therefore it had to mean either that her husband lacked something as a man or she lacked something as a woman. Her preconceptions prevented her from realizing that many other explanations were possible and that unless she explored those possibilities, unless she expressed her honest fears to her husband so that together they might evaluate the situation, she would continue to act on the basis of her erroneous beliefs—and jeopardize her marriage.

To paraphrase an old truth: the road to hell is often paved with false assumptions.

This is no less true when one makes the assumptions about oneself. A classic example is the woman who, after a number of sexual encounters in which her body seemed to her to be almost totally unresponsive, decided that she must be "frigid." The fact is that there are scores of reasons—physiological, psychological and situational —that might have contributed to her problem. At that point in her life, before her negative self-image became too deeply rooted, her unresponsiveness might have been easily remedied. But by assuming that she was "frigid"— indeed, by merely tagging herself with that pejorative and meaningless label—she intensified her fear and despair, which increased the possibility that she might suffer a great deal of unnecessary unhappiness.

Because sex is such an intensely personal matter and because most people, particularly during their impressionable early years, feel so vulnerable and insecure in relation to their own sexuality, meaningful communication about it rarely takes place. Silence, evasion or lying is the order of the day, and unquestioned false assumptions become the basis on which countless men and women try to work out their married lives. In light of this fact, what is remarkable is not that so many divorces take place but that so many marriages remain intact.

Where information about sex is made available to the public, its soundness is all too often highly questionable. What is presented as objective fact is generally colored, and sometimes distorted, by the informer's subjectivity. In the past, this subjectivity was characteristically righteous and moralizing, essentially the view from the pulpit. In recent years, the subjectivity has been that of the countercultural rebel, the supersalesman of sex.

What is needed is an understanding of sexual behavior that is based on a knowledge of *verifiable* fact, where such facts exist; on familiarity with ideas about sex and human nature that, while not susceptible to scientific proof, have the support of specialists with clinical and research experience in the field; and on sexual self-acceptance and sexual self-responsibility as the ultimate considerations.

For there are three elements that contribute to sexual functioning—knowledge, comfort and choice—and they are interlocking, mutually reinforcing elements. *To know* is one thing; *to be comfortable* with what one knows is another; *to choose* what is right for oneself is still another.

To choose to ask questions and learn the truth about sex is a personal choice. To evaluate answers is a personal necessity. To be comfortable with what one learns and to utilize what one knows in the establishment of an enduring sexual relationship is a lifelong quest.

This book by William H. Masters, M.D., and Virginia E. Johnson is intended as a contribution to those men and women who are seeking the knowledge they need about sex to make the decisions that are uniquely right for themselves. Dr. Masters is the director of the Reproductive Biology Research Foundation in St. Louis, Missouri, and Virginia Johnson (Masters) is codirector. As authorities on the subject of sex, they are unmatched in the world.

For twenty years they have devoted their lives to the scientific study of the human sexual function. In their laboratory, where they worked with volunteers to establish the physiologic nature of sexual response, and in their clinic, where they counsel couples whose marriages are flawed by sexual inadequacies, Masters and

Johnson have aimed at overcoming ignorance, myth and superstition by establishing valid and reliable facts about the physiology and psychology of human sexual expression. With the publication of *Human Sexual Response,* in 1966, and *Human Sexual Inadequacy* in 1970, Masters and Johnson joined the ranks of such scientists as Sigmund Freud and Alfred C. Kinsey, whose brilliant studies illuminated the fundamental psychosocial nature of sexual relationships.

In preparing *The Pleasure Bond,* Masters and Johnson wanted to apply the principle of preventive medicine. It is obviously preferable to avoid problems of sexual functioning than to have to treat those problems after they have developed. To this end, it seemed important to present the public with as much sound and comprehensible information as possible, to offer readers a how-*not*-to book: how not to make the mistakes that transform a naturally healthy delight in the pleasures of sexual expression into the frustrations and fears that bedevil so many men and women even today.

But what facts were most urgently needed to help couples safeguard their sexual relationships? And in what context should the information be presented? Since professionally Masters and Johnson worked with men and women whose sexual lives were already seriously distressed, the two researchers decided that it would be wise for them to meet and talk with couples who were either satisfied with their relationships or who felt that they were successfully coping with whatever dissatisfactions there were in their marriages. These discussions would then serve as the basis for the present book.

Consequently eleven symposiums were held in the period from May, 1971 to June, 1972. Five of the symposiums are contained in this volume. The husbands and wives who took part were invited to meet with William Masters and Virginia Johnson and to raise any questions about sex that concerned them. There was no formal agenda for any of the meetings. The discussions were tape-recorded, transcribed and then edited for publication. Personal details concerning the participants have been altered to conceal their identities but in every instance an effort was made to indicate their individual backgrounds. Where necessary, changes were also made in what some people actually said, to make it impossible to identify them on the basis of their comments. But all conversations remain faithful to the original remarks.

Since the symposiums were not lectures or therapy sessions, they were informal and unstructured. Whenever possible, William Masters or Virginia Johnson spoke directly to the issues raised by the participants, but in some instances—particularly in the infidelity and permissive-sex symposiums—comments were later added to the transcripts. The symposiums are dated because, given the rapidly changing climate of opinion concerning sexual behavior that has characterized this country in the last decade, it is important for observations made in spontaneous discussions to be related to the time in which they were made.

From these symposiums, Masters and Johnson selected several issues that were raised but not developed in great detail, issues that they believe to be central to the achievement of sexual pleasure, and these have been used as the basis for more extensive essays. They are introduced by segments from the actual symposiums.

Two additional points should perhaps be specifically noted. First, there are repetitions in this book. The discussion of the double standard in the introduction to Sexual Responsibility, for example, has its parallel in Chapter 4, where the subject is considered in the light of the women's liberation movement. Repetitions, when and where they occur, are refrains of basic principles that can be seen and understood more clearly only when they have been viewed in different circumstances.

The second point to be noted is that the word "marriage" means more than the existence of a license. Throughout this book, a man and woman are considered united in the true sense of the word, whether or not they have a license to live together, as long as each is committed to the other. They are not committed because they are married; they are married because they are committed.

My role in the creation of this book was as catalyst and synthesizer. Whatever my contribution, it would have been absolutely impossible without the loyal friendship and support of Sey Chassler, editor-in-chief of Redbook magazine; the editorial assistance of my colleagues Katherine Ball and Jean Evans; the dedicated cooperation of my former secretary, Doris Sherman; and, above all, not without the happy companionship of my wife Amy, to whom I am as bound by pleasure as a person can be.

ROBERT J. LEVIN

New York, New York
May, 1974

Sexual Responsibility
An Introduction

For many people, "responsibility" has the somewhat onerous connotation of carrying someone else's burden. Along with "reliability," "dependability" and "obligation," it may be perceived as a value that is oppressive and somewhat unrewarding. Unfortunately, this attitude also prevails in sexual relationships, where interpretation of sexual responsibility has been additionally prejudiced by time-honored, cultural misconceptions of sexual roles. Historically, the male has been assigned the role of sexual responsibility while the female has been confined to a role of sexual acceptance —stereotypes that show little knowledge of or regard for the natural capabilities of either sex.

It is not surprising that generations of adult men and women have found it virtually impossible to live with or live up to the sexual roles to which they were culturally conditioned as adolescents: roles which suggest that men are satyrs who ravish innocent, but grateful, females. These roles were transmitted to young men and women through innuendo and through sly, incomplete or silent response to their need to know what meaning and function sex will have in their lives.

These cultural roles were established at a time

1

when there was no knowledge of individual psycho-sexual limitations or of natural variations in male or female sexual capacity. Although they have not withstood the realities of either sexual or social needs, they remain woven into the sexual mores of society.

As individuals frustrated by almost unbelievable sexual ignorance, we cope with the disparity between our own sexual needs and our sexual roles in a variety of ways. Some people reduce all sexuality to a dirty joke, while others decry or repress anything that hints of sex. Currently, a small but clamorous number of people are immersing themselves in any or all styles of sexual expression in an attempt to break the mold of sexual inhibition and dissatisfaction. Still others just endure. Fortunately, there always seems to be a heartening number of people who, despite their cultural handicaps, are able to develop a realistic, comfortable attitude toward sex. These individuals, together with their sexual partners, have learned that sexual responsibility can be shared.

Our double-standard society, in its early stages of development, maintained a tacit acceptance of sex as a hearty source of mutual pleasure for those men and women who discovered this for themselves and confined its practice within certain prescribed boundaries. Practical, earthy levels of sexual awareness apparently fared best. Husbands and wives in the then predominantly rural society found both the need and the opportunity for achieving sexual unity within their particular life-styles.

With the advent of the industrial revolution, however, the double standard soon became the means by which men and women were separated sexually as well as socially. The concept of sex as a source of mutual pleasure (and therefore an area for mutual responsibility) faded as men and women found their lives rigidly divided by both the work ethic and social demands. As they pursued separate goals, husbands and wives lost sight of their need for one another. As an additional heritage, the omnipresent religious orthodoxies, social intolerances and ignorance of sexual matters by health-care professionals, contributed immeasurably to our culture's lack of comprehension of sexual response as a natural physiologic process, a process comparable to other natural functions such as respiratory, bowel or bladder function.

When sexual response was separated in our thinking from its rightful place as a natural function, sexual misconceptions and even taboos inevitably became integral parts of the social structure. The concept of sex as sin, and sex for reproduction only, firmly overruled the concept of sex for human warmth or sex for mutual pleasure. As a consequence, hundreds of thousands of men and women have been tied into severely neurotic or even openly psychotic patterns of behavior.

With sexual functioning firmly established in our culture as something apart from other natural processes, there were sexual roles to assign, sexual practices to establish, sexual restrictions to impose. All were done out of hand by an omnipotent social arbitration that communicated to the individual not only what his or her sexual pattern should be—but what it *must* be.

It was decided—who knows by whom?—that the male was the sex expert. Perhaps this decision evolved from man's historic role as protector and provider. Or it could have derived from a male fear of the unknown or the misunderstood sexual potential of the female. In any event, man was clearly acknowledged as the fount of all sexual knowledge. As adolescents, boys were allowed, even encouraged, to honor their sexuality. "Boys will be boys," followed by a suggestive snicker or a benign smile, became a popular cliché. After all, they did need experience, didn't they? Tacit permission was given to go-do-it, but, of course, to be circumspect. And as long as they remained "gentlemen"—didn't talk too much, didn't mention names and didn't practice on girls they might wish to marry—there was no cause for concern.

Woman's sexual role? This was another matter. During the eighteenth, nineteenth and well into the twentieth century, the woman's sexual role was even easier to define. She had none—other than that of seminal receptacle. Woman's sexual responsivity was not only denied, but actually obliterated as a possibility by male arbiters in a chauvinistic society. Everyone knew —or at least all men knew and most women pretended —that "nice" women had no sexual feelings, that respected wives only submitted in the hope of conceiving and that "those women" who freely responded sexually simply weren't the kind you married.

Intercourse was woman's burden and a true gentleman insisted upon the "marital privilege" as infrequently as possible—at least with his wife. And so, while sexual feelings and freedom to react sexually were acknowledged as male prerogatives, these rights were denounced or denied for the female.

Typical of the many decades of scientists' and physicians' negation of woman's sexual feelings is a passage from a gynecologic textbook published in the late 1950s. The editor—a male, of course—stated unequivocally that not only were women nonorgasmic, they rarely, if ever, had sexual feelings and certainly little sexual interest. And he didn't even distinguish between "nice" women and the "other kind." Yet another example of society's rigidity in the control of woman's natural sexual function is the fact that more than ninety-five percent of everything that has ever been published on the subject of female sexual response has been written by men, most of whom objectively and all of whom subjectively hadn't the vaguest idea of what woman's orgasmic experience is all about.

Until almost halfway through this century, sex was something that everyone knew the man, after marriage, was going to do *to* his wife on their wedding night. Not only did the husband believe that the wedding night was committed to his pleasure, but his wife, too, was prepared for duty—with her role exclusively that of sexual servant. The prize of virginity (real or feigned) was to be her sacrificial offering to her new husband. An unruptured hymen was not only accepted as proof positive of a wife's sexual innocence but was usually required as a symbol of her sexual ignorance and his sexual prowess. Social mores demanded that her fund of sexual knowledge, her degree of sexual experience and her evidence of sexual interest, if any, were to be defined and controlled by her husband.

In short, the prize of the intact hymen was assigned to the head of the household. It was for the taking: how, when and where obviously were his responsibility—his sexual responsibility. Our culture had decreed that brides were to be virgins. Therefore, women who had made the fearful mistake of offering this prize in prior sexual encounter must do their best on their wedding nights to conceal its loss. Yet despite having to play the role of sacrificial lamb at marriage, the virgin bride had one very real advantage over her husband: other than being available, she had no sexual responsibility.

Of course, there is the other side of the coin to the virginal bride. The culture also presumed that there was no such thing as a man with little or no sexual experience at marriage—a man who wasn't a fount of sexual knowledge. So many men who married, having only insignificant, if any, sexual experience, inwardly quaked and outwardly faked the expected expertise—and because of their discomfort, many more wives suffered.

Back then to the subject of the husband doing something *to* his wife on their wedding night. This was sexual responsibility—his to do to her; hers only to be done to. And for generations we played our culturally assigned sexual roles of expert and virgin; but sexually we hardly prospered.

Then in the 1950s, with Kinsey's good help, some light was shed on the impasse created by our sexual ignorance. As soon as we learned a little about sexual functioning, both male and female sexual roles altered significantly; men assumed a different level of sexual responsibility, and women benefited not only from male role change but from the sexual permissiveness the new knowledge brought to the marriage bed.

Professionals (still predominantly male, of course), slowly gaining confidence, began assuring the public that women not only had real sexual feelings and legitimate sexual interest, but also could and should be orgasmic—something that millions of women (even "nice" women) could have revealed had they ever been asked and been assured that their answers would have been accepted without being judged.

So the knowledgeable man who married in the 1950s and early 1960s, instead of doing something *to* his wife sexually, was prepared to do something *for* her sexually. Fortified by his newly acquired sexual wisdom, he felt fully capable of providing her with sexual release. She was now allowed to respond sexually —only on his terms, of course, but at least she had permission to respond. The culture had grudgingly consented to this change in status. Women's sexual feelings no longer need be hidden—or even apologized for— certainly no longer denied. But sexual responsibility, of course, remained with the husband. He continued to be the arbiter, he became the coach, and he remained stage center in all sexual matters. Unfortunately, in the role of doing *for* rather than just doing *to,* he had to assume even more sexual responsibility.

Woman's sexual lot improved; her role was no longer simply that of providing service. She had been granted a small part, actually more than a walk-on, in the sexual scene. But she was still expected to acknowledge her husband's natural expertise in all things sexual, particularly after he had granted her the privilege and pleasure of orgasm.

Of course, the husband's sexual burden continued unrelieved, or perhaps became even heavier. For whether he was still doing something *to* his wife or had knowledgeably switched to doing something *for* his wife, he alone carried the responsibility for achieving successful sex. The social insanity of proclaiming the male the sex expert led many a man to his functional downfall. When things went wrong in the marriage bed, automatically the fault, *the responsibility,* was his. If he was a premature ejaculator, if he was impotent or if he had a low level of sexual interest, he alone was to blame. If his wife was nonorgasmic, vaginismic (involuntary contraction of the outer third of the vagina) or sexually aversive (inability to participate in sexual activity without a feeling of revulsion), he also assumed a major share of the blame. It should be noted, however, that this degree of sexual responsibility was rarely accepted by men who culturally were conditioned in the role of "do-to" husbands; it developed, rather, as a corollary to the "do-for" concept. As time passed woman's sexual role was amplified while men strained to fulfill their new responsibilities. And still we did not prosper sexually.

How has sexual responsibility fared in the last decade? Finally, the pendulum is swinging—woefully late—but, as always, better late . . .

Has definitive research supplied sufficient knowledge of sexual functioning to significantly alter cultural concepts of sexual roles and responsibilities? Are professionals taking new looks at old problems of both male and female sexual dysfunction? And are new answers to treatment of these dysfunctions available?

Yes, fortunately. We cannot help but prosper from the recently accorded privilege of being able to evaluate human sexual functioning as accurately and objectively as we are able to research and evaluate any other natural body function.

Slowly, as secure information replaces palpable ignorance, misconception, or myth, our society is not only developing an infinitely greater comfort factor with the subject of sexual functioning, but we, as individuals, are growing from informed adolescence into more viable sexual adulthood. Today, sexual responsibility is being assumed by the individual—man and woman alike—never again to be assigned to one sex. For now we know that there is no way that a man can be responsible for a woman's sexual functioning, nor can she assume control over his sexual response patterns. In truth, there is no way that a man can "give" his wife an orgasm, or that a wife can provide her husband with an ejaculation. There simply is no way that one individual can assume responsibility for another's natural physical processes. We can't breathe for the other person, we can't eat for the other person, and we can't respond sexually for the other person.

Effective sexual functioning is something that transpires between two people. To be effective it must be done together. It is something that sexually functional couples do *with* each other, not to or for each other. So woman's sexual role has accomplished a hundred-and-eighty-degree turn—from that of sexual servant to sexual equal, all in the last ten to twenty years. There remains only for her to explore and exercise this potential and for her sexual partner to share in her experience.

While she is beginning to do so, it is not surprising to find that her initial attempts are often still grounded in the old assumptions. For example, although we lack conclusive statistics, there is little doubt that when a marriage is jeopardized by sexual conflicts, in the vast majority of cases it's the wife who seeks counseling. She may go at her husband's urging or with his agreement or perhaps without his knowledge. But in any event the implicit assumption seems clear: if sex is a problem in marriage, it's the wife who needs help.

So widespread and deeply rooted is this assumption that it goes unquestioned by most women. As a result they all too often accept—or even volunteer for—the role of scapegoat. More than once couples have come to our clinic for therapy on the basis of the wife's inability to experience orgasm, genuinely unaware that there is one important factor they aren't taking into consideration—the husband's sexual incapacity. For example, he may suffer from premature ejaculation, which at the very least contributes to his wife's unresponsiveness, if in fact it isn't the basic cause. But when first seeking help, they will have no doubt that it's the wife who requires treatment.

This traditional attitude sustains the male in a heads-I-win, tails-you-lose approach to sexual disharmony. If he is impotent, his wife worries: "What's wrong with me?" And if she is nonorgasmic, he wonders: "What's wrong with her?" He then sends her off to a family doctor or psychiatrist and hopes she will come back "fixed."

This approach is doubly regrettable. For one thing, it is almost certainly doomed to fail. A wife cannot be

treated for a malady that afflicts the marriage relationship itself, any more than she can go for lessons by herself to learn how to dance with her husband—who isn't
very graceful, can't keep time and has never enjoyed
dancing.

For another thing, therapy for the wife alone will
not only fail to solve the problem but will probably
make it worse. After all, once the doctor or counselor
has conscientiously dispensed advice and the marital
relationship remains unchanged, how can a wife avoid
feeling that she is a total failure, a hopeless case? This
further erodes her self-esteem. Consequently, there is
less chance than ever that she and her husband can overcome their sexual disharmony.

The destructiveness goes even deeper. When a
wife alone seeks help, she is conforming to the preva-
lent idea that the female role is to learn how to gratify
the male. She is expected to adapt herself, sublimate
her wishes, inhibit her desires or even distort her natural
drives so that she can please a man who will therefore
choose her, or keep her, as his mate. In the drama of
life it is only as his mate that she can play the most rewarding parts that her society assigns to females—those
of wife and mother.

To play these parts many women have paid the required price—the suppression of their sexual natures.
This price, it becomes increasingly clear, is exorbitant.
It leads to sexual bankruptcy in many marriages, and
both husband and wife understandably feel cheated.
Ironically, their dissatisfaction flows directly from the
very principle that was supposed to bring them the rewards of sex—the idea that if a young girl obeyed society's strictures and learned to accommodate herself
to the male, both would benefit in marriage.

In effect, this turns a woman into a puppet, a term
the dictionary defines as "a person whose actions are
prompted and controlled by another or others." Certainly in the past women were trained to be sexual
marionettes. But many men today belatedly realize that
being married to a female puppet is not at all what they

want. The responsive, fully functioning man wants a responsive, fully functioning wife—a woman who has discovered her natural sexual capacity and who enjoys it.

In rightfully assuming a "full voting partnership" in the sexual relationship, however, women must be careful to avoid making the same kind of mistake men have made for a long time. The mistake can be found in the remark of a wife who said in no uncertain terms that she was just as "entitled" to sexual satisfaction as her husband was. To be entitled to something means to have the right to claim it and expect that it will be provided. No matter how gently she may let him know, this wife is in effect saying to her husband: "I should be enjoying intercourse more than I am, and I would like you to do something about it."

Unwittingly and ironically, she has flipped to its opposite side the same coin the male has been using for generations, the coin of sexual service—one person is expected to satisfy the needs of the other. In the past, of course, it was the female who served the male as part of her marital obligation. Today's young women have grown up believing that sexual satisfaction is something one partner is capable of giving to the other. More explicitly, and quite logically, they believe that since, as they have been told, a wife's compliance is all that a husband needs to obtain the orgasm he wants, she should have the right to expect him to do the same for her.

Unfortunately, the coin is counterfeit. In a continuing relationship sex-as-service rarely leads to sustained pleasure and is very unlikely to bring a woman the fulfillment she desires. It is no different for the man. Contrary to one of the most widespread of all sex misconceptions, the fact is that sex-as-service has failed to reward most men with the erotic gratification they anticipated.

It has failed because it is based on fallacy—the notion that the male animal is biologically endowed to function sexually at will as long as he has a female at his disposition. And regardless of whether she is eager, indifferent or even reluctant to accommodate him, and regardless of whether she participates actively or passively, he will have the pleasure he wants.

This is a myth, one of the most deceptive and destructive ever to dominate the intimate lives of men and women. Many a man has married believing the myth and convinced that as long as his wife accepts him whenever he chooses to have sex, he will be satisfied and their sexual relationship will be rewarding. Sooner or later, however, and more often sooner than later, he learns that he was wrong. Even though his wife may willingly remain available, if all she does, or all she is permitted to do by the moral codes that govern their lives, is to receive him without responding, his satisfactions eventually fade and so does desire. Availability is not enough.

This truth is reflected in the crude and hostile jokes of men, such as the complaint that "the two most overrated things in this country are home cooking and home loving." It is reflected in the dismal number of husbands who function poorly in the marriage bed or do not function there at all. And it is directly confirmed by the testimony of those men who seek professional help with sexual problems.

What these men must learn is that if a husband is to perform effectively over the years, he requires more of his wife than that she merely be compliant. No matter how the feelings are communicated, a man no less than a woman wishes to believe that his marriage partner values him and needs him and desires him.

To the extent that his wife makes him aware that she sees him as an individual and is emotionally committed to him—not just economically dependent—she fortifies his esteem. And it is this pride in himself both as an individual and as a man that he expresses with vigor in their sexual union. If asked, she may well say that the woman's role is to yield to her husband whenever he desires her; and he may insist that he expects his wife to be willing. They may say that and even believe it, echoing old codes fashioned out of the double standard—but their marriage is in fact a contradiction of what they say.

They are not living on the basis of services duly rendered. The wife is not a servant in the home, not in the kitchen or in the bedroom. The husband is not her employer, who gets only what he pays for and must pay for whatever he wants. Their sexual relationship mirrors their personal relationship, in which each is responsive to the other's wishes, each takes pleasure in pleasing the other and each values having the respect of the other. Since emotionally stable human beings are not split personalities, how they feel about each other and how they act toward each other is essentially no different at night from what it is by day.

But the yearning of a young wife today for greater physical fulfillment than she now experiences is certainly understandable. In these transitional times, when society is slowly but inevitably learning to honor the sexuality of the female as it has always honored that of the male, women's changing expectations can be satisfied only by those men who are capable of changing their attitudes and who want to change them.

They are unlikely to be motivated by a sense of obligation. Any wife who lets her husband know that she feels "entitled" to a sexual climax and expects him to bring it about may find that even if he wants to oblige her, he will probably fail more often than not. And the more emotional pressure she exerts on him, the less physical pleasure she is likely to experience.

She will be learning the same lesson that men are beginning slowly to comprehend: sex-as-service does not produce the desired pleasure. The mistake men made was to think of the female as a receptacle. The mistake women must avoid making is to think of the male as an instrument—for she risks paying a greater penalty for her error. While a man with an unresponsive woman may still manage to secure a release of sexual tension, a woman with an unresponsive man can expect only greater tension, because his impotence will increase her frustration.

If flipping the coin to the other side is no solution, if sex-as-service is even more self-defeating a principle for the female, how, then, can a sexually emancipated woman succeed in securing the fulfillment that is her birthright?

In the same way—the only way—the male can secure his own birthright: together with a partner who is committed to the principle of mutual pleasure. More is required, of course, than simply having the right outlook, but it is indispensable as a starting point. To translate the wish and the will into the achievement, however, involves both husband and wife in the negotiation of their differences on the basis of genuine equality.

As equals they accept responsibility for mutual cooperation in the bedroom and for mutual creation of the emotional environment needed for the sexual relationship. The term "with" implies mutual cooperation, just as the terms "to" or "for" carry the connotation of active-versus-passive sexual roles. Perhaps the best means of encouraging mutual cooperation consists of communicating one's sexual needs confidently and openly to one's partner. Free flow of both verbal and nonverbal communication between cooperating sexual partners is the cornerstone of effective sexual function. In essence, accepting sexual responsibility means informing and cooperating: one partner must never presume knowledge or attempt to control the other partner's sexual needs.

Conversely, mutual cooperation also includes the necessity of an ear constantly attuned to a partner's expression of sexual interest. It matters little how clearly a partner sends a message of sexual need, if one's own reception of the message is confused or prejudiced. The willingness to send and receive is as vital in sexual communication as in any other kind of communication. Each partner is sexually responsible for keeping both capacities in good working order.

In recent years, there has been a more social interpretation of sexual responsibility that bears at least passing scrutiny: that of responsibility for conception.

The sense of commitment between partners does not end with their mutual concern for the pleasures of sexual encounter but carries over to include their mutual obligation in exercising control of conception or accepting responsibility for the results of their union—pregnancy.

The introduction of contraceptive information into our culture approximately forty years ago helped to liberate the woman from her role as sexual servant. Whether one is committed to the contraceptive technique of "rhythm" or to that of the "pill," or to any step in-between, sexual parity would never have been possible without the opportunity that contraceptive knowledge alone provides for both sexes to assume full responsibility for every potential of sexual interaction.

To repeat: sexual responsibility has a twofold implication in today's world. Primarily, we are responsible only for ourselves in our sexual commitments, for full communication of our sexual wants and, subsequently, for physical expression of our sexual drives. Also, we are committed to remaining fully attuned to partner communication and to the cooperation necessary to enable one's partner to satisfy his or her sexual needs. Secondarily, our sexual responsibility extends not only to full obligation for pregnancy, but to adequate control of conception.

The potential rewards from parity of sexual roles are limitless. For a man, alleviation of the fears of sexual performance that were so ingrained in his socially assigned role of doing to or for his wife, inevitably will be of major consequence to his sexual function. And the freedom to be and do sexually as a full partner will immeasurably improve the quality of a woman's sexual expression.

But the largest dividend will come to the culture. No longer will sex be accepted as a thing apart, an isolated entity, a sexist privilege or an exploitable commodity. With each individual assuming responsibility for himself or herself alone, sex finally will be returned to the only position from which it can be viewed with

comfort, and experienced with reliable fulfillment—
that of a natural function.

VIRGINIA E. JOHNSON and
WILLIAM H. MASTERS, M.D.

St. Louis, Missouri
May, 1974

ONE

THE MARRIAGE THEME

1

Young Marriages
The Search for Sexual Pleasure

Early in 1970, Dr. William II. Masters and Virginia E. Johnson decided to conduct symposiums on sex and marriage with young couples. Their decision was in line with their concept of preventive counseling —the more widely they could disseminate accurate information about sexual functioning to young husbands and wives, the more likely they were to prevent marital problems from occurring in the early years of marriage as a consequence of ignorance or misinformation.

The first symposium was held in New York in May, with five couples who had been married two years or less. Muriel and Sam Gordon, both twenty-four years old, were native New Yorkers. Muriel was a copywriter at an advertising company and Sam was taking a graduate degree in sociology at Columbia University. They had been married for one year. The Jamesons, Nancy and Ted, had been married for two years and had a ten-month-old daughter. Ted, who was twenty-seven, was a life insurance salesman; his wife, who was twenty-five, worked as a substitute teacher until the birth of their child. Charles and Jean Gallagher, twenty-six and twenty-five respectively, had been married for

19

eighteen months. They worked for two different publishing houses, he as an editor and she as a secretary. Peter Stillman, thirty-one, and his wife Sheila, twenty-four, had been married for almost two years. Peter was a dentist and Sheila attended art school, where she studied lithography. Harold and June Snyder had been married for a little more than a year. He was twenty-six and worked for the New York Telephone Company; his wife was a year younger and worked in a midtown bookstore.

BILL MASTERS: For a number of years Mrs. Johnson and I have been interested in counseling young couples. In our experience, however, premarital discussions almost always center on contraceptive methods. Making this information available is useful and important, but we found that it did not enable us to move toward our primary goal—learning how to help couples avoid sexual problems wherever possible. Obviously it is better to prevent a problem than to treat it after it has become acute enough to keep a marriage from developing in a healthy, harmonious way. So we hit upon the idea that there might be more value in postmarital discussions with couples who have been married from six months to two years or so.

VIRGINIA JOHNSON: After they have experienced some of the pleasures of living together—and some of the wear and tear.

BILL MASTERS: In a relatively new marriage it's natural that a number of questions should arise. How do we compare to other people? What kinds of behavior are matters of choice? How can we handle particular problems? Unfortunately, it isn't easy to get frank and reliable answers. There are taboo areas, subjects that some people believe shouldn't be discussed. Therefore it's hardly surprising that the commonest cause of marital incompatibility is simply misinformation. Well, we don't have any taboo areas here today. Ask any questions you wish; we'll answer them if we can. Who would like to begin? (*After a moment's silence he smiles and says*) Or are you all experts?

JUNE SNYDER: Is there any good way to say, "I don't feel like it," aside from the old headache routine?

VIRGINIA JOHNSON: I'm afraid there is no magic formula, but it may help to keep some considerations in mind. Two persons are involved, and it's important for each to become aware of the other partner's needs. If you really don't feel like it because physically or emotionally you feel incapable of responding, say so. But say so with love and not rejection.

The situation, after all, is inevitable. Two human beings with different needs, different moods, a different sense of timing—it simply isn't possible for the two of you to find your desires always dovetailing perfectly. But how can the two of you reconcile those differences in a spirit of love? (*Emphatically*) It depends less on what you say in any particular situation than it does on the climate of your marriage. If most of your sex experiences with your husband have been good ones, if you have let him know that you as a woman enjoy him as a man, then he should be able to handle the disappointment of an occasional no without feeling rejected.

BILL MASTERS: We would hope that a wife would understand a comparable response on her husband's part.

HAROLD SNYDER: It's not what you say, it's the way that you say it.

JUNE SNYDER: It's not what I say, it's the way that he hears it! (*Laughter and several participants talk at once.*)

VIRGINIA JOHNSON: It's both, really, isn't it? That's what communication is all about—and *there's* a word we'll be using often this afternoon. But right now I'd like to consider an issue that lies beyond the question of how to say no. After all, it wouldn't matter too much how we said no if it didn't matter whether we were ever asked again. Besides, isn't it perhaps better to say no for the right reasons than to say yes for the wrong ones?

Being asked, being wanted—and, on the other side of the coin, wanting and asking—this is of central importance in a marriage. This is what must be safeguarded. Each of you must feel free to approach the other and express a physical desire, to express it with some urgency, if that is how you feel—in a word, to importune. And this freedom can be achieved only if both partners are confident that no matter which one initiates the sexual overture, the other will respond lovingly—listening, touching, holding—even though the invitation to intercourse may have to be declined for compelling personal reasons. Declined not with annoyance or anger, but with warm consideration for the outcome of this moment in their relationship.

MURIEL GORDON: A wife should have the same right to ask for sex as her husband, isn't that true?

VIRGINIA JOHNSON: The same *privilege,* of course. But there is a slight difference. A female, no matter how liberated she may be, is often more reluctant to deliberately express her sexual desire, and for what she *assumes* to be a good physiological reason. She usually waits for some signal from the male before she makes an overture because she has been led to believe—and therefore really fears —that any indication of her sexual interest might place him in the position of wanting to give something he may be physically incapable of producing at the moment. In trying to protect him from what she anticipates *may* happen—the inability to have an erection—she sometimes manages to eliminate that very stimulation which he would benefit from: knowing that he is sexually desired.

BILL MASTERS: I think we can put that problem aside for now by simply assuming that when either partner approaches the other under mutually acceptable circumstances, sexual functions will follow. *If it doesn't,* then the greatest mistake in the world is for either partner to persist and force the issue or to feel rejected. You should always let your partner know if you're in the mood. Always. Provided that you remain sensitive to your partner's responses, you can't importune too much. You can importune too little.

NANCY JAMESON (*hesitantly*): Do you think it's healthy or acceptable or whatever word you might use, to push . . . (*Starting again*) If two people are timid, or *one* person (*laughter*), don't you think they should surge forth and try something different anyway? Because then they'll sort of feel better for having tried it even though at the time it may not have seemed such a good idea.

VIRGINIA JOHNSON: Well, Nancy, I don't think they should grit their teeth and close their eyes and say, "I will, I will, I will!" But on the other hand, it seems desirable for a couple to want to evolve, to experiment together, to move toward experiences that will enrich their relationship.

BILL MASTERS: Such an approach can open up an incredible spectrum of sexual responsiveness.

VIRGINIA JOHNSON: But don't expect to like everything. Don't expect everything to represent *you*—

BILL MASTERS: Not only shouldn't you expect that, but for heaven's sake don't reject something you haven't tried, saying, "I know I won't like it." Or don't turn away after you've tried it only once— that's a big mistake. You have no idea what you're going to like or dislike until you've had some experience. And I don't know what "some" means, but I know it means more than one!

PETER STILLMAN: Is there any such thing as normalcy in sexual relationships? Or is it up to the individuals and whatever they're comfortable with?

BILL MASTERS: Our basic concept is that any sexual practice taking place in private between consenting adults is acceptable. And by "consent" we don't mean in writing or anything like that. Mutual consent implies that the practice is mutually enhancing, mutually pleasurable or does not occur at either partner's expense.

SHEILA STILLMAN: Some things, I just don't think I could handle them.

BILL MASTERS: Certainly. These particular feelings are always a problem in terms of initial anticipation of something unfamiliar or something which seems contrary to your established values. You approach it with some trepidation. Take manual or oral stimulation, for example, both areas of some concern. How should it be handled? How may it affect intercourse in a relationship? Will it become the preferred way of sexual expression instead of just a variation on a theme? I can answer the last question by telling you that this rarely happens. And for what it may be worth to you, I'll point out that in general the higher the level of formal education people have had, the more varied are their sexual practices.

SHEILA STILLMAN: But what do you do if you know that your partner would like to try something new and yet it makes you feel uptight?

BILL MASTERS: Why do you feel uptight?

SHEILA STILLMAN: Well, maybe just because you've never done it before.

VIRGINIA JOHNSON: Can't it be, perhaps, because you're afraid of being graceless or tasteless? (*Sheila nods*) You see, with sex we can't suddenly start something new and strange just because we've heard about it or because our partner suggests it. Because *it*, whatever "it" may be, then becomes something to be done, an act to be performed instead of a moment to be experienced.

Sex, after all, should be a spontaneous expression of your personality, how you feel at a particular moment. To turn it into a performance, as something with a goal, where you start here and do this, this and this on some kind of checklist, is to lose the capacity to express your most private self. Instead of making your goal to perform with grace and good taste, make it to be yourself: "I'm me, I feel a little scared and foolish, but I'd like to know what other experiences are like." That's the first line of communication—if you're not in touch with yourself, you can't be in touch with anyone else.

But once you're aware of your thoughts and feelings, let your partner know them. If you're afraid, say so. Perhaps together you can discover what you are afraid of and why, and perhaps your partner can help you find ways of overcoming your fears gradually. Then as you move along the way, you will be acting in accordance with your feelings, not in spite of them. And in time you should be able to include in your lovemaking all that you now enjoy, the sharing and exchanging that is warm and familiar and understandable, as well as this wild, mad . . . *it* over here.

SHEILA STILLMAN: Sometimes it's hard to get the words out.

VIRGINIA JOHNSON: But there are so many easy, simple ways to communicate without words! A touch, a glance, a sound, can say a great deal.

CHARLES GALLAGHER: A sigh is as good as a paragraph.

JEAN GALLAGHER: If your husband listens! (*Her husband shakes his head and grins.*)

BILL MASTERS: It's important to understand that this interaction between husband and wife, this spoken or unspoken communication, is crucial to sexual stimulation. There are two basic sources of stimulation. When you approach your partner and please her with a touch, the greatest reward that comes to you is her pleasure in the approach you took. Her pleasure, communicated to you, stimulates you. The second source of stimulation is, obviously, when your partner approaches you. Both sources stimulate you sexually; both sources bring you pleasure. Fundamentally if you think of any technique of sexual approach as a giving of yourself to *get back* from your partner—

VIRGINIA JOHNSON: It's a delightfully selfish thing!

BILL MASTERS:—it becomes very self-centered. And a

moment's reflection should make clear that orgasm itself, male or female, is entirely a self-centered I-me proposition.

VIRGINIA JOHNSON: Because at that moment you are totally involved with your own experiences. But such self-realization is a real compliment to your partner, of course, since your pleasure has been produced by the relationship between you.

JEAN GALLAGHER: Isn't it enough of a compliment to a man if his wife has a completion of orgasm? We've discussed this, and he feels it might be better if I said something during orgasm . . .

VIRGINIA JOHNSON: To identify the occasion?

JEAN GALLAGHER: Right. But I was just enjoying what was happening to me at that moment and I didn't want to lose any of it.

BILL MASTERS: You have to realize that even men with a great deal of experience can't always identify the onset or the duration of the female orgasm. Now, women don't have the same difficulty; you're jolly well aware when the man is orgasmic. And let me ask you—do you not thoroughly enjoy that moment?

JEAN GALLAGHER: Yes, I do.

BILL MASTERS: Your husband deserves the same privilege. He wants to be aware because it's incredibly stimulating for a man to have an orgasmic woman in his arms. That doesn't mean you have to say, "Now, George!" But if you can find a way to communicate the intensity of your feelings, you may discover that instead of detracting from your experience, you may have intensified it.

VIRGINIA JOHNSON: Even if talking is put off until shortly afterward, it helps to share the experience. You don't have to intellectualize it to death. But a little descriptive communication of what it was like will help your husband associate that with what he himself felt and observed. And the next time he may be more sensitive, more aware of your responses, and he'll know what he needs to know. That's how you develop your own private signal system, your own way of communicating without words. Then when you're caught up in that self-centered moment, when you're subjectively enjoying your own experience—as you should be—your partner can share your pleasure and be stimulated by it.

NANCY JAMESON: When you were talking about the I-me, selfish sort of relationship, I just didn't understand. I don't think it's that way at all. I don't think it's a case of "I'm going to please my husband so I can get pleased." Don't you believe that one person can really be trying to please the other?

BILL MASTERS: Certainly. But let me clarify something here. We were not talking about an I-me *relationship*. And we weren't talking about sex play either. We were talking of the actual orgasmic experience only. That is an I-me situation.

SAM GORDON: Words seem to be getting in our way. When we talk of giving of ourselves to get something back from our partners, it sounds like backscratching: "I'll do this for you if you'll do that for me." It sounds conditional. But I don't think you mean it that way. My giving is unconditional. My giving is my pleasure. I am not giving because I expect my wife to give something back; I am giving because I get sexual pleasure from it. Is that what you mean?

BILL MASTERS: Exactly. Still, the issue involved—and I think it's important to chew on it until we understand each other—is that while the entire mode of sexual stimulation certainly is one of giving, the fact remains that *as you are giving, you are also getting*.

SAM GORDON: I see. Because if I weren't getting, I would eventually stop giving. I'd have lost the incentive of my own pleasure.

BILL MASTERS: Right.

VIRGINIA JOHNSON: It may also help to look back to the not-so-distant past. As part of our sexually repressive Victorian heritage—

BILL MASTERS: The sad truth is that people in this country paid more attention to Queen Victoria than her own people ever did. (*Laughter.*)

VIRGINIA JOHNSON: —women are brought up to be passive. They are expected to serve the man. You know: "I want nothing for myself—just to please you." Any vestige of that philosophy has to be resisted, because it keeps a woman from experiencing her own potential for pleasure and from discovering her own wants and needs.

BILL MASTERS: And it minimizes the man's pleasure. A nonresponsive woman is a nonstimulating partner.

JUNE SNYDER: Maybe I'm getting the wrong message, but it seems to me that all we're talking about is enjoyment and pleasure. Is that all there is to sex?

TED JAMESON (*teasing*): Is that bad? (*Laughter and several people talk simultaneously.*)

VIRGINIA JOHNSON: If I understand you correctly, June, you want to know whether sex hasn't some meaning or value beyond pleasure alone. I hope you aren't underestimating the significance of pleasure—and by pleasure I don't mean fun. I mean the authentic, abiding satisfaction that makes us feel like complete human beings. We don't experience pleasure in *anything* we do if it fails to fulfill us in some fundamental way. So the question isn't whether there is something more important that lies beyond pleasure. The question, it seems to me, is: What important considerations *precede* pleasure? What personal values have to be satisfied before sex can be experienced as a natural pleasure?

BILL MASTERS: Don't ever forget that above everything else, sex is a natural function, as natural as breathing, as universal as eating. And whenever we engage in any natural function in a satisfying way, we experience pleasure. This is no less true of the sexual function, and we have a sound basis for believing that pleasure should be a natural and desirable consequence.

But no physical function is purely physical. They all are subject, more or less, to outside influence. They all are subject to cortical control. That is, the cerebral cortex, which most people refer to as the brain, influences sexual behavior just as it does almost all other physical functions.

Take breathing, for example. If you walked out of this hotel and came close to being hit by a cab, what would happen? You'd start breathing fast. Yet you weren't running or exerting yourself. Fear alone made you hyperventilate.

Emotions, you see, obviously influence natural functions, and this is particularly true of sex. When you engage in sexual intercourse, you're doing what comes naturally, and pleasure too should come naturally. When it does, there are no further questions to be asked. When it doesn't, then questions are in order.

VIRGINIA JOHNSON: It's when we fail to achieve pleasure that it becomes important to understand our fundamental needs and desires. They grow out of ideas and perceptions that have the power to stimulate us erotically. They turn us on. For one person a touch may be the most erotic experience imaginable if it occurs at the right time, in the right place, with the right person. For another it may be a specific sexual act; for another, a word; for still another, giving comfort or being comforted.

Because such things can spontaneously generate erotic feelings, we value them. They make up what Dr. Masters and I call the sexual value system. Each of us has a unique sexual value system that helps us distinguish what matters a great deal from what doesn't matter much at all. And what *really* matters are all the ideas and perceptions that make sex work effectively for us as individuals. They free us to enjoy it.

Some elements in our sexual value system may be intensely private, but others are shared by many people. One of the most universal values, no doubt, is the idea of conception. There probably isn't a single one of you young women who hasn't had the thought at one point in your life that sex is for the purpose of reproduction. You may have rejected the thought or accepted it without question. But in any case you probably recognize the feeling of being sexually stimulated that comes from the idea of your giving a child to a man or receiving one from him as a result of intercourse.

Today, however, we no longer consider producing a baby each year to be the only way to define ourselves as women. Married or not, we want to live full lives, to be individuals in our own right. For those who are wives and mothers, it isn't enough simply to *be* wife or mother. What counts is the *kind* of wife or mother we are, the quality of our relationship with husband or child.

Our sense of purpose in life no longer comes primarily from matrimony or maternity. It comes from how we relate to the people who are important to us. The way we express ourselves sexually—our most intimate way of relating to another person—reflects how we value ourselves, how we value the other person, how that person values us. It reflects all the things that mean warmth, love, affection and security to us—and which we therefore seek and cherish. It reflects, in a real way, some of the purposes and meaning of life.

Sexual expression that ignores these values gives us no sense of purpose in what we are doing. And this often leads to a loss of interest in sex or to functional disability. After all, any meaningless act takes away some of the meaning of life itself, and meaningless sex is no exception.

I hope that in a reverse way this partially

answers June's question. Sexual pleasure doesn't exist in a vacuum. It flows from the mutual fulfillment of wants and needs by a man and woman who are physically and emotionally committed to each other. Sex for them confirms their deepest values. The existence of pleasure testifies to the quality of their relationship.

BILL MASTERS: This does not mean that sex is the be-all and end-all of marriage or living. We do not believe that. We simply think it plays a vital part and perhaps a crucial one. After all, cóital activity can be the ultimate communication between a man and a woman. If you are successfully using sexual expression as a means of mutual enhancement, if you have a reasonably effective marital bed, then in addition to the physical release and the physical pleasure each of you affords the other, you both have, in effect, a secure home base. You have a place where you can safely "cuss and discuss" those issues that are of major importance at the time. You rarely have this kind of emotional security if you don't have the security of reasonably effective sexual functioning. A marriage can survive without it, but usually, though not always, the marriage proves to be a relatively poor one.

VIRGINIA JOHNSON: Without the ability to communicate sexually, the marital relationship has a wide gap in it, and most often this gap contributes to the breakdown of other kinds of communication. It's that simple.

SHEILA STILLMAN: Would you say that there is good communication if a husband and wife sometimes make love for different reasons? I mean, suppose it's an emotional thing on the one part and physical on the other?

BILL MASTERS: Is there anything objectionable in that?

SHEILA STILLMAN: I don't know. There are times when I feel much more emotionally in need than physically. Isn't it perfectly all right for me to go

ahead and just find the emotional satisfaction I
want even though I know it would be more stimulating to my husband if I reacted more physically?

VIRGINIA JOHNSON: Of course, it's all right. Both you
and your husband must be completely free to express what you want and feel what you want every
time.

NANCY JAMESON: And knowing there is complete trust
between the two of you. You're completely attuned to each other's wishes, knowing that you
have moods and that you're a different person
with different needs at different times.

PETER STILLMAN (*dubiously*): Can any couple ever
really be completely attuned to each other?

VIRGINIA JOHNSON: Well, being attuned is not magic.
It's communication. It's something you participate
in by identifying with another person and sharing
with that person and learning how to reconcile
your private, intimate thoughts and feelings with
those of the other person.

BILL MASTERS: Being attuned results as well from good
nonverbal communication.

VIRGINIA JOHNSON: And being attuned is the key to
an important point. Sexual expression isn't necessarily a matter of yes or no, to bed or not to bed.
Sexual expression exists on a continuum. It includes a very wide range of behavior. It means
reaching out just to touch, drawing close to share
a mood, developing it or letting it drift. It means
enjoying the sexual *feelings* of the moment without necessarily turning them into an invitation or a
request or a command.

But being attuned also means sensing when
the mood is right to take the next step, and then
you should be free to respond in the way that
feels best for you. To be able to say, "This time
I'm going along for the ride." Or not even say
it; just feel it. Or to be demanding—and, if it
goes wrong, to communicate and say, "Look . . ."

SAM GORDON: Isn't it natural sometimes not to be completely *with it?* To be a little removed? Sometimes I even find I'm sort of watching . . . (*Abruptly*) Is there anything wrong with that?

BILL MASTERS: There probably isn't anyone who, while having intercourse, doesn't become a spectator for a time. On occasion we watch what we ourselves may be doing or what our partner is doing. It's perfectly natural to consciously observe the procedure; in fact, it's quite stimulating to do this now and then.

What is important is the *degree* to which we assume this spectator's role. In some cases, being the spectator on occasion may reflect a detachment from any emotional involvement. This too is natural and no cause for concern. But it does cut down on the *input* of the stimulus. For instance, if you are the spectator during sexual activity, some degree of your wife's pleasure and excitement doesn't really get through to you, which means you lose that stimulation. And to a degree your own pleasure is dulled because you're not lost in the experience—you're observing. I am *not* saying that you experience no pleasure at all. I'm just saying that some of it is blocked. A level of perception is blocked.

This becomes critical in cases of sexual dysfunction. For example, suppose the male has trouble achieving or maintaining an erection. In that circumstance both partners have fears. Whenever the wife approaches her husband he worries: can I? will I? And then there is his wife's fear: will he? can he? or am I going to be left hanging?

MURIEL GORDON: Is it my fault?

BILL MASTERS: Do I contribute to the problem? Am I pushing him too much? And in that case, when dysfunction crops up, the *fear* of performance rather than the pleasure of performance becomes dominant. Then one really becomes a spectator. Because both partners are off in the corner, watching to see what happens. Usually nothing does.

PETER STILLMAN: When the male cannot sustain himself in the long run—what is the main cause?

BILL MASTERS: Are you asking about the male who loses an erection without an ejaculation or who ejaculates too soon?

PETER STILLMAN: Too soon.

BILL MASTERS: Premature ejaculation is very difficult to define. But our concept of it, basically speaking, holds that if a man maintains control long enough to provide the opportunity for his female partner to achieve satisfaction approximately fifty percent of their coital opportunities, he cannot be considered a premature ejaculator. Now, there are certain circumstances under which any man may tend to function in such a rush that his partner is unsatisfied. Suppose he has been away for a couple of weeks. The first time after that he usually has trouble. He may have similar trouble during his first encounter with a new woman. These are classic situations.

But if the problem is a consistent one within the marital unit, there is a technique to remedy matters. When this technique is used lovingly by husband and wife together, almost every man can learn self-control. It is simple enough to put into practice easily but too complicated to describe in detail right now.

HAROLD SNYDER: You said before that sex is a natural process. To not want it—is that unnatural?

BILL MASTERS: On occasion or for a long period of time? It's perfectly natural on occasion—sometimes you're just not hungry. If it lasts two or three weeks, though, it may be time to give the matter some thought.

HAROLD SNYDER: Say it lasts a month.

BILL MASTERS: Sexual tension exists in the body just as the appetite for food exists. If sexual desire is lacking, we would first want to check for a physical disability, just as we would if a person went too long without feeling hungry. Let me point out, however, that in one respect sex is like no other physical process. It is the only physical process that can be denied indefinitely, even for a lifetime.

VIRGINIA JOHNSON (*to Harold*): It is one thing, of course, for someone with reasons that are valid for him or her deliberately to condition himself to set it aside. But if you're talking about someone who suddenly finds that now there is no interest where there *was* interest before, and if there seems to be no physical explanation, then the answer may lie in the cares and concerns that are draining his energies.

SHEILA STILLMAN: Is this problem—you know, lack of desire and all that—is it the same for a woman? If she's busy with the house and the children and she's just beat . . .

VIRGINIA JOHNSON: Of course that's going to affect her responsiveness! How could it not? There's probably no young mother in the country who wouldn't know what you're talking about. (*Sheila's husband reaches over with a smile and pats his wife's hand, which starts the others laughing.*)

NANCY JAMESON: I don't know whether this pertains to what Sheila just said, but isn't it a fact that women have their strongest sexual drive at a later age than men? What is it—eighteen to twenty-five for men and twenty-five to thirty-three for women?

BILL MASTERS: That's a reflection of the old Kinsey data.

NANCY JAMESON: Is it true? I'm just curious.

BILL MASTERS: It's not a physiological fact but a sociological one. It's culturally induced.

VIRGINIA JOHNSON: Perhaps one of society's ways of protecting young girls from the risk of pregnancy was to teach them that they had no sexual feelings; they were given all the moral precepts to make sure they remembered the lesson. Boys were permitted—even encouraged—to have sexual feelings, so they got off to a head start. Girls took longer to catch up, that's all. It's cultural, not biological.

NANCY JAMESON (*persisting*): The reason I asked is that I had been told by other women that immediately after the birth of a baby, your sexual desire wanes—probably because you don't want another child in nine months!—but then the desire comes back even stronger. That's how it was for me. When we were trying to have a child, we were trying so hard it was pretty terrible, but once I was pregnant, it was great. Then after we had her—we have a daughter—it waned, but now it's even better than ever. So I wonder whether this isn't one reason why women have stronger sex drives when they get older?

BILL MASTERS: The question is too complex to answer in detail today, because it involves both psychological and physiological elements. So permit me to put aside the issue of whether sexual desire occurs at a later age for the female and I'll concentrate on the physiological aspects of female responsiveness after childbirth.

Many women in a relatively happy marriage are not fully responsive sexually until after the birth of a first baby, and there is a physical reason for this. Sexual responsiveness for a woman, just as for a man, is inevitably accompanied by a concentration of blood in the pelvis. The amount of blood supplied to the pelvis changes through pregnancy and childbirth, and this affects responsivity—especially a woman's awareness of sexual feeling.

From about the third to the sixth month of pregnancy there is usually a high sexual-demand level. You seem to have noticed that, Nancy, and it was a happy contrast to the period when you were first trying to become pregnant, when you forced yourself to make the effort. But you mentioned a waning of desire after childbirth—and this reflects, among other things, the fact that your ovaries weren't functioning yet. The ovaries stop functioning at about the second or third month of pregnancy, and they don't start again until anywhere from six weeks to three months after you've given birth. If you nurse your baby, it may take an extra month or six weeks.

What does all this add up to? Well, it means that sexual demand can be expected to return a couple of months after childbirth, and when it does, it may well be stronger than before because now you have a greatly increased vascular supply to the pelvis, much greater than you ever had before.

CHARLES GALLAGHER: My wife and I have been talking about having a baby, and she keeps telling me that she isn't sure she wants to start a family. But it seems to me she's kidding herself and she really wants me to decide that we *will* have one.

BILL MASTERS: I certainly don't want to find myself stepping into the middle of a battle (*laughter*) but I'll say this. Somewhere along the line, Mother Nature talks to every female. There is, I'm convinced, an innate female demand to reproduce. Some women, of course, make a deliberate commitment, for their own valued reasons, to certain goals in life that preclude motherhood. But the demand to reproduce is real; it's a tremendous instinct. It may not be too much of a factor for many women when they are twenty-three, twenty-four—but when thirty-three or thirty-four rolls around without pregnancy, the gal looks in the mirror and says, "Well, how much time do I have, oh Lord?"

SAM GORDON: When a man says that at thirty-three or thirty-four, he has something entirely different in mind! (*Laughter and considerable overlapping conversation.*)

VIRGINIA JOHNSON: It's popular, I know, to point out the differences between men and women, but I have to tell you that from the beginning of our work, what has impressed us most have been the similarities, not the differences, between the sexes.

BILL MASTERS: Not only physically but emotionally—and we're talking specifically about sexual functioning. Men and women are incredibly and constantly similar. Oh, there are a few basic—

VIRGINIA JOHNSON: —happy—

BILL MASTERS: —basic and happy biological differences that we all enjoy. (*Laughter.*) And there are a couple of other differences that are far less obvious. For instance, there is no question that the human female is infinitely more effective as a sexual entity than the male ever dreamed of being. Her potential capacity to respond to effective sexual stimulation is almost unlimited.

VIRGINIA JOHNSON: Nature simply built her that way.

BILL MASTERS: This is her *natural* facility. On the other hand, if the male capacity to produce sperm is compared to the female capacity to produce eggs, it is plain that the male is infinitely more fertile than the female ever dreamed of being. By comparison she is an astonishingly sterile creature!

The other difference that I want to mention is just an interesting sidelight. Recently, as you may know, there has been a good deal of research on sleep patterns. In our laboratory we have observed husbands and wives to see whether they move differently in their sleep, depending on whether they have or have not had orgasmic release. Observers discovered that in the first hour after sleep, the postorgasmic female usually moves nearer the male. If he is removed from the bed, the sleeping female still reaches for him, and in one out of every two cases she will settle in his place.

Would anyone care to guess about the behavior of the male?

TED JAMESON: He moves into another bed. (*Laughter and a few wives talk simultaneously.*)

BILL MASTERS: Not quite. The man stays put. Of course, we're talking in terms of percentages. This differential response was not universal. But the indications seem reasonably clear and quite fascinating—that the female, the postorgasmic female, has a subconscious need to relate, to remain *in touch* with her partner. The male does not need to relate physically to the degree that the female evidences.

VIRGINIA JOHNSON: There may be a physiological factor operating here. As we mentioned a moment ago, the woman's natural capacity for repetitive sexual response is far greater than that of the man. The fact that she reaches out for him in her sleep while he tends to stay where he is may be a reflection of a difference in their sexual capacities. Even in sleep she may seek to continue sexual interaction while he is satiated and seeks nothing more. On the other hand, her sleep behavior may reflect her acceptance of the traditional female role of being sexually receptive rather than indicating any active desire. But I'm afraid that this discussion, as interesting as it is, is based on speculation and has taken us away from the more immediate and very real concerns that young couples are encountering in marriage.

TED JAMESON: I was just wondering . . . does a marriage work out best over the years if the husband and wife place more emphasis on the emotional than the physical side? Because after you've been married for a while, making love just isn't the same sensational thing it used to be when you were dating. So you have to deal with it differently. You learn to appreciate it for what it is—an act of communication. It's part of what keeps two people together. But you don't expect it to be the way it was in the beginning.

VIRGINIA JOHNSON: *Nothing* feels the same way it did in the beginning—and some things become better than they were then! Of course, the first flush of excitement, the first taste of the unknown, this is always memorable and can never be duplicated— and I am not talking about sex alone. The first dance, the first kiss—the first time is unlike any other that follows. And yet, because a later experience often unfolds out of an earlier one, it can prove to be more mysterious or more wonderful than the one before.

It's a cliché that we become older and wiser, but clichés are often true. And "wiser" simply means that we can do more things, do them better—and appreciate them more.

It's no different with marriage. I don't want to sound like Pollyanna—or like Methuselah, either!—but let me assure you that marriages can become deeper and richer and more intense over a period of time as your commitment to each other becomes reinforced by all the experiences, good and bad, that you share. This isn't true for all marriages, of course, it may not even be true for *most* marriages. But it has proved true for some marriages—and since that is the case, why shouldn't it be possible for yours?

All I'm trying to say—and saying it poorly, I'm afraid—is that marriages may grow, or fail to grow, depending on whether the husband and wife develop greater trust in each other, greater confidence in themselves and greater pleasure in their relationship—their emotional *and* their physical relationship—because they are really two sides of the same coin. The existence of sexual pleasure testifies to the quality of that man-woman relationship. It adds a dimension to your marriage and makes life itself more rewarding. If you and your husband are vital, growing individuals, different today from what you were yesterday, and if you can communicate this growth not only emotionally and philosophically but also sexually, your marriage, over the years, will remain vital and creative.

2

How Conciliation Becomes
Another Word for Marriage

JUNE SNYDER: Is there any good way to say, "I don't feel like it," aside from the old headache routine?

VIRGINIA JOHNSON: I'm afraid there is no magic formula, but it may help to keep some considerations in mind. Two persons are involved, and it's important for each to become aware of the other's needs. . . . Two human beings with different needs, different moods, a different sense of timing—it simply isn't possible for the two of you to find your desires always dovetailing perfectly. But how can the two of you reconcile those differences in a spirit of love?

Few couples would have any trouble understanding exactly what a cynic meant when he said that marriage, as a part of life, is like a duel being fought in the midst of a battle.

To a considerable extent, it could hardly be otherwise. Even as individuals we are often at cross-purposes with ourselves, waging inner battles as we struggle to resolve confused or contradictory intentions and desires. With marriage, the problem is inevitably compounded. No matter how obliging by nature a husband and wife may individually be, they must expect to engage in a

41

certain amount of disagreement as they try to reconcile their personal wishes so that together they can pursue the goals they share. What is more, culturally conditioned attitudes toward sex and sexual identity could hardly have been better designed to insure conflict between man and woman.

But for those men and women who basically accept and respect one another as independent and equal human beings, differences can be a stimulus for growth rather than a threat to happiness. A sharp point of disagreement can prod them into testing their feelings and thoughts and beliefs, thus possibly bringing them to a deeper level of understanding.

These feelings, thoughts and beliefs reflect values that the individual, from childhood on, is continually crystallizing out of the totality of his or her personal experiences. Originally the experiences have no direct association with the act of sex. They are simply memories attached to happy or unhappy feelings. They may be linked to a parent's actions, for example, or to a favorite teacher's counsel, a passage from a novel, a scene from a movie or the derisive laughter triggered by a dirty joke.

Through the drift of emotions in imperceptible ways over a period of time, these memories become sexually charged. They acquire the power to define for the individual the circumstances which make intercourse something to be actively enjoyed or simply endured or even dreaded, and to be remembered with good feelings or bad feelings—or indifference.

Thus every individual evolves a unique set of needs that have to be met if satisfying sexual feelings are to result. In a sense these needs, these factors, might be considered prerequisites to pleasure; our term for them is the sexual value system. At baseline, it includes all the considerations—the time, the place, the mood, the words used, the gestures made, the thousand and one little signals that a man and woman send each other with or without language—that the individual requires in order to respond emotionally, to let feelings come to the surface.

It also includes—and this is very important—those elements that permit the individual to be comfortable with those feelings. For example, a man might have a desperate need to be held, to be touched and stroked, and this is a requirement that he, as an individual, must have fulfilled if he is to be stimulated sexually. But if it happens, will he then accept the touch with pleasure? Or might his response be blocked by guilt or embarrassment? Or plain discomfort? After all, if the pure physical fact of being touched was an automatic turn-on, there would be daily orgies in the subways!

Another example would be the woman who is with the man of her choice, when the time and the mood are both right, and she wishes he would do X—whatever her particular X might be—but she cannot tell him to do it or signal him to do it because, in her system of values, that would be "unromantic." And if she forced herself to tell him and he then did what she asked, she might be completely unresponsive, turned off by any of a dozen ideas: he didn't really want to, a woman shouldn't tell a man what to do, a real man wouldn't obey a woman that way, and so on. All these considerations are part of what makes up her sexual value system.

For a man and woman who want to satisfy each other's needs without sacrificing their own, a delicate process of accommodation is required. Even in an exemplary marriage, differences in temperament and spontaneous feelings make it certain that at times a husband and wife will find themselves emotionally at odds. With or without words, one partner may signal a wish to make love, for example, and the other partner either ignores the signal or counters it, saying, in effect: "I'm not in the mood." Often the refusal is tempered —not now, not here, not that way. And there is the "yes" that means "no," communicated in a veiled message that means: "All right, if you insist."

No matter how the response is phrased, whether it expresses outright refusal or conditional acceptance, it puts an emotional discrepancy in sharp focus. The feelings of the husband and wife are in conflict. Perhaps the disagreement arises because one of the two likes to use four-letter words during intercourse while the other partner finds them discordant and abrasive, or perhaps one of them wants to make love occasionally on the spur of the moment, in unlikely places, while the other cannot relax except in the security of their bedroom. But no matter what the specific argument may be about, the problem is more than just a difference in preference. The real issue isn't making love; it's feeling loved. Although the wife may never say the words, she is thinking: "If he loved me, he wouldn't insist." Or else: "If he loved me, he would be understanding enough not to ask." And the husband thinks: "If she loved me, she wouldn't refuse."

The emotional stakes are higher than is generally realized, a fact that is underscored by the bitterness and hurt feelings that quarrels over sexual differences often generate. But these differences can be successfully negotiated, in ways soon to be discussed. The negotiation will be simpler, however, and the outcome more certain, in cases where husband and wife share the same fundamental convictions about sex. Success becomes more problematical for the couple with a basic disagreement in philosophy, particularly if one partner holds conventional views and the other takes an unconventional approach.

Major differences divide the latter couple. Should the wife accommodate her husband and accept the traditional female role, for instance, or is she equally free to express desire and initiate sex? Must intercourse be reserved for a customary time and place—in bed at night, on certain days of the week—or can it be enjoyed whenever and wherever the mood dictates? Should the physical embrace be restricted to the familiar positions and practices—with the woman supine, the man prone above her, and foreplay intended to facilitate penile penetration of the vagina—or should the sexual exchange be adventurous and experimental, utilizing every imaginable method of stimulation and every available orifice?

Obviously if a man and wife hold diametrically

opposing views on such questions, they will have difficulty compromising and their sexual relationship will be a trial for one or both of them. It is unlikely, however, that any substantial number of marriages fit this pattern. It represents the extreme. But in countless marriages, including those where husbands and wives are essentially of the same mind about sex, whether conventionally or unconventionally so, conflicting feelings about intercourse on any given occasion are the rule, rather than the exception, and rarely are they easily resolved.

How such conflicts are handled is one of the crucial factors in establishing the prevailing atmosphere of a marriage. A negative approach to this vital problem creates defensiveness and resentment on the part of one or both partners, undermining their relationship. A positive approach leads to the openness and trust that strengthen the bond. The difficulty, of course, lies in understanding the difference between the two approaches and, what is even more difficult, implementing that understanding.

Negative approaches to sexual conflicts are characterized by fear, hopelessness or ignorance. Fear, for instance, impels some couples to minimize their dissatisfactions and to tell themselves that if they are just patient enough, the problem will go away. (A young wife, whose husband rarely makes love to her and who even on those occasions is unable to bring her any measure of enjoyment, may console herself for years with the belief that "nature" would soon assert itself.) Other couples may acknowledge the problem but become defensive about it, each partner seeking personal reassurance in the belief that "it's not my fault"—an attitude that produces nothing but anger and endless recrimination.

In its most paralyzing form, fear expresses itself by the denial that any problem exists, or by a refusal to face the problem even after it has become apparent. Just as there are none so blind as those who will not see, so there are none so frightened as those who will not concede their fear. They cannot be helped because they do not seek help, nor would they accept it if it were volunteered. Only when their misery overwhelms their fear can they make an effort to break out of their trap. Some escape through divorce; others resort to extramarital affairs; and still others seek therapy.

In one case, for example, a couple came for treatment because the wife had never experienced orgasm. It soon became evident from their personal histories that the husband had problems of his own. He was often impotent. But that was not how he saw himself—his self-image was of a virile male who, because of fatigue or having had too much to drink, would on rare occasions be uninterested in sex. It was his wife, he insisted, who could not function sexually; he himself did very well, thank you.

His wife confirmed his description of the situation. Although this would seem to fly in the face of logic— surely she must have been aware of his failures—the truth is that she saw his impotence *as her fault* and she therefore agreed with him that the problem was hers and hers alone.

No effort was made to persuade the husband or wife that they both might be deceiving themselves. Instead the husband was told during one counseling session that when he and his wife had intercourse that night, he was to permit his wife to assume the superior position. He was given those instructions with full awareness that this variation, which ran contrary to his picture of himself as the dominant male, would put him under considerable tension and thus make it unlikely that he could perform satisfactorily.

The following day he reported that he had in fact failed to have an erection, and he quickly explained that this happened because he had eaten too much at dinner. He was then told that his failure had been anticipated, that it resulted from having been under emotional stress, and that his inability to perform was, for him and under those circumstances, a natural reaction. He was reassured that this did not demean him as a man nor prove that he was sexually incompetent.

It did, however, demonstrate two things: that under stress he reacted as a human being, and that he was subject to occasional impotence.

Once his fear of being something less than a man could be recognized for what it was—an adolescent image of the male as a sexual athlete—he was relieved of the need to deny the existence of his very real problem. He could acknowledge failure when it occurred and, seeing it in perspective, he could concentrate on learning to cope with his emotional tensions. The calmer and more confident he became, the more certainly his body asserted itself—and the more readily his wife responded. She had been as much a victim of his tensions as he was. Once she was set free of the fear that she was the cause of their sexual unhappiness, she was free to let a sense of physical pleasure rise to the surface of awareness and culminate naturally in orgasm.

Some couples make no attempt to deny the existence of a sexual conflict—on the contrary, they may fight openly about it—but they proceed to handle matters in ways that are just as self-defeating as total denial would be. One wife, for example, endured almost total frustration for years, furious with her husband because, as she saw it, "he didn't know how to do 'it' right." Nevertheless she continued to engage in sex whenever he made a request. "I feel used," she admitted, "but I also feel that I'm doing my duty. He supports me and the children, and if this is what he wants, that's what I do."

Like many women, she thought she was solving her marital problem by doing whatever could be expected of her as a wife, accepting a conventional, subservient role. But the solution solved nothing; instead, it made a bad situation worse. Over the years her anger intensified, and her husband, who genuinely regretted his inability to be more sexually effective, became increasingly impotent. Once in a while, however, he got back at his wife without being fully aware of what he was doing. On occasions when it was transparently clear that she did not want to have intercourse but grimly agreed to it anyway, he found himself able to prolong his performance almost indefinitely.

A simpler, but no less negative, approach to sexual conflicts is taken by couples who use stereotypes to explain away all their difficulties. If a husband and wife cannot agree on how often to have sex, for instance, empty generalizations make it easier for them to accept their differences. The wife can reassure herself that it is all her husband's fault because, as everyone knows, "the more you give a man, the more he wants." And her husband remains confident that his wife's lack of enthusiasm is no reflection on him because, as everyone knows, "most women really don't have much interest in sex."

Such stereotypes, incidentally, are remarkably versatile. They can be used to support opposite decisions. If most men have sex on their minds almost all the time, a woman can either justify refusing her husband when she chooses to because it will make him more eager the next time—or justify obliging him as an act of kindness since he can't help being in a state of perpetual desire. Her husband, on the other hand, can either accept her refusal as evidence of her female nature—or else he can refuse to take no for an answer since that same female nature requires a man to assert himself if there is to be any chance of a response.

False though they are, such sentiments are relied on by countless couples to suppress anxiety and to avoid having to search for the underlying source of their discontent. With this kind of sedation, some marriages can struggle along for years. Others cannot—and it is difficult to say for certain which outcome is the more unfortunate.

One other ill-advised approach should be mentioned. A couple may openly acknowledge to each other that their sexual relationship is far from perfect and both agree that they want to do whatever they can to increase their pleasure. Their unity of purpose starts them in the right direction—but they immediately take a wrong turn. They pull sex out of context; that is, they consider the physical act of intercourse as something in and of itself, a skill to be practiced and improved. The usual analogies are with dancing or tennis —but such comparisons are misleading. Sexual intercourse is not just a skill to be mastered, an activity to exercise the body, or a game to be played. At certain times and under certain circumstances, any of these elements may dominate the total experience. But to reduce sex to a physical exchange is to strip it of richness and subtlety and, even more important, ultimately means robbing it of all emotional value.

Less pleasure, rather than more, is the almost certain outcome for a man and woman who make the mistake of compartmentalizing sex as a physical act. As a hypothetical example, and one that is not as far-fetched as it might sound, consider the husband who decides that his wife's inability to have more than one orgasm is an indication that in some way she still isn't totally free in the acceptance of the pleasures of her body. Since she is both a curious and suggestible person, she thinks it is a good idea when he suggests that she use a vibrator as a means of going into training, as it were, for bigger and better and more frequent orgasms.

Incorporated in this one decision are two important errors.

The first, of course, involves pulling sex out of context. The fact that the husband wants his wife to experiment with a mechanical device appropriately symbolizes what the two of them are doing to their sexual relationship. Instead of seeing it as an extension of their marriage, reflecting how they feel about themselves and each other and expressing their particular needs on any given day, they are turning it into a performance. They are transforming themselves from participants into spectators, watching themselves having intercourse. This means that the wife cannot relax and enjoy her sexual feelings because she will be straining for more than one orgasm—if she can have any at all under the artificial circumstances that she and her husband are imposing on themselves.

The second error is of a different order. The husband is acting as the authority for his wife. Her concurrence does not alter the fact that he is using male standards and male attitudes as guidelines for female sexual behavior, something no man should presume to do. Even if by chance he happens to guess right, what he is doing is wrong—because his wife then comes to conclusions on the basis of her husband's reasons, not her own, and the damage to her self-confidence can be incalculable. For if he has in fact guessed right, and if she follows his suggestions and achieves greater responsivity than in the past, she must believe that he knows more about her sexual feelings than she does —and this is absolute nonsense.

Exactly the same situation prevails when a wife tells a husband what he is thinking or feeling or should do. Where sex is concerned, no partner can ever be the authority for the other.

Each partner must accept the other as the final authority on his or her own feelings. In affirming that principle, a man and woman have taken the first step toward achieving sexual harmony in marriage. They are telling each other that they acknowledge and accept without question the fact that they are individuals, separate but not separated, different but not dissimilar, and that their happiness must flow both from the delight they find in their differences and the security they derive from their similarities.

This is not a conviction too easily attained, especially for young men and women. In growing up, the emphasis was never on what they shared or on an appreciation of the differences that distinguish them as male and female. On the contrary, considerable emotion was invested in sharpening the sense of difference and in using that difference as a way of defining themselves sexually. If girls like to talk, then a boy's taciturnity is an assertion that he is a male. If boys like to compete, then a girl's cooperativeness marks her as a female. Each sex defined itself by deliberately choosing *not* to think or feel or behave like the other.

With such a heritage, it is no simple matter for

a married couple to overcome the prejudices of the past and to understand that the differences between them are essentially no more and no less than the differences between any two individuals. As long as the old attitudes persist, however, as long as a man and woman use the differences between them as a way of separating themselves to prove that they are male and female, their marriage is likely to remain at best a working partnership. In those circumstances, conflicts are threatening and are consequently avoided or denied. To do otherwise would seem to put the partnership in jeopardy.

But for the man and woman who accept conflict as offering an opportunity for growth, much depends on whether they have developed an adequate system of communication. To say that disagreements can revitalize a relationship leaves open the question of how the disagreements are expressed. This is particularly true when sex is the issue. How indeed can a husband and wife adjust their discrepant physical needs and at the same time reinforce their marriage bond?

They must first realize that a sexual conflict is not a problem in need of a solution. It is a situation that requires resolution. These are two entirely different approaches, promising radically different outcomes.

Suppose a husband wishes intercourse four times a week while his wife welcomes it just twice. Arithmetic suggests a simple compromise of three times a week. But the idea is, of course, ludicrous. The husband will still feel frustrated; the wife might feel imposed upon; and neither one would have learned anything about the other's feelings. If that were not enough, there remains the final incongruity: the real difference between them has nothing to do with numbers. Frequency of intercourse is almost never the true issue.

Had this couple been able to communicate with each other, they could have explored the situation they were in. Their goal would not have been to determine how many times to make love each week but to discover, if possible, their true feelings on the matter. Literally hundreds of alternative factors might have been operating for each partner. The husband might have felt that he was failing to excite his wife, that he was in need of more care and warmth than usual, or that he felt especially loving and filled with energy. His wife might have felt oppressed by financial pressures, or unhappy because she had put on weight, or preoccupied by her new job. For this couple to ignore these matters and discuss instead the frequency of their lovemaking, would be to talk in an emotional vacuum.

Even if they fully unburdened their feelings, they would still have to deal with the fact that the husband's sexual needs were, at least for the present, greater than those of his wife. But their basis for approaching each other would be entirely changed; the problem would not be one of taking or demanding versus not giving or submitting—it would be that of finding the best way to express care and concern for each other and to meet the needs of whichever partner was under the greater emotional strain.

This kind of communication is not easy to accomplish, but it can be achieved by any couple willing to make the effort and to abide by two principles. The first calls for *neutrality;* the second for *mutuality*.

The neutrality principle requires both husband and wife to assume that past sexual discord will not necessarily repeat itself in the future, because each partner is motivated to try to change. Each, in brief, credits the other with good intentions and the will to implement those intentions. Each accepts full responsibility for what he or she does—or fails to do—in making the effort to act differently. And each individual accepts responsibility for functioning sexually, and does not hold the other accountable for the body's responses. If a man and woman are to have a good physical relationship, each must strive to be *responsive* to the other, not *responsible* for the other.

The second principle, that of mutuality, requires all sexual messages between two people, whether conveyed by words or actions, by tone of voice or touch of fingertips, to be exchanged in the spirit of having a common cause. Mutuality means two people united in an effort to discover what is best for both. In attempting to reconcile differences in their sexual needs and desires, they must avoid what lawyers call "adversary proceedings," in which each person tries to prove that he is right and his opponent is wrong. (It remains right vs. wrong even when other terms are used, such as healthy vs. unhealthy, should vs. shouldn't, uninhibited vs. uptight, and everybody-does vs. nobody-I-know-does.)

By contrast, the principle of mutuality calls for both partners to accept the idea that if a sustained—and sustaining—physical relationship is desired, no conflict involving sex can be resolved on an either/or basis. Often, of course, one partner may be in a position to impose a decision on the other. Most frequently it is the husband, taking authority in matters of sex as the traditional male prerogative or as simply another instance of the tune being called by whoever pays the piper. But almost as frequently the decision is imposed by the less emotionally stable of the partners. Such is the tyranny of the neurotic over the normal that a person who suffers from persistent depression, chronic psychic exhaustion, free-floating anxieties, the need to be a martyr or any other similar mental afflictions, generally succeeds in coercing a considerate partner to yield in sexual matters.

A man and woman who interact as equals, however, must understand that if sexual disagreements are habitually settled in favor of one partner's wishes, at the expense of the other partner's feelings of personal comfort, the ultimate penalty will be paid by both of them. Suppressed resentment or unhappiness tends to short-circuit sexual feelings, and desire goes dead. This was described by a man who had come for therapy with his wife, after fifteen years of marriage. For more than thirteen of those years, the wife had never been orgasmic but had tolerated perfunctory acts of intercourse. Then she read a book that convinced her that she had a right to expect full satisfaction. She became increasingly unhappy, however, as her efforts to reach a climax proved unsuccessful. Her husband, too, became unhappy. He also began losing his ability to have an erection or, if he achieved one, to maintain it for longer than a minute or two.

"She *should* want an orgasm," he said, "and if she could have it, so much the better. But after a while this one desire, what I call an obsession, dominated the sex act. My desires and everything else became subordinate to this one particular thing, so what was there in sex for me to look forward to? In other words, sex became sexless."

It would be simple to say that his wife had made him impotent. But that would be just another instance of making one partner (in this case, the wife) *responsible for* the other partner's inability to function sexually (the husband's impotence).

Her real failure lay in not being responsive to her husband's emotional state. His failure lay in not signaling his growing dismay. Their sexual distress was the consequence of their failure to communicate, their failure to approach their undeniable problem in a neutral, non-fault-finding way, and their failure to be motivated by *mutual* concern.

It would have been an impressive accomplishment if they had managed otherwise. For this unhappy couple—and for so many like them—neutrality and mutuality were almost impossible. They had accumulated frustrations and hurt feelings over the years, piling them up like bricks to build a wall of anger until eventually they lost sight of each other. The wife blamed the husband for her failure to enjoy sex, a blame he meekly accepted. And in their bedroom they silently argued their case, a plaintiff and a defendant without a judge or jury, wondering why they could not come to a satisfactory conclusion.

To speculate about what they might have done is pointless. In reality, given their particular life histories, and especially in view of the wife's severe emotional deprivation during childhood and adolescence, there was little they themselves could have done unassisted, and they were wise to choose therapy. But suppose, in a comparable situation, neither partner had had a crippling childhood, and suppose, too, that they had been married only a few years. What might they have done to forestall a sexual crisis?

They would have talked. Communication doesn't just mean talking, it's true, and talking doesn't necessarily mean communicating. Nevertheless, as has already been pointed out, a husband and wife who find themselves troubled by sexual frustration are going to have to say so. Each must disclose his true feelings in first-person-singular terms: I think, I feel, I wish, I need, I'm afraid—clear, candid statements that relieve one partner of having to guess, usually wrongly, what the other is experiencing. And on the opposite side of the coin, both husband and wife must resist the temptation to interpret each other: you think, you feel, you want, you need, you're afraid—opinions which, no matter how accurate they may be, put the other person on the defensive and set the stage for conflict.

Such honest communication is not a simple achievement. It is more than just a play on words to note that talking about sex is, for many couples, easier said than done. Some reasons are obvious. Cultural inhibitions, internalized over the years, do not disappear overnight; they create an atmosphere in which self-consciousness blocks self-disclosure. In the same way that men and women conceal their naked bodies because they have been taught to do so—and, more important, because they are afraid they may be physically unattractive—they also conceal their sexual feelings because they are afraid those feelings may be emotionally unappealing to their partners.

In addition, they may be reticent because they lack a comfortable vocabulary. Clinical words can prove chilling and vulgar words can prove disruptive in the kind of talks that take place, not during sexual encounters but in times of reflection and emotional communion, when a man and woman are struggling to be reflective and truthful. Some people, of course, are completely at ease with crude language, but for a considerable number of men and women, and particularly

those who are accustomed to expressing themselves
with discrimination, blunt terms are inadequate to con-
vey the shades of meaning that matter a great deal in
exchanging confidences.

Talking is certainly not the only way of communicating about sex and it is not necessarily the best way;
words can mislead as well as illuminate, and there can
be many a slip between implication and inference.
Nevertheless for most people, most of the time, talking
is an indispensable line of communication, and the fact
that the line goes dead when sex is the subject means
that in marriage a considerable amount of important
information remains shrouded in silence.

Assuming, however, that each partner sees the
situation through the other's eyes, the next step is to
improve matters—to negotiate the differences that
threaten to deprive the couple of the gratification they
both want. Negotiating differences, however, is not a
matter of bargaining or setting terms. Negotiate, in
these circumstances, reflects its definition as meaning
"to move through, around or over in a satisfactory way,
as in dancing." And the purpose of negotiation is
conciliation. (Conciliate is derived from the Latin
conciliāre, meaning "to bring together, unite," a term
that seems singularly appropriate.) Business negotiations end with a conditional contract which states,
in effect, "If and when you do X, I will do Y." Sexual
negotiations end with a trusting commitment which
states, in effect, "I will do my best to do X because I
know you will do your best to do Y."

If such expressions of willingness to change are
to be anything more than the empty promises characteristic of couples who are making up after a quarrel,
they must be translated into *reciprocal* action. Generally speaking it is not enough for just one person to
make the effort. Under those circumstances, what may
seem to be passive acceptance of change on the other
person's part is actually disguised passive resistance.

A husband and wife, for instance, can agree that
she has been much more eager for sex than he has and
that, without intending to, she has made him more re-

sistant than he would otherwise be. He says that if she makes an effort to restrain her expression of desire, he will take the initiative more frequently than he has in the past. Each understands the other's feelings; both express a determination to change their habitual ways of interacting.

Soon enough, however, it becomes evident that while the wife is holding to her promise, the husband's response is something less than impressive. From the wife's point of view, intercourse occurs with frustrating infrequency. Again they talk; again they resolve to do better; and once again the husband's actions fail to match his intentions. Plainly his avowed wish to improve his sexual relationship with his wife is not a truthful representation of his deepest feelings. For reasons which he himself may not understand, he is not actively committed to conciliation. He is, in reality, resisting it.

The commitment requires each partner to try—and to keep on trying. It is the effort itself that means so much, even when success is not immediately achieved. If, in the previous instance, the husband tries to reach out to his wife, no matter how ineffectually or stumblingly, the effort will tell her, without a word, that he cares about pleasing her and values their sexual bond; at the very least he will spare her the feelings of rejection and anger that must otherwise turn her completely against him. In fact, the struggle to do what is obviously difficult is often more impressive evidence of emotional commitment than the actual achievement. The struggle is a measure of devotion; the achievement is not necessarily so.

But simple tenacity of purpose is not the entire answer, either. The process of sexual negotiation hinges, to a considerable degree, on how failure is handled. What a man and woman need of each other is the security that comes from knowing that occasional failures will not be used against them—they will not be ridiculed, scolded or punished. On the contrary, the failures will be not his or her but *theirs*.

A brief illustration concerns a man whose physical

motions during intercourse are not to his wife's satisfaction. Because he moves too rapidly and forcefully, in a rhythm and with movements that are not in harmony with her own, she finds her responsiveness impaired. Finally she tells him what is wrong, and he immediately wants her help in changing the ways he uses his body. Although the first few times he blunders and reverts to old rhythms, she corrects him with her hands, and soon he improves. The intimate mood is never shattered. Navigating these tricky emotional currents requires that each partner be constantly aware of the other's efforts.

This can be seen more clearly by contrast with other kinds of responses that might have been made. The wife might have been condescendingly patient ("Well, dear, I'll be glad to show you once more") or annoyed ("Clumsy!") or discouraged ("Oh, not again!"). The husband might have been angry ("Don't tell *me* what to do!") or critical ("You don't know what you're talking about") or deflated ("I'm sorry, but can we try again later?"). Or each might have remained silent, the wife with her hands motionless, and each could have assumed the worst—the husband, that nothing he could do would ever satisfy his wife; the wife, that her husband cared only about his own pleasure.

Variations on the script are almost limitless, but the underlying point is that a successful approach is a creative act, and the credit belongs to both partners. Conversely, any failure would be a joint failure. Each would have failed to meet the other's needs in the most painful of all circumstances: when each feels himself or herself to be alone, uncertain and exposed—and desperately in need of help and reassurance. (This may cast some light on the reason why an effective sexual relationship contributes so much strength to a marriage. It is not simply because of the physical pleasure the husband and wife experience, important though that is. It is because of the powerful sense of emotional well-being that comes when each partner knows that at times of greatest vulnerability, the other can be relied on to provide warmth, comfort and protection.)

What this means, in terms of the husband who was trying to harmonize his rhythms with those of his wife, is that on an occasion when his efforts would prove unsuccessful, she would understand that the failure was in part her own. She might not say so in words, but if she communicated an awareness of sharing the responsibility—of having failed to let him know when his movements started going wrong or of failing to make the effort to encourage him to move differently or of failing to cope with feelings of frustration and annoyance—she would at least have given him the confidence to try again.

One cautionary note: any individual's level of sexual tension—the power of the sex drive—is not easily changed by conscious decision, and it is important for both partners to take this into account. To a large extent, the strength of the sex drive is influenced both by cultural values and by the individual's unique experience growing up in that culture. But apart from these influences, there seems to be an innate level of sexual drive that varies from person to person. Why one person is born with a stronger drive than another, science has not yet determined.

Consider, for example, a woman who was born with a comparatively mild sex drive and whose experiences while growing up did nothing to intensify that drive. For her, sex in marriage is satisfying as long as it expresses warmth and tenderness and as long as she feels that her husband needs and values the love she is capable of giving him. And if, with good judgment and equally good luck, she has selected a man whose personality, attitudes and sex drive complement her own, she can have a genuinely happy marriage.

Very few couples, however, start out perfectly matched. The question is whether a husband and wife can learn to respect and accommodate themselves to differences in the strength of their sexual desires. Suppose, for example, that this young woman with limited sex drive marries a man whose enjoyment of sex depends to some degree on the intensity of his partner's enjoyment. In the beginning his pleasure inevitably will be somewhat tempered by his wife's low-key·responsiveness.

If these two are to achieve a compatible sexual relationship, they must reach a mutual understanding of their individual natures. They must accept the fact that variations in sexual drive do exist, that neither partner should apologize to the other for having more or less sexual energy, that one is not "better" or "worse" than the other. The husband must make his wife feel that he accepts her nature for what it is and that any regret he may have about her inability to experience a more intense degree of sexual pleasure is genuine regret, not dissatisfaction. The wife in turn must make her husband feel that her muted response is not a reflection on his skill as a lover or in any way a personal rejection but her natural expression of sexual fulfillment. Thus instead of acting as two separate individuals with contrasting—or even conflicting—standards of sexual behavior, they become a couple who honor the sexuality of their marriage.

Limited sexual responsiveness is, of course, often enough true of the male. The same principle applies— an acceptance of variations in sexual natures. This means rejecting the idea that the husband is any less a man because his sexual needs are less urgent than his wife expected, and it also means rejecting the idea that the wife is at fault because she fails to stimulate her husband to greater activity.

The strength of the sexual drive can change over a period of time. It is not fixed at a permanent level. A woman—and, of course, a man—may become more responsive; physical needs may surface more frequently and with greater intensity. If this happens, fine. But it doesn't mean that there was anything wrong with that person before the change occurred. It simply indicates that the sex drives of this particular individual were stabilized at a lower level as a result of any number of factors, such as limited experience, personal problems, family demands and social pressures. As these things change, so does sexual behavior.

In trying to resolve their sexual conflicts by changing their ways of interacting, a man and woman can be easily discouraged. If their occasional and inevitable failures result in criticism or a loss of self-esteem, sooner or later the confidence that is needed to keep trying will evaporate and all efforts will stop. Continuation depends on encouragement, and the acceptance of failure as a shared responsibility is encouraging.

The ability of both partners to share responsibility is additionally encouraging, if only because it is pre-eminently realistic. Each is prepared to take into account the fact that both of them are not only fallible but temperamental, that they cannot and do not always act as they would like to, and that apologies are acceptable after something has gone wrong.

This is an act of faith and it is crucial to the establishment of sexual conciliation. To expect or want or need something of another person, and to let that person know this truth, is to be open to disappointment or denial. But as long as the disappointment or denial is not a deliberate act on the part of the trusted person, as long as it can be seen as a reflection of such things as forgetfulness, impatience, lethargy or unhappiness, the hurt can be accepted or at least put in perspective. And when forgiveness is later asked for—and given—sharing has taken place. Trust has been reaffirmed; openness to each other has been maintained; and the ongoing process of sexual accommodation can continue.

There is no formula for success. No script can be provided for couples who want to use conflicts as a means of discovering new dimensions of themselves and their partners and thus enhance their physical relationship. Nor are there any shortcuts that will expedite the process of achieving genuine intimacy. But if the principles of neutrality and mutuality are used as guidelines in the negotiation of sexual differences, there is every reason to be optimistic about the outcome.

And this much is certain: all experience gained in resolving conflicts creates the facility for dealing constructively with future conflicts—which are inevitable. Conciliation is another word for marriage.

3

Young Marriages
How the Double Standard
Influences Sexual Pleasure

In June, 1970, a second group of young couples joined in a symposium in St. Louis. They were all in their middle or late twenties, had no children, and like the first group, had been married less than two years. Jerry Dollinger was an architect and a native Bostonian; his wife Diane, who had lived all her life in St. Louis, taught high school English. Steve Laird was a musician and at the time was playing piano with a rock-and-roll band. Betsy Laird worked in a local bank. The Saxons were both writers—but only Julie, a newspaper reporter, had seen her work in print. Philip had written one unpublished novel, was working on a second. Doug Hughes and one of his brothers were partners in an electrical engineering company. His wife Marjorie, a secretary, was recovering from an automobile accident and not yet ready to return to her job.

BILL MASTERS: In meetings that Mrs. Johnson and I have had with young couples like you, we keep being told that in this "enlightened" age the double standard is disappearing.

JERRY DOLLINGER: Hallelujah!

BILL MASTERS: Yes, hallelujah. But actually the truth is that time after time we find people saying one thing and doing something else. They believe what they're saying, all right, but they're not looking very carefully at what in fact they really do. Certainly you young people talk more freely; you communicate better. You accept the subject of sexual functioning with much more aplomb. And yet there seems to be an awful lot of residual double standard in your generation too.

VIRGINIA JOHNSON: Is this true for any of you? Are there things you believe a man is permitted to do, for example, but for a woman it's "thou shalt not"?

STEVE LAIRD: As a kid I was taught that sex was something you just didn't do, but if you did, you picked girls who weren't "your blood," as my parents used to say.

BETSY LAIRD: I remember my parents telling me that good girls don't do those things. They'd remind me every time I dated the same boy more than once. So I necked and petted, and my mind kept saying it was pretty silly to go to a certain point and then stop just because Mommy and Daddy said it's not right. But I went along with it.

JULIE SAXON: I'm besieged by the double standard. I'm absolutely in a mire of residuals! (*Laughter.*)

VIRGINIA JOHNSON: Why, do you suppose? Because of the memory of things you've been told? Or admonished for?

JULIE SAXON: I can't recall that my father or mother ever said, "Wrong! Nasty! Dirty! You'll get warts on your hands!"—or whatever. (*Pauses as others laugh, then continues*) My mother was a sensible woman; she would never have wanted to instill any kind of fear. And I didn't go to church, so I don't think it came from that. It must have come —I cannot pinpoint it, but it must have come from a very puritanical attitude among my friends in junior high and high school, when sex really started to matter.

VIRGINIA JOHNSON: Was it presented on a competitive basis?

JULIE SAXON: "It just wasn't done." That's how it was said. The good girls versus the tramps—and the tramps went all the way. They put out.

JERRY DOLLINGER: The vernacular of the fifties!

DOUG HUGHES: What Julie says, that's how it was in my town too. You'd take one girl behind the barn because you knew she'd go, but you went to the dance with Mary Jane, who was as pure as the driven snow. (*Laughter.*)

JULIE SAXON: It was a kind of thinking nobody *had* to teach you. You got it by osmosis. If you were a girl, you grew up believing sex was dirty and awful.

DIANE DOLLINGER: I guess I was lucky. At some point my mother must have said *something* about sex, but I don't remember what she told me. What I do remember is that she made me feel it was a marvelous thing to be a girl, and she was always very accepting and very nice about my seeing boys. Every once in a while she'd get paranoid about a particular boy and she'd say she wanted me home early because she didn't trust him. She'd be right. But she never gave me any bad attitudes toward sex.

JULIE SAXON: My parents gave me all these books to read and they talked to me. But they weren't talking about the actual act of intercourse. They were talking about what it means to have a period, how a baby grows in the womb—and so you got to know all the diagrams but you never knew what went on in between, how it all connected together. (*A general chorus of agreement.*)

DIANE DOLLINGER: My friend Wendy told me about the facts of life before she left for summer camp. We were both ten, and I was absolutely horrified. I said, what happens if you're doing it and you have to go to the bathroom? She said she didn't know but if you wanted a baby, you had to do it. And then we shook hands and she went to camp. And that was the last specific thing I ever heard.

JULIE SAXON: I remember when my girl friend first told me what French kissing was. I thought, That's *disgusting!*

DIANE DOLLINGER: You'd really have to be crazy—why would anyone go and do a thing like that!

MARJORIE HUGHES: I don't think my attitudes come from my friends. I'm still stuck with a fair share of double-standard residuals, and they come directly from my mother. But she had some help from the nuns, too, with patent leather shoes and all that! (*Laughter; several people talk simultaneously.*)

STEVE LAIRD: I know a lot of girls who went to Catholic school, and they had two favorite stories. One: They were instructed never under any circumstances to wear patent leather shoes because the boys could look at the shoes and see a reflection of what was under their dresses. (*Laughter.*) Second story: The girls were warned that if they were ever at a social function, they should never sit on a boy's lap unless they first got a telephone book and put it on his lap and then sat on top of the book!

BETSY LAIRD: In high school the nuns told us that when we took showers it was best to wear towels all the time, which we could not understand. How could you dry yourself with a towel that you wore under the shower?

DOUG HUGHES: I've had such a Catholic upbringing that I'm not happy unless I feel guilty in a lot of ways. (*Laughter.*) I remember that in the seventh grade we found a book in the library that described everything. We knew it all already, but it was reassuring to read it, actually written down in a library book. We had a kid in the neighborhood who didn't believe it, though. He said, "Ah, come on!" For months he just wouldn't accept it, and he had six brothers, too. "My mother?" (*More laughter.*) In high school—it was a Catholic high school —things were more relaxed. All the priests knew what was going on, and every now and then they told you that you were going to hell.

BILL MASTERS: How did that affect you?

DOUG HUGHES: For a long time I believed that the act of intercourse was dirty. My whole experience with it—not being married—meant being reminded that it was all dirty. And since I couldn't understand how it could be dirty only if it was out of marriage, I thought it was more or less dirty even when you *were* married.

BILL MASTERS: This is, unfortunately, an all-too-familiar story. I want to emphasize, however, *in the strongest possible terms,* that although we have been discussing orthodox Catholic influences, there are any number of similar myths, misconceptions and sexual taboos that have been perpetuated through Jewish and Protestant teachings. And for the occasional adolescent or teenager who is hypersensitive to the authoritative suggestion that "sex is sin," the long-range effect can be devastating. It can cripple the ability to function sexually as an adult. But let's get back to what you were saying, Doug. How much of the old attitude—that sex was dirty—would you say still persists in your thinking?

DOUG HUGHES: Very little—or none, really. (*Hesitating*) But can you ever be sure that you've got rid of all traces of what you used to believe? You might be unaware of your real feelings.

BILL MASTERS: For example?

DOUG HUGHES: Well, I was just thinking about something. When we were growing up, the most sinful thing wasn't intercourse. Not for a boy, anyway. What you really felt guilty about was masturbation. Now we know better, and if you asked us whether we think there's anything wrong with masturbating, we would all probably say no. But would we feel comfortable admitting that we masturbate occasionally? I doubt it; I wouldn't. So I think old feelings stick with us longer than we realize.

BILL MASTERS: Most married men masturbate at times. They don't do so with the same frequency that prevailed during their teens or during the years that preceded the establishment of a more or less regular coital pattern, whether in marriage or not. But there are circumstances when the male has a high incidence of return to masturbatory tendencies, even though he has a partner who theoretically is available. When she is not available, when husband and wife are physically separated, the function of masturbation seems clear enough. But there are other circumstances in which it serves a similar need. It is not uncommon, for example, for masturbation to be utilized during the wife's menstrual period, particularly if at this time either partner feels negatively predisposed to intercourse. Masturbation may be utilized during illness or the last stages of pregnancy or the first month or two after childbirth. And then there are occasions during the normal course of marital life when suddenly it just seems like a great idea to the male—or the female, for that matter. Obviously, the same principles should apply to the woman as to the man. And I know of no harm at all in this.

VIRGINIA JOHNSON: There is one other consideration I can think of, and it involves the stabilization and preservation of a valued partnership. Here is a way of satisfying extraneous sexual need without making excessive demands on the relationship. It enables a woman to cope with her tensions at a time when, because of special concerns, she feels she cannot involve her husband, or she chooses not to. Once she comes to terms with the fact that this does not take anything away from her marriage, it may help keep the relationship in balance. For a number of women this is not an infrequent experience.

BILL MASTERS: That's a good point. Fundamentally this kind of situation exists when a marital unit is not sexually dysfunctional but the partners have different sexual tension levels. This difference in levels is found in an incredible number of cases and is often balanced by masturbation, which permits the partner with the higher tension level to relieve that tension occasionally and ease up a bit. It may be the husband who needs relief; it may be the wife.

JULIE SAXON (*dubiously*): Do you think that's a healthy situation?

BILL MASTERS: Keep in mind that we are talking about occasional incidents. If we find an established masturbatory pattern of some significance, we then look into the relationship itself.

VIRGINIA JOHNSON: When we counsel husbands and wives who have serious problems, we introduce the concept of mutuality. This requires them to be sensitive to inevitable differences in their individual needs and to be willing to meet and satisfy those needs *together*. In the circumstances we have been describing, this means that the couple must accept the fact that their sexual desires and capacities are not always going to match perfectly.

JERRY DOLLINGER: Now, that's what I call a fact of life! (*Laughter.*)

VIRGINIA JOHNSON: Yes, and the important question is how a couple handles that particular fact. If at a given moment one partner's needs are on a slightly higher level, we would encourage him—or her—to ask for the other's cooperation so that together they can enjoy making it a mutual sexual experience without putting performance pressure on the partner who is not quite so turned on. This can be a rather happy solution, because it uses the very differences that might otherwise have come between two people to bring them together.

DOUG HUGHES: I would think that for some people this would be more difficult than just to have relations.

BILL MASTERS: Why?

DOUG HUGHES: Well, it goes back to what I was saying before. It's all right to play house when you're a kid, and it isn't too bad to play doctor. But God help you if you're caught playing with yourself! (*Laughter; several participants talk at once.*)

MARJORIE HUGHES: To this day there's still no lock on the bathroom door at your parents' house.

DOUG HUGHES (*grinning*): Nobody ever bothered explaining why, but I'm sure my older brother stayed in there too long one day so my father got rid of the lock. Anyway, it's hardly surprising that you feel guilty about doing anything like that. But it's different with intercourse—for boys, at least. And once you're married, you *know* it's all right to enjoy sex. Society gives you a license so you can do it whenever you want—even *before dark*. (*Laughter.*) But masturbation is still a no-no.

BILL MASTERS: Let's be clear about this. Many married men and women masturbate on occasion, for good reason and with no harm done. We discussed some of the circumstances—sickness, separation, impulse, what have you?—and I will add a medical reason. We know that many women will masturbate with the onset of their menstrual cycle if they are having dysmenorrhea—severe cramps. An orgasmic experience frequently will relieve the spasm of the uterus and the cramps will disappear. Many women learn this trick. Does it work for all? Of course not, but it helps some women and so they masturbate periodically, which seems sensible.

Now, when we suggest to couples who have different levels of sexual tension that the partner with the lower level can—and should—help the partner with the higher level to achieve release, we are not discussing masturbation per se. We are discussing sexual stimulation, the various modes by which one partner gives pleasure to the other. If either partner rejects the idea of providing or accepting release this way, we continue our in-depth interview until we find out, if possible, the basis of rejection. Then we try to negate that attitude.

In attempting to overcome any sense of rejection by either partner, our usual approach is to make a major issue of the naturalness of sexual functioning. This includes stressing the fact that sexual functioning is a total body response and that this response generally can be enhanced by *any* form of physical stimulation. We find that a significant percentage of individuals who object to a particular form of sexual play do so on the basis of preconceived ideas. These individuals are frequently intrigued by the concept but are concerned with how it will be received by the partner, or they may even be concerned with what other people might think. If they are given an adequate explanation of the naturalness of any form of sexual expression, by persons whom they accept as authorities, they feel they have what we call "authoritative permission" to indulge in the particular activity.

VIRGINIA JOHNSON: Very often we find that negative attitudes are based on myths or half truths or irrational notions carried over from childhood. In a surprising number of cases, all it takes to change those attitudes is for a minister or doctor, for example, or for an older, well-regarded person to say to the individual, "My wife and I have enjoyed doing this all our married life." And suddenly it becomes a perfectly acceptable practice, especially for young people.

Incidentally, I might add one point about the cooperation of partners with different sexual tension levels. Often the woman feels that it's completely all right for her to release her husband but she doesn't feel the same about the reverse situation. There may be any number of different reasons for such an attitude, but one of the commonest is that she is afraid such a request might undermine her husband. It might make him feel that he is inadequate, that he isn't capable of pleasing her. In fact, he himself may have communicated that idea to her. Here is another double-standard residual—

a reflection of the traditional view of the woman's role, with the culture assigning her the responsibility of meeting the man's needs.

STEVE LAIRD: And now Women's Lib says it's up to the man to meet the woman's needs—or else! (*He makes the gesture of cutting his throat.*)

BETSY LAIRD: Oh, Steve, don't exaggerate!

VIRGINIA JOHNSON: I'm afraid we don't have the time now to debate Women's Lib. But in passing I'd like to say that it seems unfortunate to lump everyone together under a single, catch-all label like "Women's Lib," when the fact is that there are different groups with different philosophies and different goals. Some are doing important work while others, I'm afraid, are just tilting at windmills.

But let's not lose track of the issue. According to the familiar double standard, the man was sexually active, the woman sexually passive. She served his needs. Today this master-servant kind of sexual exploitation is no longer acceptable, but the answer to the problem doesn't come from reversing roles. It's not either/or; it's neither/nor. In most marriages today the goal of both partners is to be neither master nor servant. But, of course, it's more easily said than done, because the sexual relationship is a subtle one, delicately constructed out of the needs and desires of two human beings who individually may not—probably do not—know fully what those needs and desires are. Their marriage is like a bridge from one to the other; somehow they can cross back and forth on it but they're not entirely sure just what is holding it up. And so if they arbitrarily decide to pull out one support and replace it with another, they may find the bridge in danger of collapsing.

To be more specific, let's suppose that the change they want to make in their relationship— the support they want to replace—concerns sexual initiative. Traditionally this was the male's privilege—to initiate or invite or suggest or request a physical response. This was his right because he was a man, and the exercise of that right proved he was a man. For the woman, naturally, it was the reverse. By exercising her right to respond or to refuse, she proved herself a woman.

Today we are in transition, and we'll assume that a young couple don't want to live in accord with that traditional standard. But can they make progress toward sexual equality without undermining the sexual relationship itself? In considering the problem I'll speak for the woman, which is all I'm entitled to do.

Suppose that a young woman has grown up, as so many still do, in a comparatively traditional climate. Her father, brother, boyfriends, teachers and, in another way, her mother, older sisters, aunts, all have unwittingly conspired to make her see herself as being most female when she is most responsive or receptive to the male sex. This is her chief frame of reference as a girl. In all her plans and dreams where boys are involved she sees herself as *being* pursued, *being* desired, *being* enjoyed. Diane, I see you shaking your head.

DIANE DOLLINGER (*flustered*): Oh, it's nothing! But—well, I was just thinking. I'm a pretty liberated woman; I don't remember ever having had any real sex hang-ups. Whatever I did, I enjoyed—more or less enjoyed. And whatever I enjoyed, I did. But what you just said is so true. As a girl I never felt it would become me to be physically aggressive toward a guy. If he wanted me, that was fine; and if he wanted me at the same time I wanted him, I would have to hope he could get the right cues from me.

VIRGINIA JOHNSON: The traditional outlook. And do you still see things that way?

DIANE DOLLINGER: No.

VIRGINIA JOHNSON: When did it change?

DIANE DOLLINGER: In my marriage I've learned to be much freer.

VIRGINIA JOHNSON: Did it happen as soon as you were married?

DIANE DOLLINGER: No, it took a little while. The change started before we were married. My husband is just that kind of man.

VIRGINIA JOHNSON: That's the point I was about to make. You see, if we take a girl with a basically traditional background, we can be almost certain that one of the things that turns her on is being pursued. The chase is delightful, and it has erotic value for her because being pursued intensifies her sense of herself as a *female person*. Both words count. She is happy with herself both as a female *and* as a person.

It would be pointless to tell this girl at this stage of her life that sexual equality gives her the right to take the initiative at times. Because the moment she tries, she probably will discover that when she is physically aggressive, the chase isn't the same exciting, self-confirming thing it used to be. On the contrary, it may even leave her feeling dissatisfied and unhappy with herself.

Now, this doesn't mean that she can't change and eventually be comfortable in a situation where she at least shares the initiative and where she participates more actively in a relationship with a man. She *can* learn and she *can* change. But she needs time to allow her deepest feelings to adjust to these new values, to make them part of her sexual value system.

She also needs to have the right man—or men—in her life at the time this is happening. After all, we're not talking about an intellectual abstraction. We're talking about flesh-and-blood human beings trying their best to work out their lives together as male and female. Here, by the way, the traditional female role helps the woman. Socially and culturally it is perfectly acceptable for her to be the pupil. So if she is fortunate enough to have the right man teaching her to take the initiative when the time and the circumstance and the mood seem favorable, she can be far more comfortable in the learning role than the man may be if the situation were reversed—if she were teaching him to accept her as an equal.

BILL MASTERS: From the male point of view, the problem is basically functional. If he is to perform at all, the situation must stimulate a spontaneous or voluntary physical response. This response is easily aborted, by fatigue, worries, fear, illness—you name it. Failure can result if the male perceives the female as threatening him, even if in fact she intends the opposite. She may, for example, take off her nightgown before getting into bed, a gesture she intends to be stimulating and flattering, letting him know that she would be happy to join him. But if he sees this as taking the sexual initiative, as making demands on him, he may feel threatened. He may then be unable to perform and, inevitably seeking an excuse, he will be furious with her for having taken what he sees as an aggressive step.

This is not an extreme example; it is a situation we encounter frequently in our clinical work. The man is taking a traditional double-standard attitude. A man with this philosophy is unlikely to take kindly to having his wife teach him other ways. In therapy, however, he can be introduced to new concepts. He may then perceive his wife's action quite differently, and he may account for himself very well indeed.

PHILIP SAXON: Don't you find this kind of thing truer of older people?

BILL MASTERS: Yes, pretty much as you'd expect. But you see it with surprising frequency among younger couples too—particularly after marriage. Marriage apparently does seem to change one's outlook. I don't say that it *should,* mind you—just that it does. When a man looks at a woman, that's one thing. When he looks at the same woman, who is now his wife, it's something else. If he's a latent double-standard man, you'll know it, all right.

JULIE SAXON: It's a silly example, but . . . Well, men are supposed to have all these sexual fantasies and women aren't. But I happen to fantasize everything. I conjure up passages from *The Story of O,* I run parts of movies through my mind—I guess I have the richest sexual-fantasy life, probably, on the face of the earth! (*Laughter.*) Which I happen to need but my husband thinks is wrong.

BILL MASTERS: Not at all.

VIRGINIA JOHNSON: Well, you mentioned earlier that you had all sorts of residuals of the double standard, attitudes that you had got from your peers. Fantasizing is simply your way of breaking that down.

PHILIP SAXON (*ruefully*): She's got a schedule that she refuses to reveal to me! She knows what's going to be playing every night. (*Laughter.*)

JULIE SAXON: I don't think that I have to tell him. I mean, it's *my* thing. I don't feel I should have to tell him what I've used. It's embarrassing.

BILL MASTERS: It shouldn't be.

JULIE SAXON: Well, it is. That's part of the residual.

VIRGINIA JOHNSON: I can certainly understand that. But I would enjoy hearing you say that on occasion you can put it aside, that you use it by choice, not necessity.

JULIE SAXON (*lightly*): I decide in advance whether I'm going to need it.

BILL MASTERS: All of us use fantasy, to a greater or lesser degree. It is a form of self-stimulation. It helps us move from where we are to where we want to be, when the occasion warrants. In that sense it is a bridge and can be very useful. We can see that if we apply it to what we've been discussing—guilt and the double standard. Julie's fantasies help her advance from the old double-standard thou-shalt-not morality to a single standard of permissibility.

In this respect, Julie symbolizes what is happening in society at large. Social changes are unquestionably altering the traditional sexual relationship between male and female. The female is achieving greater equality, although I suspect at a much slower rate than most young people think. Traditions that evolve over centuries do not disappear overnight. But if today's changes are to continue and become culturally entrenched, it is up to young people like you to incorporate these changes in your own marriage patterns.

VIRGINIA JOHNSON: As the woman seeks to become a more active partner she must understand and accept the nature of sexual response. Any woman who demands the right to her sexual climax the way she demands equal job rights is simply ignorant of sexual physiology. In achieving equality she must preserve those aspects of herself as a female that the male has learned to value—because his physiological response is dependent on them. This does not mean that she has to pretend or tease or manipulate or submit or play any of the thousand and one roles written for her in the past. Instead of playing parts she must be herself—the female self. And since sex is not a matter of one person but of two, she has to be the kind of woman who appeals to the man who appeals to her. She has to give, as he has to give, if together they are to get the pleasure from each other that they both seek.

BILL MASTERS: What the man must understand is that he has everything to gain. Until now he has been playing a stereotyped part too—whether he felt like it or not, he was supposed to be tough, unemotional, giving orders and assuming all responsibility. Well, if you translate those terms into the sexual relationship, they may—and often do—work against him. To some extent they can deprive him of enjoyment. They diminish his chances of experiencing the kind of total body response that intercourse offers. If he has never experienced it, of course, he doesn't know what he's missing. But once he does, he's jolly well likely to want it again. In the long run, the trend toward sexual equality should mean a great deal for both male and female. As she assumes a share of the responsibility for making something happen between them, her self-esteem should rise, and with that should come an intensified capacity for pleasure. And as the male is relieved of some of the pressure his pleasure too should be increased—and, within physiological limits, his performance as well!

MARJORIE HUGHES: Wouldn't you say, though, that some people expect too much of sex?

VIRGINIA JOHNSON: You mean that they expect every encounter to set off fireworks?

MARJORIE HUGHES: Well, yes, that sort of thing, too—but more than that. (*After a moment's hesitation*) Judging by some of the things I read these days, it seems to me that people are forgetting that there are other things in life besides sex and that if you want to have a happy marriage, it's just as important and maybe more important to do a good job of running your home and taking care of your children.

BILL MASTERS: I couldn't agree with you more that it's very important for any woman who chooses to be a full-time wife and mother to work hard at that and do the best job she can. What I do question, though, is why you seem to feel—at least, this is how it comes across to me—that sex is like recreation, something to enjoy if and when you have finished the work that must come first.

MARJORIE HUGHES (*with a smile*): More like dessert. (*Laughter.*)

VIRGINIA JOHNSON: The analogy with food is overused, perhaps, but it may be helpful here. Fruit is a good dessert, for example, but it also serves as an appetizer and as a soup—or as a salad for the main dish. And there is nothing better than eating fruit on the spur of the moment, just because you feel like it. What I'm saying, of course, is that sex should not be categorized, should not be made into a "thing" that is reserved for a specific occasion or a specific use. And having said that, I hope you'll put the dessert analogy aside and just keep in mind the point that Dr. Masters was making— there is a danger of letting everyday chores and responsibilities come between you as husband and wife, so that you are always postponing the pleasure of having each other's company because there is work to be done.

BILL MASTERS: It would probably amaze you to know how many husbands and wives become sexually dysfunctional as a result of the so-called work ethic.

PHILIP SAXON: Suppose a couple has the kind of problem they just can't settle themselves? Something . . . my friend, for example, tells me that he and his wife are having trouble. I don't know what kind of trouble, exactly, but he's let me know that he's not happy with their sex life. In fact, he knew we were coming here today and he asked me to ask you what he should do about it.

BILL MASTERS: First of all, *he* can't do anything about it. Neither can his wife. But *they* can. Let me make a few specific suggestions.

They can begin with a telephone directory. If they want medical consultation, the first step is to call the local medical society and ask for a referral. In some large cities there is a community medical society; if not, there will certainly be a county or state medical listing. Looking them up requires a little persistence, since the name may appear under the name of the city, county or state or be listed as the medical society of the city, county or state. The telephone listings might come under the medical society heading—Medical Society of Such-and-such or under the county heading: Such-and-such County Medical Society. These societies accept the responsibility of making appropriate referrals.

JERRY DOLLINGER: But what do you say on the phone —"*Help!*" (*Laughter.*)

BILL MASTERS: They can always begin by saying hello. (*More laughter.*) Then, if they are like most people, they will probably feel uncomfortable and find themselves groping for the right words. Well, they will find it much easier if they are simple and matter-of-fact. They might say something along these lines:

"We believe we're faced with a problem of sexual incompatibility. We would like to consult a physician about this matter. Are there any individual physicians in this area who have dealt with such problems in the past? If so, we would like a recommendation. If not, can you direct us to any other professional person who can be of assistance or who can put us in touch with a reliable authority?"

The medical society will refer the couple to someone who on the basis of his professional experience is considered capable of handling such matters. He may be a psychiatrist, an obstetrician, a gynecologist, generalist or urologist or he may come from some other field of medicine. Rarely will he be a specialist in the treatment of sexual dysfunction, because until now medical science has not developed this kind of training. The medical society referral will therefore be made on a pragmatic basis, selecting someone on the basis of his known interest and previous experience.

There is another way. Your friends may prefer to get a reference from their local family service organization—one can be found in cities and counties across the country—so that they can talk with a trained social worker. In general these counselors have had a great deal more clinical experience with marriage problems than the physician. They also are professionally knowledgeable about other specialists in the marital field—psychiatrists, psychologists and marriage counselors in private practice.

A third possibility is for them to ask their local priest, rabbi or minister. The clergyman himself may not be the person to do the counseling—some members of the clergy are trained to handle problems of sexual incompatibility, but most are not. But he has probably been asked for similar guidance before, and if he does not know who your friends should consult, he can certainly come up with suggestions by making inquiries of his own.

If your friends have no association with a church or synagogue, they might turn to their lawyer for a recommendation. He is bound by professional codes of confidentiality, so that they don't have to be concerned about local gossip, and he should have enough knowledge of the community to be able to evaluate its counseling resources.

Two general warnings: First, the single greatest mistake any distressed couple can make is to discuss their problem with friends or neighbors.

Second, no matter how difficult the search for help may be and despite the fact that even professional help is no guarantee that a couple's sexual problems can be resolved, the effort *should* be made. What are the choices, after all? Either to live out the years in a miserable marriage or to get a divorce—or to solve the problem and enjoy the pleasure, in bed and out, that the couple expected to have when they got married.

4

What Men Stand to Gain from Women's Liberation

DIANE DOLLINGER: As a girl I never felt it would become me to be physically aggressive toward a guy. If he wanted me, that was fine; and if he wanted me at the same time I wanted him, I would have to hope he could get the right cues from me. . . .

VIRGINIA JOHNSON: . . . Here is another double-standard residual—a reflection of the traditional view of the woman's role, with the culture assigning her the responsibility of meeting the man's needs. . . . Today we are in transition, and we'll assume that a young couple don't want to live in accord with that traditional standard. But can they make progress toward sexual equality without undermining the sexual relationship itself?

The increasing acceptance of American women as independent persons is an irreversible process. And the final outcome seems clear: women will join men as full partners.

This prospect evokes uneasiness and even anxiety in many people, women as well as men. Change is never more unsettling than when it raises questions about fundamental matters that have always been taken for granted. And few matters seem less open to question than the nature of sexual identity and the importance of differences between the sexes. Both women and men are thus understandably disturbed to find themselves confronted with the possibility that much of what they believe about the female sex may be inaccurate or untrue. The new outlook introduces a disconcerting and troubling element into their world.

Such alarm is groundless, based for the most part on confusion and misconceptions that need clarification. Not all aspects of the problem can be dealt with in this limited space, but several important considerations can be raised as a contribution to the dialogue now going on between women and men all over the world.

A primary and rather obvious distinction must first be made. The common basis on which men and women cooperate in society at large is not the same as the unique basis on which a specific couple coexist in private. The two worlds are separate realms of experience with radically different requirements for success —performance at work, fulfillment at home—and they involve different risks and rewards. For any woman determined to develop her independence beyond traditional lines, there is no possibility of weighing the consequences without taking into account whether the steps she takes will influence the life she leads in public or in private. The Liberation Movement possesses a different significance in each of these worlds. To overlook this distinction is to blur the meaning of the movement and to transform any discussion of the matter into a futile debate.

Both worlds, of course, do interact. A self-assured woman who works on a basis of equality with male colleagues, for example, is likely to find it easier to establish a personal relationship with a man based on mutual needs than if she were in the usual subordinate position at work, dominated by males. This highly complex crossover effect—from public to private life— deserves further careful study. All that can be noted now is that public attitudes influence private relationships.

Our intention here is to focus on the private relationship in an effort to trace some of the ways in which the equal rights movement may affect the intimate man-woman bond. For this, after all, is the crux of the matter. While feminism today is moving forward with all the fervor of a fad, for how long will women continue to pursue the principle of sex equality if it does not lead to emotional fulfillment in their private worlds? And fulfillment for the overwhelming majority of women requires an enduring relationship with a man.

Militant Women's Liberation advocates may deplore that fact, but a fact it remains. Marriage is now more popular than at any time in the nation's history. Two out of three Americans of marriageable age are married; more marriages were performed in 1970 than any year since the 1946 postwar boom; and the number of marriages continued to rise during the first nine months of 1971, the last period to be studied. These statistics alone refute those social observers who, with no sociological evidence to offer, have been prophesying the decline of marriage.

Furthermore the statistics do not reflect the full extent to which men and women choose to be united as couples, since living together without being legally wed seems an accelerating trend. All things considered, we have ample persuasive proof that the man-woman bond still plays a crucial role in the lives of individuals of both sexes—and appears likely to continue in importance in the future.

If some of the leaders of the women's movement make the strategic mistake of attacking marriage as part of a male plot to keep women under control, they will almost surely find themselves out of touch with most other women. Any attempt to persuade the average woman that she too has an important stake in the outcome of the present campaign to extend women's rights will fall on deaf ears if that campaign projects the concept that equality and independence are assets only for the unmarried and the childless.

Such a misconception is regrettable. The emancipation movement has much to contribute to society as a whole, but it cannot succeed without widespread support from the general public, men as well as women.

Before the feminists can hope to win over any substantial number of the opposite sex, however, they must first find ways to convince most members of their own. The nonconformist minority must be joined by the traditionalist majority.

But what have Liberation spokeswomen to say to a woman who dreams of having a husband, a home and a family? This woman wants to know what part, if any, sexual equality can play in helping her to find happiness in the world she shares with friends and family.

Her questions are simple, personal and practical. If she is single and acts with more self-reliance and initiative than most men are accustomed to, and she wants to be accepted as a person first and a female second, she may wonder whether her attractiveness will be diminished. If she selects a job not usually performed by a female, makes friends with men as naturally as with women, and accepts premarital sex as a healthy consequence of emotional commitment, will she jeopardize the future she desires?

Or if she is married and has as much to say as her husband in making decisions that concern them both, if she chooses to work or be of service in the community even though this takes her out of the house during the day, and if she makes it clear that she enjoys being an active partner in marital sex, she may worry about undermining her marriage.

There are good reasons to believe that such fears are groundless. By disregarding outdated social stereotypes and searching instead to discover what she can do and wants to do, a woman improves her chances of becoming a happier and more fulfilled person—and this improves her chances of achieving and maintaining a rewarding marriage.

This is a general principle, of course, and what happens in any given case can never be predicted. A woman can always make an unfortunate choice of partner, for example—although such an error of judgment is less likely if she respects herself as an individual in her own right. Secure in her identity as a female, she won't feel compelled to marry to prove that she is a woman; confident of her worth as a person, she won't be vulnerable to the man who needs to dominate a woman to prove his masculinity.

In seeking a partner to marry or to live with, she will be looking for her male counterpart: a man who rejects the sex stereotypes that prevail in society, who will accept her as his equal and will prize her individuality. With such a man she can avoid the trap in which so many wives are caught, where roles are assigned on the basis of sex alone, where both man and woman act on cue in standardized ways according to a script written centuries ago, no matter how awkward or compromised they may feel, and where, barred from the kind of sharing relationship that would extend their sense of themselves as individuals, they live out their lives locked side by side in separate cells labeled His and Hers.

Any woman who has the will and the courage to break out of the cell that historically has been considered appropriate for females, a cell comfortably padded with privileges, has something of tremendous value to offer a man—the key to his own prison door. For wherever equality of the sexes exists, and especially in the intimate world of marriage, liberation of the female liberates the male.

This can be seen with striking clarity in the sexual relationship. Traditionally sex has been something a man does to a woman. During a considerable period in history this arrangement served its purpose. It offered the man release from physical tension whenever he needed it so that he could concentrate on earning a living for himself and his family. And it resulted in pregnancy and children for the woman, which represented justification of her existence. Under these circumstances most husbands could perform adequately because nothing was required beyond a brief coupling. They themselves were led to expect little pleasure from marital sex; and their wives, none at all.

Attitudes began changing in this century in response to complex social and cultural influences. Men —and, to a lesser degree, women—began hoping to achieve sexual gratification in the marriage bed. Since they still adhered to the old active-male/passive-female philosophy, however, a woman could not cooperate sexually without compromising her standing as a respectable woman, in her husband's eyes as well as her own. And because she could not contribute her own sexual feelings, success depended entirely upon the man.

Over the years, pressures on him increased. At first he was expected only to be gentle and considerate; then, to make his wife feel loved and desired; next, to assure her of an orgasm, possibly simultaneous with his own; and finally, to trigger a whole series of orgasms. It is only fair to point out that these were not female ultimatums. Most of them, in fact, were articulated by male writers—novelists, psychotherapists, sexologists and the like—whose recommendations often depended more on imagination than on research and were influenced more by prevailing cultural beliefs than by secure, scientific knowledge. They envisioned the sexual function less as an authentic expression of a total relationship than as a personal achievement test with specific performance goals.

Their unrealistic sex-performance standards, which filtered into the expectations of many men and women confused by shifting ethical and moral codes, were still based on the insidious notion that sex is the mark of the man. This lopsided approach to the sexual relationship persisted through the 1940s, fifties and even the sixties, despite the fact that more and more young women were rejecting the double standard, accepting—and even initiating—premarital sex.

Sex with affection was their byword, and they saw it as part of an exchange. If they could learn to be more open, more flexible and more encouraging, they would then be rewarded with male performances guaranteed to deliver ecstasy. They did not realize that this attitude was simply a new variation on the old theme of active-male/passive-female; they didn't understand what it meant to be a full and equal partner.

In that sense they are no more liberated than their mothers, and today's young men are under greater pressure than ever before. In the past, men at least had escape hatches. Inexperienced females had a limited ability to respond, were further inhibited by fear of pregnancy and settled, not ungratefully, for warmth and tenderness in place of passion. But once morality and birth-control methods evolve to a point where the woman feels free to grant herself permission to enjoy sexual relations, she turns to a particular man to make good on the promise made in his name by the male sex in general—to deliver pleasure on demand. What acceptable excuse can he offer if he cannot produce the promised delight? Whom can he blame but himself?

Thus sex often looms like Mount Everest before many a man—he is expected to reach the peak, pulling his partner up with him, and, if he is married, to do so with regularity. If intercourse does not proceed according to plan most of the time—if it does not reach the five-minute mark, for example, or does not include the programmed orgasm—a man may come to believe that he is sexually incompetent. No wonder some husbands, unwilling to make the effort or to risk being considered sexually inadequate or perhaps impotent, retreat behind the defense of indifference.

What a great many men and women must learn is that they cannot achieve the pleasure they both want until they realize that the most effective sex is not something a man does to or for a woman but something a man and woman do together *as equals*.

This deceptively simple truth points to one of the most valuable contributions a woman can make to a man's ability to function effectively, from which she, of course, benefits. The sexually liberated woman learns, among other things, the importance of being free, as men have always been free, to express openly the full range of her sexual excitement and involvement —the delight of wanting and being wanted, touching and being touched, seeing and being seen, hearing words and uttering them, of fragrances and textures, silences and sounds. Her spontaneous feelings, spontaneously communicated, stimulate her partner and heighten his tensions, impelling him to act on his own impulses.

Whatever she gives him returns to her and whatever he gives her comes back to him.

More than half the pleasure of the sexual experience depends on a partner's response. If there is virtually no reaction at all, or at best passive acceptance, the emotional current steadily weakens and eventually flickers and goes dead. In too many marriages the wife may never say no but never really say yes—and then is puzzled later in life that when she goes to bed, her husband stays up to watch television.

But even saying yes—and meaning it—is not the answer. Active participation does not consist of merely initiating matters which the man is then expected to complete. The woman who wholeheartedly commits herself as an equal in the sexual union is involved in continuous response to her husband's changing needs and desires, as he is involved in hers. Like him, she values freshness and variety and from time to time willingly experiments with the many modes of arousal as an expression of her personality and mood of the moment, not as an artificial contrivance to resuscitate flagging desire.

The responsiveness of both partners is based on their mutual acceptance as vulnerable human beings with unique needs, expectations and capabilities. The wife does not assume that her husband wants what all men are supposed to want. Sensitive to what he says or reveals without words, she responds to his actual feelings at a specific moment—and she counts on him to do the same for her. Emotional needs, which vary with the mood, time and place, are not labeled "masculine" and "feminine." If he enjoys it when she manifests a strong sexual urge, that is fine; and if—as inevitably happens at times—their needs are not complementary, they will gently make their way to the best solution they can negotiate, not as representatives of two different sexes but as two separate partners united by a mutual concern.

Together they succeed or together they fail in the sexual encounter, sharing the responsibility for failure, whether it is reflected in his performance or hers. While conclusive proof is still lacking, there are firm grounds for believing that the female who esteems herself as something more than a collector's item, who has a positive appreciation of her biological nature and enters into sex as a free and equal partner—and who is as responsive to her partner's needs as she wants him to be to hers—will do more to eliminate male fears of functional failure than all the therapy in the world.

But a woman cannot be sexually emancipated without first becoming personally emancipated. If she is nothing to herself, she has nothing to give to anyone. For such a woman, to give herself to a man is to give him nothing, and so she expects nothing in return. Sexually she receives him and perhaps considers herself useful, as an object is useful.

The more she sees in herself and values herself as a person, however, the more able she is to establish an equitable relationship with a man. Thus before any woman can play a constructive role in a man's life as an equal, before she can join him as a partner, contribute to his sexual pleasure and, by sharing it, relieve him of some of the performance pressures placed on him by society, she must have a strong sense of who she is and what she can do and of her worth as a human being. She must have pride in herself as an individual who happens to be, and is happy to be, a woman.

She cannot achieve this goal by wishful thinking or her own solitary efforts; she does not exist in a cultural vacuum. In her earliest years her personal integrity is best served if it is safeguarded by those closest to her— parents, relatives, teachers, friends—and if somewhere, somehow, the outside world permits her to glimpse examples of what she can become, if she chooses to make the effort. The very society that currently tries to bribe her with special privileges to accept subordinate status also offers her a chance, no matter how small, to struggle toward independence and equality.

This is no less true outside the realm of sex. An interesting example of how husbands who accept their wives as equals gain from being united in a mutual effort can be found, surprisingly enough, in the trucking industry. On long-distance hauls, where the drivers must operate in pairs so that one can spell the other at the steering wheel, a small but growing number of husbands and wives have been teaming up. Less than ten years ago the idea would have been inconceivable. For it to be happening today in an industry generally regarded as a stronghold of male chauvinism is striking evidence that the principle of equality of the sexes is spreading more rapidly than is generally realized.

The advantages of such a joint venture—to the couple as a pair, to the husband as a man and the wife as a woman—seem transparently clear. By sharing the driving they reject the old, stereotyped division of labor into "a man's job" and "woman's work." Since both receive salaries, they reject the traditional view that only the man should be the provider. The husband, secure as a male, accepts his wife's cooperation in carrying a burden that, as life-insurance statistics make shockingly plain, literally has cost other men their lives. Thus not only can a couple like this enjoy being together —they also can enjoy being together longer.

The wife, no less female for driving a truck, gains the security of a closer relationship with her husband, strengthened by sharing responsibilities and sharing experiences. Knowing that she is respected for what she can do, valued for what she contributes, and appreciated for the woman she is, her sense of her self cannot help flourishing.

She may never have heard of the Women's Liberation Movement, but she exemplifies it. And if an image is needed to characterize the relationship between husband and wife today, perhaps it can be found here: co-drivers of a vehicle taking both to the same destination, each trusting the other to help steer in the direction they want to go, traveling together because they do not want to be apart.

This is the significance of the Liberation Movement today. For in the past it was only the most exceptional women in the most exceptional of circumstances who could transcend the rigid limitations placed on their sex. Today, and certainly tomorrow, that opportunity must be available to women with less privileged backgrounds—and this can happen only if the social structure itself is changed so that discrimination is not enforced by law and only if public opinion and private attitudes can be changed so that discrimination is not perpetuated by a "gentleman's agreement." These are the obstacles which women in the vanguard of the struggle for equality must concentrate on eliminating.

This struggle, which is echoed in discussions and arguments in homes all over the country, is too often conceived in terms of a misleading image: two on a seesaw. Power is the pivot, and if one sex goes up, the other must come down. What women gain, men lose.

But the sexual relationship itself shows the analogy to be false. What a man and a woman achieve together benefits both—the very quality of life, *as it is individually experienced*, can be immeasurably augmented by a fully shared partnership.

5

Why "Working" at Sex Won't Work

MARJORIE HUGHES: Judging by some of the things I read these days, it seems to me that people are forgetting that there are other things in life besides sex and that if you want to have a happy marriage, it's just as important and maybe more important to do a good job of running your home and taking care of your children.

BILL MASTERS: . . . Why [do] you seem to feel—at least that is how it come across to me—that sex is like recreation, something to enjoy if and when you have finished the work that must come first?

A young couple go away for a vacation, leaving their children with the wife's parents. Although neither one has said a word to the other, both husband and wife hope that having some time to themselves will be all they need to overcome the sexual dissatisfaction that has arisen between them. She has been achieving orgasm less and less frequently, and he has been troubled by a diminished physical drive.

To their delight, the vacation proves a complete success. Their problems fade away and they find themselves responding to each other with an intensity that both had secretly feared they had lost forever. When they talk about it, they agree that the explanation is obvious: because the children aren't around to interfere, because he isn't distracted by business matters and she isn't fatigued by household tasks, they have the time and energy they need to enjoy themselves physically.

Many American couples look forward to vacations for this very reason, and become resigned to the fact that when they return home, the distractions and obligations of daily life will resume and take their inevitable toll on sexual pleasure. What they do not realize is that they are accepting without question the principle that *being productive is always more important than being pleasured, that work comes before play.* This assumption has its roots in the old Calvinist philosophy which took hold in this country during colonial days. The Calvinists preached that work redeemed the believer, but that indulging in pleasure, especially the pleasures of the flesh, brought eternal damnation. Work as virtue and play as sin proved to be an intimidating and tenacious doctrine, even for people who were not Calvinists. It may be hard to believe that any vestige of such a joyless outlook could persist today, three hundred years later in our affluent, leisure-oriented society. But old attitudes and myths die hard, especially where sex is concerned. Often they may seem to disappear, only to turn up again in a different guise.

This can be seen in the influence of the work ethic on sexual attitudes in contemporary Western society. On the surface, considerable change has taken place—many people are increasingly reluctant to make a job all there is to life and more willing to accept sexual pleasure as part of their birthright. But for many others, there has been no change or else the apparent change is illusory. In the first case, a person still assigns the highest priority to work and the lowest to sex. In the second intricate case, a person may assign sex a high priority only to approach intercourse as though it, too, were a performance task to be mastered and measured—an ironic and unfortunate reapplication of work-ethic standards.

Individuals cannot be neatly categorized, of

course, and most people live with overlapping—and even contradictory—beliefs and attitudes. But it may clarify matters to briefly examine a few more or less typical examples of the various ways in which some men and women today attempt to synthesize their sexual feelings and their attitudes toward work.

The traditionalist stands at one extreme. To him, work means redemption and anything else is wasteful, if not immoral. Sex is for procreation, not pleasure. A man and woman who share this philosophy, fortified by their religious convictions, ought not be seen as caricatures. Measured by their own values, they can and often do live full, rich lives.

The situation is not the same for couples less totally committed to religious principles. When they assign the highest priority to work and the lowest to sex, they do so for materialistic reasons. In effect they turn the work ethic upside down. They do not work in order to live. They live in order to work. They are the husbands and wives who search endlessly for ways to occupy their time and use their energies profitably: making more money, advancing in a career, improving homes, accumulating possessions, engaging in community affairs—in short, doing anything that feels like work, which affords them the only justification they can accept for their lives.

A sexual relationship has little chance of flourishing between a wife to whom polishing the floor takes priority over sitting in the room and talking, and the husband who busies himself polishing the car instead of driving off with his wife for a quiet hour together. Such a couple, of course, may be hiding behind work to avoid confronting their sexual problems. (The husband who spends as much time as he can at the office and the wife who is "too tired" to have sex at night are all-too-familiar figures in American life.) But it is also likely that the couple may honestly be unaware that simply talking and being together could have any bearing on sexual pleasure. They may just think of sex itself as a job to be done, at the appropriate time and place.

Such an outlook is basically antisexual. The husband and wife cannot be comfortable with their sexual natures and are too insecure to permit free expression of sexual feelings. When coitus takes place, they prefer it in silence and the less emotional involvement, the better. If, deprived of emotional sustenance, the sexual impulse eventually withers and dies, either partner or both may secretly feel a sense of relief.

For other couples another pattern of sexual deprivation develops—not from antisexual attitudes, but from misuse of the principle of self-discipline. This is the most insidious element carried over from the work ethic to the sexual relationship. The mood of the individual is expected to be subordinate to the task at hand. It could hardly be otherwise. How many people, for example, wake up happy and eager to start the day's work? Except for those who are fortunate enough to be doing what they really want to do, men and women must disregard their feelings about the tasks at hand to get them done well and efficiently. This is as true for the woman in her home as it is for a woman or man in a factory or an office.

Such self-discipline takes its toll. Let a man at the office keep his emotions under tight rein eight hours a day while he concentrates on getting his work done, let a woman at home do the same for twelve hours a day—or far longer if she has an outside job as well— and the transition to becoming an individual who acts according to spontaneous and authentic feelings becomes difficult. For some persons it becomes impossible.

Even under the best circumstances, however, the work-ethic principle of self-discipline exerts an undesirable influence on sexual response. If nothing else, it exists as a force to be overcome; some effort is required by a man or woman seeking to regain freedom of sexual expression. A husband, for example, wanders into the kitchen, moved by an unexpected wish to touch his wife. He hugs her from behind, as she stands at the sink; she smiles perfunctorily and tells him that dinner will be ready in twenty minutes; and he nods and returns to the television set. Neither partner may be particularly disappointed by the sequence of events because neither one realizes that both of them are creatures of habit who have unwittingly arranged their intimate emotional life to conform to patterns established by impersonal on-the-job conditioning.

For them to have behaved otherwise in the kitchen, to have enjoyed a moment's pleasure even though it might interfere with the task at hand, would have required making a conscious effort to alter the habits of a lifetime. The wife would have had to stop herself from reacting as though her husband was just getting in her way, that he was expressing sexual affection in the wrong place and at the wrong time. And her husband would have had to summon his own convictions so that if his wife failed to respond to his touch, he could gently but firmly remind her without words that a loving gesture has its own priority.

Such a change in conventional attitude is not easy to accomplish. It is most difficult for those individuals who have not been privileged to learn, as they grew up, that sexual feelings in their fullest expression deserve to be protected in a kind of sacrosanct domain. Even in a disciplined scheme of living, with a husband and wife who by nature and upbringing need always to be efficiently organized, it is possible to include protected time to be alone together—not necessarily in order to engage in intercourse but simply in order to have the freedom to respond as man and woman in a natural, unpressured and unscheduled way.

For couples who do not honor their own sexuality, the capability to interact freely is never developed because it is not valued. Being alone together doing nothing is precisely that: doing nothing. They feel they are wasting time.

For men and women who do not accept and value their sexuality, however, the problem lies in understanding that the very part of themselves that they must discipline for purposes of work—their true emotions at any given moment—is the part that needs to be free of discipline if their sexual relationship is to flourish. It is striking to note that during vacations, the one time when it is socially approved for people to do what they feel like doing at the moment they feel like doing it, nonorgasmic women frequently become orgasmic and minimally functional men are frequently revitalized.

This was the case with the young couple mentioned earlier, who went off on vacation without their children. The absence of daily worries and intrusions will surely contribute to the resurgence of sexual vigor —but beyond that is the fact that when a husband and wife are vacationing, they feel free of the presumed cultural requirement to discipline their feelings. The impulse to touch, for example, can be immediately translated into touching; the wish to talk becomes a conversation that can take its own time wandering where it will; being silent and lying side by side is experienced as an intimate unity. All this and more can be profoundly sexual.

Husbands and wives who fail to gain this insight, who persist in the belief that sex should be scheduled for a specified time and place and that physical desire, like the capacity to work, is subject to will power, run the very real risk of returning home after a fulfilling vacation only to find themselves sexually unresponsive again.

In sharp contrast to individuals who use the work ethic either to avoid sex or devalue it, are those men and women who place a high value on sex but unwittingly approach it with a work perspective. Sex, like work, becomes for them a matter of performance. They always have a goal in view: ejaculation for the man, orgasm for the woman. In their view, sex is a purposeful activity and intercourse is its objective. If this goal is accomplished, the job has been satisfactorily handled.

Such an outlook logically enough includes an emphasis on quantity of achievement as a measurement of quality. If the man performs skillfully enough, for example, the woman may have several orgasms— and as they see it, two or three are obviously superior to one. If the woman performs skillfully enough, the man may be stimulated to respond several times in one night.

Sex for them is not a way of being, a way of expressing the mood of the moment, a way of nourishing a continuing emotional commitment. It is always a single incident. Goal-oriented sex concentrates on this moment and this act. It demands gratification now, and gratification is returned only through attainment of specific sexual goals.

Goal-oriented sex is usually self-defeating. As the result of a constant demand for performance, which can blot out emotional appreciation of what is actually happening, sex interest is soon lost. At first there may be extraordinarily intense excitement of the senses. But a steady decline in sensual responsiveness is all but inevitable, because the power to evoke excitement by purely physical, tactile stimulation is subject to the law of diminishing returns.

The first time a hand touches a body, the sensation may be explosive—nourished by expectations of what is to happen. By the tenth or twentieth time, however, if the expectations have not been fulfilled, the hand will probably be just a familiar physical presence with a considerably diminished capacity to evoke the desired response. And by the fiftieth time, even a demanding touch may have no positive effect whatsoever. It may even evoke aversion.

But place that touch in the context of an emotional climate in which two persons are together simply because they enjoy being together, arrange the time and circumstances to permit them to express the feelings of a man and woman who, as caring human beings, kindle sexual pleasure in each other quite apart from the act of intercourse; and then a hand's caress results in more than just tactile stimulation. Then touch acquires emotional meaning.

Sex in a warm, emotionally committed relationship may change in character and sexual response may become diffused after a while. It may not always reach the peaks of excitement that are sometimes experienced by a man and woman in their early, experimental encounters. But other dimensions of sexual pleasure may be discovered—the familiarity that is comforting, the safety that allows complete vulnerability, and the deep-

ening sense of emotional intimacy, among other pleasures. In contrast, the peaks that occur in goal-oriented
sex decline steadily thereafter—to be achieved again,
if at all, with a new partner, and then another.

This observation should not be interpreted as a
condemnation of goal-oriented sex, if that happens to
be all an individual desires, finds available or is capable
of achieving. *Sex as a goal-oriented performance is the
usual substitute when sex with emotional commitment
either fails to develop or is deliberately avoided.* How
many people succeed in the quest for a relationship
of mutually shared emotional involvement, married or
not? For marriage does not automatically make the
difference. On the contrary, in too many marriages sex
is goal-oriented, a one-dimensional demand for momen-
tary gratification. This is one of the reasons so many
couples complain of sexual boredom. Like workers on
an assembly line, they go through routine motions and
produce predictable results. They are following directions, not expressing feelings.

They want to know, for example, how many times
a week they should have intercourse. If everybody else
has it three times a week, then they should have it
three times a week. Three times is right and proper;
anything less means that something must be wrong with
them—and anything more means that something quite
different is wrong with them.

Numbers are useful to them in still another way.
If one partner has a lower level of sexual desire, numbers are a convenient way to limit the other partner's
demands. "How much do I have to do?" these individuals are asking. It is, of course, the work ethic all
over again.

Boredom also results from what might be called,
and with some justice, specialization of labor in the
bedroom. This, in effect, is the consequence of stereo-
typing sex roles. Each partner handles his or her particular responsibility. The husband, for instance, is
expected to initiate sex because both he and his wife
believe that is the man's "job." Thus the sequence of
events becomes completely routine and the sexual re-

lationship sooner or later becomes perfunctory—and then objectionable.

The solution for avoiding such a deterioration might seem to some people to be obvious: have the wife take the sexual initiative with equal frequency. Such a solution, however, is a perfect example of the work ethic in action. Directing the wife to take the initiative in a certain percentage of their sexual encounters merely reinforces the notion that sex, like work, can be improved by an improved technique. If only she learns to perform more tricks, or her husband learns more tricks, or if there is a "proper" assignment of sexual activities—and, most important, if they get better instructions and practice hard—everything will be fine.

This simply is not true. No formula answer is possible. Each partner must feel free to discover his or her unique way of expressing wishes, desires and needs as they occur, spontaneously and naturally, never by assignment on the basis of being male or female, never by the numbers according to a book.

It is often said that couples have to work at making a success of marriage. The term seems unfortunate, particularly in relation to sex. If there is one thing they should not do, it is to work at the relationship as though it were some kind of task. Yet this is the burden of the message carried by a discouraging number of books on the subject. In fact, two sociologists of the State University of New York at Buffalo, Lionel S. Lewis and Dennis Brissett, at the conclusion of a critical analysis of books that advise couples on ways to improve their sexual lives, noted that "sexual play in marriage has indeed been permeated with dimensions of a work ethic. The play of marital sex is presented by the counselors quite definitely as work."

More often than not, these books do a disservice to troubled couples. Husbands and wives seeking greater sexual happiness need less, not more, emotional discipline; less, not more, deliberate direction of their efforts. If they have anything to discover, it concerns themselves as unique individuals and the privileges and responsibilities of their relationship. They have to learn to trust each other fully and to be vulnerable, one to the other, and to let their feelings unfold in their own way at their own time. They must learn to communicate, not simply with words, but also with a touch or a glance that needs no explanation.

Above all, a man and woman must learn to be present to each other—not just to look, but to see; not just to hear, but to listen; not just to talk, but to commune.

TWO

VARIATIONS ON THE MARRIAGE THEME

6

Extramarital Sex
Who Gambles—and Why?

In April, 1972, five women and three men met in New York to discuss their extramarital relationships. Justin, twenty-seven, was the personnel director for a large company with its main office in Connecticut. His wife did not know, as far as he was aware, of his affairs. Leah, who was in her early thirties and the mother of two children, had let her husband know of her affairs. She had what she called "a drinking problem" but felt that it was now under control. Celia, twenty-five, was the mother of a little girl; shortly after this symposium was completed, she filed for divorce. Oliver, who was in his late thirties, had been brought up as a strict Catholic. He was the sales director for a chain of department stores. Jessica, married for twenty-three years, was a part-time golf instructor. Alec, forty years old, had been married for eighteen years and had two teenaged children. He was a certified public accountant. Dagny admitted to being "about forty," was married to a literary agent and had two volumes of poetry published. Naomi, not yet forty, was married to a television producer. They had no children and Naomi, a photographer, traveled extensively for several months each year.

BILL MASTERS: We would like to begin by having each of you tell us about your premarital experience and then about your first extramarital affair. Justin?

JUSTIN: Well, I had substantial premarital experience. And when I felt I was ready—sexually—to get married, I did.

BILL MASTERS: How old were you when you had your first sexual experience?

JUSTIN: Fifteen.

BILL MASTERS: And when you got married?

JUSTIN: Twenty-three.

BILL MASTERS: During those years before marriage, did you have an active sex life?

JUSTIN: Sort of, between fifteen and seventeen. But from seventeen to twenty-three, I had one sustained relationship.

BILL MASTERS: What happened after your marriage?

JUSTIN: I didn't immediately go outside my marriage. I had thought, as the saying goes, that I had sown all my wild oats. But after about six months I found myself becoming more and more involved with other women. In my type of business—I'm in the employment business—I interview people constantly, and they'll reveal their secrets and inhibitions to me because I have a way of putting them at their ease. And I become very involved with them. I can get a genuine affection for an individual very easily and very quickly.

BILL MASTERS: Do you use your profession as a source of sexual opportunity?

JUSTIN: I'm afraid so. (*Smiling*) It's kind of a fringe benefit.

BILL MASTERS: The first time that you moved outside your marriage, were you concerned at all?

JUSTIN: What do you mean, "concerned"?

BILL MASTERS: Were you concerned that it might affect your marriage?

JUSTIN: Not at all.

BILL MASTERS: Were you filling a need that was not

met in your marriage or was it just something apart, a separate capsule?

JUSTIN: Something apart. To this day I still feel nothing lacking in my marriage sexually. But I guess you could say I am very egotistical or that I have to prove something to myself continuously.

BILL MASTERS: One last question. How long have you been married?

JUSTIN: Three years.

VIRGINIA JOHNSON: Leah, what can you tell us about yourself?

LEAH: I think I'm a chronically distressed individual. (*She hesitates*) I had a very bad experience when I was about ten years old. I was sexually molested.

BILL MASTERS: By a member of the family or a stranger?

LEAH: A stranger. I was actually abducted in a car and sexually abused. I remember having nightmares about it for many years. (*She shakes her head*) At sixteen I met a boy and fell madly in love and became pregnant, and the boy was forced to marry me.

BILL MASTERS: Who did the forcing?

LEAH: My mother. My father wasn't told about it until afterward. Before I became pregnant, everything was fine, and I thought I loved him and he loved me. After I had the child, though, it was terrible because I was totally rejected. The marriage lasted two years—he was in the army, so we weren't together very often—and we had it annulled when I was nineteen. I stayed with my family until I was twenty-three, and then I remarried.

Looking back, I realize that when I married my second husband I felt desperate. I wanted marriage very much because it meant a certain amount of freedom. And now that we've been married ten years, I find myself in the same predicament—I still want freedom very much.

BILL MASTERS: How long after this second marriage did you look for someone else on the outside?

LEAH: After seven years. I've had two affairs in the last three years.

BILL MASTERS: Does your husband know?

LEAH: I told him about the last affair two weeks after it started. But my husband still loves me and still wants the marriage to work. I have to add that I have never achieved sexual climax. I have a sex drive that my husband feels is definitely based on the fact that I have never achieved climax—it's what drives me on. At least, I think so now. I didn't before. I've been through psychiatrists, Alcoholics Anonymous, quite a bit of things. But I never thought until the last year or so that my problem might be sex.

I've lost a good job because of my affair. I made it very blatant, and now I can see I was asking to be caught. So here I am at thirty-three, and I really don't know where to go or what to do. Because I know what I'm doing is not right for me or for anyone involved with me.

VIRGINIA JOHNSON: When you say you wanted to be free—do you have any sense of what you want to be free of?

LEAH: Well, I've always felt pressured; I was an only child. And I have two children now, and a great deal of responsibility. I've always felt I had a lot of responsibility and I've always fought it—I'm no martyr. I've done what I've wanted to do, but with a certain amount of guilt.

VIRGINIA JOHNSON: And with a price.

LEAH: I'm willing to pay it. My cliché is: you play, you pay.

BILL MASTERS: What decided you to play? What were you looking for?

LEAH: Initially I wanted some kind of freedom—or maybe I was just reacting as I always did under pressure, objecting to having responsibilities. In many ways I think I am still the naughty little spoiled child, and I was doing something you're not supposed to do.

BILL MASTERS: Did you think that in further sexual experience you might find this release you're talking about?

LEAH: Not really.

VIRGINIA JOHNSON: Is it just that having the experience represents a certain freedom?

LEAH: I think so.

BILL MASTERS: What triggered your first extramarital affair? Can you tell us what started it?

LEAH: It was built-up frustration, year after year. A while ago I found a letter I had written my husband, who likes to talk about the tides of life rising and falling, and I had written that if we couldn't work out our problems, I was going to sink because I just couldn't go on treading water. I just cannot stand still in a relationship; I have to go out and meet the waves. I like my husband very much but I don't have the feeling a woman should have toward a man. Even when a relationship lasts a long time, there must be some spark, *something* that ignites it.

I know I'm attracted to a certain type of man who is nothing like my husband. Why did I marry him, then? I think I pleased everybody by marrying the person I did. I know I finally pleased my parents. But I'm pleasing myself with this other person. I know his shortcomings but it's worth it.

BILL MASTERS: In what way is it worth it?

LEAH: It gives you a sense of freedom because there are no restrictions and no responsibilities. It's definitely a trip into fantasy-land.

VIRGINIA JOHNSON: What do you draw from the relationship that is important to you?

LEAH: I feel much more a woman. It makes me more of a total person in my own eyes.

VIRGINIA JOHNSON: Can you take this back with you into your marriage?

LEAH: No, I can't. (*She sighs*) I've heard that having

an affair will make a marriage better, that it will
do something for you, that it will give you a glow
or a new insight into your problems. But for me
it's like living a double life.

Virginia Johnson comments: It has been said before but seems worth repeating that it would be pre-
sumptuous for Dr. Masters or myself to interpret in a
clinical way any of the remarks made by the men
and women who participated in these symposia. They
did not come to be interrogated or analyzed, and our
knowledge of the personal details of their private lives
is too limited to permit even tentative evaluations of
their behavior. But to a considerable extent their comments are familiar; they echo remarks made by other
men and women who have come to St. Louis for help,
and on this basis some observations can be offered.

Leah, for example, is like other women who come
of age belatedly. Ironically, such women often seem
quite grown-up as children. The fact is, however, that
they have simply learned how to behave in a way that
pleases adults and they are grown-up more in appearance than reality. They do what is expected of them
—but their behavior is usually no reflection of how
they really feel. They may not even know how they
feel, so well-trained are they to do what is required.

This pattern is found among boys as well as girls
but culturally it is more characteristic of the female,
because she is taught to be "good," which means being obedient, cooperative and reasonable. This kind of
upbringing deprives children of the opportunity to explore their own attitudes and ideas, to forge a sense
of personal identification by trying alternative ways of
behavior and discovering which of those ways feels
better, produces better results, and in the end leads
more frequently to satisfaction.

On these terms, Leah never had a chance to find
out who she really was. Even if there had not been
the trauma of being molested as a child, her inability
to experiment as she grew up—because of her concentration on pleasing her parents—would have limited

her sexual development. This was compounded by her mother, who, in time-honored fashion, let her daughter know that female sexuality was a secret, if not a shameful, matter to be discussed among women but concealed from men—a lesson implicitly conveyed by the mother's collusion with her daughter to keep Leah's father from knowing that she was pregnant.

Consequently women like Leah grow up believing that sex is something not to be spoken about openly, if at all, and certainly not to men. Even in marriage these women remain tongue-tied when the subject of sex arises and they have no way of communicating with their husbands. Not that sex has to be expressed verbally—on the contrary, to a considerable degree it is far better to have these nuances exchanged without having to resort to lengthy conversations on the subject. Nevertheless, if a woman feels that all her sexual desires or disappointments cannot or should not be shared with her husband, whom she does not expect to understand her feelings, there is almost no way for the two of them to overcome obstacles in the path of sexual satisfaction.

Leah is looking for freedom but the freedom is not simply to enjoy extramarital sexual affairs. The affairs are a symptom of a deeper need to learn who she is—not just a wife, not just a mother, but, in her own terms, the "total person" that she feels herself capable of becoming. All too often such women believe that their affairs are merely a search for the sexual gratification that they are not experiencing in their marriages. In this sense, they too are victims of the idea that sex and sexual intercourse is a separate function of the total human being, quite apart from the rest of their existence. They act as though the analogy of sex and food is meant to be taken literally: if there is nothing to eat at home, they can go out to find a restaurant that will satisfy their hunger.

It is a regrettable confusion because, despite the legitimate ways in which the sexual appetite can be compared to hunger, sexual satisfaction depends in the final analysis on more than the mere availability of a physical partner. This is even more true for women than men—again, for cultural reasons—because they have been taught to be more sensitive to circumstances, to be more responsive to subtleties of emotion, and to require more of a partner than just his physical presence, if they are to experience the pleasure they rightfully seek.

One further point is worth making: if Leah understood that what she really is trying to do is to find herself, she might succeed in using her affair in a more constructive way. If, with her lover, she could learn how to establish a satisfying relationship, one that gave her a sense of personal fulfillment, and if a sense of guilt did not prevent her from bringing that new awareness with her back into the marriage, she could try to get her husband to join her in creating a comparable sense of pleasure in their emotional and sexual lives. Failing in that, she might then have the courage to divorce him. Either way, she would be constructively utilizing the extramarital experience as a means of learning what it is that she really wants from life—and how to achieve it.

VIRGINIA JOHNSON: Celia?

CELIA: I was married when I was twenty-one, right out of college, to a boy I thought I was in love with—just the person I thought was good for me and whom I thought I could make very happy. But from the first moment that we experienced any privacy, I was unhappy.

I think I married too young, but I also felt, as soon as I had lived with him for a while, that he just wasn't for me. But I managed to pretend —we lived together for four years, very miserably, not enjoying any kind of sexual life. And then, quite accidentally, a few months ago I met a man —really a boy—and I started having an affair with him.

At the beginning I used to enjoy sleeping with him, because I felt that I was pleasing somebody and I was with somebody who was also pleasing me. Besides, it was illicit and exciting and very transient. But recently I broke it off because it began to dissatisfy me. It turned out that the fact that it was extramarital had no meaning for me. I mean, for years I felt guilty about wanting to sleep with another man, even though I never did. When I finally did it, I didn't feel the guilt I expected. I just felt that I had gotten married too young and I didn't like being tied down.

BILL MASTERS: Tell us about the sexual experiences you had before your marriage.

CELIA: Well, I had a lot of experience, none of it very good. The first time I was fifteen, and it was a mess—a feeble, unhappy mess. I didn't know what was going on. After that, I slept with quite a few boys that I liked. But it was only after I met a boy whom I trusted and whom I thought I was in love with, when I was seventeen and had been dating him for three years, that I was able to learn something about what enjoyable scx felt like, even if I didn't have an orgasm.

When I met the boy who is now my husband, I was immediately drawn to him physically. But in spite of my excitement, I never did achieve orgasm. I'm not sure whether it was because I didn't know what I was looking for or whether he just didn't know how to help me. Right now I think a lack of emotional motivation has made it impossible for me ever to enjoy sex with him. When we read your book, *Human Sexual Inadequacy,* we studied it and worked on making things better but I just couldn't get very far.

VIRGINIA JOHNSON: Is your husband still quite committed to you?

CELIA: Until recently, yes, and very, very distressed at the fact that I wasn't satisfied with him. I mean, whatever I tried to hide came through in bed, and there's just no hiding anything there, I guess.

Virginia Johnson comments: Of all the recent notions about sex that have been given publicity in recent years, none is more harmful than the idea that a poor sexual relationship can be "cured" by learning technique from a book—any book. In this case, Celia has put it very well when she said that "there's just no hiding anything there"—meaning in bed. An emphasis on the importance of technique is characteristic of so much that passes for advice about sex today. Nothing good is going to happen in bed between a husband and wife unless good things have been happening between them before they got into bed. There is no way for a good sexual technique to remedy a poor emotional relationship. For a man and a woman to be delighted with each other in bed, both must want to be in that bed —with each other.

Celia, like so many young women of this generation, is a female in transition. She believes, intellectually at least, in her right to sexual pleasure—but she doesn't know how to go about discovering it. This is because, like Leah, she isn't fully sure of who she is. Her early sex encounters illustrate this point. She was able to function physically, apparently without too much guilt, but she never learned to function emotionally—that is, she never felt free or secure enough to be able to try to find out why intercourse consistently proved to be emotionally unrewarding. She was sufficiently emancipated to engage in sex but she was still a prisoner of the past in the sense that she believed that sexual satisfaction was something that would happen all by itself, and that it was up to the young man to supply it.

Basically this is what happened when she met the man she later married. She describes herself as being physically aroused by his presence, which means simply that he stood for something that she found pleasing— either in his physical appearance or his manner or his social attributes. Her excitement, therefore, was almost completely a reflection of her romanticized notion of what she thought that he represented. But the man himself, as she describes their relationship, proved a disappointment. She did not experience the sexual gratification with him that she had anticipated, just as she had not experienced it with the other young men in her life before him. This disappointment can be attributed to her husband only in part; it is always conceivable that his knowledge of sex and of female responsiveness was inadequate. But it must also be recognized that Celia herself is responsible for her failure to communicate with him in such a way that they either improved the satisfactions of their total relationship, including sexual intercourse, or ended their marriage.

Many young women today are living—or trying to live—in accordance with two conflicting and often contradictory sets of rules. One set refers to the traditional relationship of a man and a woman. A woman chooses as a husband the man who makes the best possible match that she can hope for; she judges this by his background, his education, his family, his ambitions, and it may even include her estimate of him as a potential father.

But contemporary standards include her right to be a sexual person, someone for whom sexual enjoyment is part of the bedrock on which her marriage must stand or fall. Many young women today believe this intellectually but have yet to translate it into emotional terms. Had Celia done so, she would have accepted as a fact that this particular young man was not someone with whom she could anticipate having a future that included sexual pleasure. At the very least, she would have determined not to become married to him until together they had achieved the kind of physical relationship that held the promise of being rewarding for both of them.

This is not simply a matter of experiencing orgasm, although that is an important part of it. It refers to the totality of their feelings about each other as physical individuals, the degree to which each is delighted by the sexual embrace of the other, and the extent to which each is concerned with the pleasure of the other. If living together, as so many couples now do, is to prove socially advantageous, it will do so because it enables men and women to go beyond the novelty of exploring sexual freedom to the point where they are genuinely caught up in discovering how they feel about each other as individuals, not simply as male and female partners who need each other to engage in intercourse.

VIRGINIA JOHNSON: Oliver?

OLIVER: Well, I'm thirty-six, and I've been married for thirteen years—and up to five years ago, I was into drinking in a big way. Prior to marrying I had slept with probably three or four women—I can't really remember—all the way from a swinger in Tokyo to a high-school sweetheart. I had my first extramarital activity two or three years into the marriage. My wife and I were living in the West Village—it was very bohemian then, and I fancied myself some sort of gay blade. So I decided, I'm going to get laid somewhere. And I did. And I kept on doing this for probably eight years. It was very easy—just: "Hi, come on, let's go. Fine!" Boom.

VIRGINIA JOHNSON: At what age did you marry?

OLIVER: I was twenty-three, she was twenty.

VIRGINIA JOHNSON: Was there any element of boredom in your marriage as you embarked on the first extramarital opportunity? Was there any need to find more of yourself in some way? Or was it really as light and offhanded as you suggest?

OLIVER: I think marriage was something I just wasn't prepared to handle then. I was like a child, and it was fun to run away. Each time I'd give myself good reasons, though—she doesn't like me, I'm unhappy, we'll get divorced and all that nonsense. Since I quit drinking, though, there's none of that.

VIRGINIA JOHNSON: You're saying that the reality of responsibility, of commitment, suddenly hit you at that time?

OLIVER: Yes.

VIRGINIA JOHNSON: How have things changed since then?

OLIVER: When I stopped drinking, I became aware of a whole new kind of sober sexuality with my wife, so the extramarital activities sort of went down.

Being in the sack with my wife and being sober was an incredible experience. But now we've entered the stage where we're living apart in a sense during the week, and I go home on the weekends —that arrangement seems to be the best for us.

Two weeks ago, my wife for the first time slept with someone else. She called me and said she was freaked out, and indicated that she really needed me. So I went up there and was really surprised that my attitude was one of wanting to comfort her. Instead of throwing a fit, which I probably would have done four or five years ago, I just said, this is wonderful.

VIRGINIA JOHNSON: You mean she was upset by her own action?

OLIVER: She felt that the experience was—let's see, what word did she use—"unclean." She didn't like the guy really; she didn't intellectually have anything in common with him, but she was lonely. So there we are, thirteen years into the marriage.

VIRGINIA JOHNSON: Had she been aware of your sexual activities outside the marriage?

OLIVER: She claims not, but I really can't believe that there wasn't some awareness. I mean, if I had been as busy as I'd claimed I'd been, I'd be president of something, for Christ's sake. And I'm not.

Bill Masters comments: It is important to be aware that Oliver's attitudes are more complex than they might seem. Certainly the procedure of choice at the moment that his wife needed his reassurance was to provide comfort, as he did, particularly in view of his own history of multiple extramarital affairs. In addition, however, since he now finds his wife tremendously more attractive in every respect, he would want to be helpful and supportive, if only to protect his relationship with her, from which he now obtains valued benefits. Finally, although he does not acknowledge it, he may be expressing guilt. He could hardly help wondering whether his absence at home was one of the key factors in pushing his wife into having the kind of distasteful extramarital incident that she since described to him, and so some responsibility clearly rests on his shoulders.

Whatever Oliver's real feelings were about his wife's single act of infidelity, his remark that he found it "wonderful" that she had finally taken this step is characteristic of men who want the scales balanced in some way so that they feel justified in continuing to have outside sexual relationships. This kind of man, incidentally, is often likely to cajole his wife into taking part in swinging. Characteristically, he thinks of this as a way to have his cake and eat it—but often becomes dismayed if he discovers that no matter how reluctant his wife may have been to engage in such activities, she may very well find it more rewarding than he himself does. At that point, he is only too eager to terminate the experiment.

VIRGINIA JOHNSON: Jessica?

JESSICA: I was brought up in Boston in a puritanical background, and I managed to be a virgin when I finished art school and came to New York.

VIRGINIA JOHNSON: At what age?

JESSICA: Unbelievable—at nineteen. Then I met my husband. He's a lawyer. And we had real sex together, and that was an unbelievable thing. I loved it, I really loved it. But after I got married, I just could not accept being married to one man, and that's when it started.

My husband is marvelous, just marvelous. But I really don't love him. My extramarital relationships are much more wonderful. I've had relationships with a lot of men and I still do, and everyone is different and everyone is marvelous.

But the peculiar thing is that in the last few years I've changed—I'm just not the same person I was. I've known one man for fifteen years, and I've loved him very much—it's always love, by the way—but now I seem to have the need for another lover as well. Now it's not love with one, but love with two. I've never had the two together, but I've loved them both. . . . Sex is just such a thrilling, marvelous thing for me.

VIRGINIA JOHNSON: Is it ever confusing for you? Do you ever have any sense of leading a double life?

JESSICA: No.

VIRGINIA JOHNSON: Wherever you are, you are you?

JESSICA: Right.

VIRGINIA JOHNSON: And you never were able to experience this excitement even for a little while in your marriage?

JESSICA: Only for a very little while, a very little while. My husband hasn't gone to bed with me for ten, twelve years. He doesn't have any sexual desire whatsoever. He's a marvelous person—brilliant guy, great lawyer, you know, the whole bit—but no sex whatsoever. I've tried, I've tried awfully hard on vacations and everything. He just can't . . . he's sick.

But I've done the most marvelous thing I've done in my whole life with my new lover. He was almost impotent and I helped him. He's the greatest lover in the whole world now.

VIRGINIA JOHNSON: How long have you been married?

JESSICA: Twenty-three years.

VIRGINIA JOHNSON: Was there any indication at the beginning that your husband had less of an interest in sex than you had expected?

JESSICA: Oh, no. Before we got married, he was a great lover. And after we got married, he was a great lover for a couple of years, and that was it. He has a real deficiency, I think. I mean, he just doesn't get sexually aroused. He gets more aroused by a legal brief than . . .

VIRGINIA JOHNSON: Did anything happen that you're aware of that changed things?

JESSICA: Not really. He's not a very stable guy, he really isn't. I went for analysis for five years; he said he couldn't afford it for himself.

BILL MASTERS: You don't describe your outside relationships as a substitute for your marriage. They come through to me as an entirely additional phase of your life. Is this the way you visualize it?

JESSICA: Right, absolutely right. My husband is a very intellectual and stimulating person, and I love to live with him. We play a lot of golf, I'm very physical. And, you know, that's part of it. He's interested in me, and I just want to help him— but I can't.

BILL MASTERS: To what extent is your husband aware of your extramarital affairs?

JESSICA: He's not aware at all.

BILL MASTERS: You're sure?

JESSICA: Absolutely.

BILL MASTERS: How do you manage the time commitment without causing concern on his part?

JESSICA: He gives me free rein all day.

VIRGINIA JOHNSON: To your knowledge, has your husband ever gone outside the marriage?

JESSICA: Not really, no. I may have suspected it once or twice, but I doubt it seriously. I know he's not physically capable of doing it.

VIRGINIA JOHNSON: But you've found that your particular compromise is very comfortable?

JESSICA: Very comfortable, very comfortable.

VIRGINIA JOHNSON: If you had a choice, would you change it? If by some magic wand your husband could become a composite of all the men you have known, would you—

JESSICA: I think it's too late.

Virginia Johnson comments: There are some women—and Jessica may be one of them—who are self-contained and self-assured in a way that is more commonly associated with men. Such a woman is able to establish a sexual identity and to have a code of values that sustains her despite the fact that the life she leads runs counter to the traditional pattern—and she accomplishes this without any bravado or dramatic gestures to call attention to herself (gestures which would, of course, reflect her need to solicit approval and admiration, and thus belie her apparent emancipation).

A woman like Jessica is the counterpart of the man whose wife is genuinely disinterested in sex. There may be very good and valuable rewards for these individuals in their marriages and they work out what seems to be a satisfactory compromise, in which sexual satisfaction is achieved outside the marriage and yet a strong emotional bond ties the husband and wife together. But it must be kept in mind that this is testimony from only one of two involved persons. Without being able to discuss the matter with both partners, it is impossible to evaluate the extent to which deceit and self-deception enter into such an agreement. This woman's husband may very well be pretending not to know about his wife's outside affairs and she in turn may be pretending to herself that he doesn't know. This is not to say that in some, but certainly very few, marriages a man and a woman cannot work out an arrangement of this kind. But unless both partners are interviewed, there is no sure way of learning whether one of them is not in fact being hurt, and perhaps badly hurt, by the behavior of the other.

In those cases where a successful arrangement is accomplished, it is all the more impressive, given cultural pressures, when the wife is the person who finds herself sufficiently strong to move outside the marriage in search of sexual satisfaction and to do so without any evident neurotic behavior. In any event, Jessica's last comment makes it clear that this is a way of life that has not only evolved successfully—it is a way of life that she has almost designed and which she does not really wish to change. This indicates, at the very least, that some sense of her self-esteem is dependent upon being free of the customary rules that apply in most people's lives. It may very well reflect a reaction to her early upbringing, which she described as "puritanical." Any sexual code that restricted her activities would seem to her a throwback to those earlier times, when she was not free to express her own sexuality, and her present behavior is an affirmation of her independence.

Bill Masters comments: From a male point of view, this is clearly a marriage of convenience. Assuming that the wife's report is accurate, the husband emerges as a man who is not only impotent but who is too much involved with his image as a male to be able to admit the truth—that he is afraid of having to perform sexually. Like a great many other professionals —physicians, dentists, psychologists, and so on—he refuses to seek help for sexual inadequacy because he is afraid that in doing so, he would lose status in his wife's eyes. He feels, as most of these men do, that his professional accomplishments and skills should in some way protect him against the distresses of sexual dysfunction.

Most men in circumstances similar to those being described here are, at the very least, suspicious of their wives' activities. Particularly if these men are intelligent and educated, their tendency is to be secretly relieved that their wives find ways of being sexually gratified outside the marriage. These men share attitudes with wives of previous generations, who accepted as a fact their husbands' extramarital affairs but insisted that those affairs be kept discreet.

Sure awareness is not always conscious, of course, and it can best be described as self-deception. It represents a human being's efforts to keep his feelings in some kind of emotional equilibrium. As long as such an individual derives genuine satisfactions from being married, he—or she—is a living illustration of the old adage that there are none so blind as those who will not see.

BILL MASTERS: Alec?
ALEC: I was married when I was twenty-three. It'll be
      eighteen years in June. My wife and I had a very
      good physical relationship before we were married
      and since we were married—it was out of sight
      last night. . . . But the idea of other women was

just something that always seemed to be in the back of my mind.

It was about seven years into the marriage before I actually slept with another woman. And this has happened with about seven people during the last ten years. In some cases, we only slept together two or three times. Just about every relationship I have had has been with somebody that I have known quite well, that I am fond of. After we have a sexual relationship we seem to have a deeper friendship. We find out more, we pretend less, and it seems to open up more possibilities. Many of these women are close friends of both my wife and myself.

BILL MASTERS: Do you usually make the approach?

ALEC: It has varied. I guess I must in some way seem receptive to the idea, but I think in most cases the one who makes a specific suggestion or the first one to reach out is the woman. By and large I will not approach somebody unless I feel completely sure that she is receptive. I travel a great deal and I don't, with very rare exceptions, find myself in bed with a girl in Los Angeles just because I happen to be in Los Angeles. I see no sense in that kind of sex.

BILL MASTERS: What sexual experience did you have before you married?

ALEC: Well, approximately three years with my wife as a regular thing before we were married; two years with prostitutes in the Army in Japan, and there were three girls in college.

VIRGINIA JOHNSON: Would it be accurate to say that you feel the sexual part is simply another dimension of a friendship?

ALEC (*nodding*): That's pretty close. However, I sometimes wonder how my friendships would be interpreted by other people.

BILL MASTERS: You described the termination of your extramarital sexual experiences as more or less friendly. Is this true?

ALEC: Well, of the seven women, I am still in touch

with six. And if I were to be alone somewhere with any one of them, and if the circumstances were right, we'd probably go to bed because it's the friendly thing to do. Most of them call me regularly—not that they call me daily—but we are in touch the way you would be with a friend. We'll have lunch together. But there's only one who made me feel anywhere as good as my wife does; and if I had to choose one woman just for a sexual relationship, I would choose my wife because sexually she and I know where we're at.

VIRGINIA JOHNSON: And you enjoy it when you're there?

ALEC: Absolutely.

VIRGINIA JOHNSON: Give us a sketchy idea of your background. Are you an only child or one of several? How would you describe, in general terms, your parents' attitudes?

ALEC: I have one older sister. My parents were solid middle-class New Yorkers. My mother was and is very rigid in certain of her attitudes. She was always prudish, for instance, about being undressed in front of my father—this sort of thing. But when I was a boy, my father wished me the best of luck and told me what to get in the drugstore. I think I grew up pretty relaxed as far as sexual behavior is concerned. As a matter of fact, at no point in my life have I ever felt that I had any kind of sexual problem. (*Dryly*) Of course, it *would* be a problem if my wife finds out what I'm doing.

BILL MASTERS: Your wife has no idea about your extramarital activities?

ALEC: I am totally convinced she is completely unaware that I have ever been involved with anyone.

BILL MASTERS: Do you think that your wife has had any extramarital activities?

ALEC: I don't believe so. But then again, I'm sure she doesn't believe I have, so . . . (*He shrugs.*)

BILL MASTERS: Let me ask another question. Would it bother you if you found out that she had?

ALEC: I hope not.

BILL MASTERS: I didn't ask you that.

ALEC: I think it wouldn't. (*He hesitates*) But many years ago I had a friend who believed in having affairs, and he came home one day and found his wife in bed with some man, and he divorced her on the spot. And I said, how could you do that; and he said, if it happens to you someday, *then* tell me what you would do. I frankly feel, and I hope, that I wouldn't mind but it would depend on the reason that she was doing it. If she were having an affair because there was something wrong with me, that would probably upset me. Or if she were having an affair to spite me, because she found out about my affairs. But if she was in bed with someone because it seemed like a good thing to do at the time and she was enjoying it, I would think, I would like to think, that it would not bother me.

Bill Masters comments: This is perhaps the most sophisticated approach to infidelity that a man can have. He says that he doesn't wish to take the chance of being rejected so he simply waits for the woman to make the first move. In cases similar to this one, and on the basis of the available evidence here, sex is approached in a rather relaxed and casual way. For the man, the satisfactions are both physical and social—but there is little or no passion involved. This is an advantage as far as infidelity itself goes, since it minimizes the possibility that any affair will develop into more than a casual relationship. But it is simultaneously a disadvantage, on the personal side, because it indicates a possible incapacity for deep feeling, emotional as well as sexual.

Although it is always risky to make assumptions based on such limited testimony, it does seem probable that Alec has a rewarding enough relationship with his wife so that he is not driven by any overwhelming physical or emotional need to have affairs with other women. In fact, his extramarital affairs seem to be as much a reflection of his curiosity about other women as an expression of sexual need. Furthermore, his control over the situation—and this includes not only making the women come to him but also restricting his partners to women who belong in his social circle and who are friends of his wife as well—is another indication of an approach to infidelity that is more French in character than American, in the sense that it is almost a game played according to very definite rules. This kind of behavior is often found among very wealthy families, where sex outside of marriage is permissible as long as no one takes it seriously.

BILL MASTERS: Your turn, Dagny.

DAGNY: I've been married for many years to a brilliant, charming and very disturbed man. He has had fantasies, sexual fantasies, about me being in bed with somebody else, of me having an affair with somebody else. And when he found out a year ago that I actually *was* having an affair, he flipped completely and threatened to kill the man and threatened to kill me. It's only because I'm not in love, no longer in love, with my husband that I can see him very objectively.

BILL MASTERS: You're not in love with him?

DAGNY: No, but my lover is the same kind of man, threatens all sorts of violence. There's a pattern, I guess.

VIRGINIA JOHNSON: Is this the only extramarital affair you've ever had?

DAGNY: The only one that has lasted over a long period of time.

BILL MASTERS: How long have you been married?

DAGNY: We have lived together for about twenty years, and been married about fourteen years. My husband did not want to marry me. But I pressured him. I pressured for marriage because of a child who was getting old enough to know we were living together outside of marriage, and I pressured for it because I was deadly afraid that my son would be taken away from me, that my father would find out. I pressured for marriage for all these reasons, and for a lot of other conventional reasons. And finally he said, "I will marry you because you're pressuring me; but from the moment I marry you, I will be unfaithful."

BILL MASTERS: Did he put this threat into action as far as you know?

DAGNY: The next day, as far as I know.

VIRGINIA JOHNSON: He wanted to prove his point.

DAGNY (*emphatically*): He wanted to prove his point and he did.

BILL MASTERS: Nevertheless his reaction to your affair was so extreme?

DAGNY: With all his very expansive personality, his aplomb, his charm, he has a terrible insecurity which shows itself in impotence in business, in impotence in sex, and so on, and this was the final blow. And the final blow had also to do with the fact that my lover was his best friend. My husband is not capable of having intimate relationships with many people. And this other man is the one person with whom he had been intimate: the one person to whom he would tell his little infidelities, his big infidelities, his erotic fantasies.

BILL MASTERS: How far into the marriage before you had this affair?

DAGNY: I had started it even before I was married.

BILL MASTERS: Did you have much premarital experience?

DAGNY: For several years I was almost promiscuous. Instead of being the actress I wanted to be, the writer I wanted to be, the anything I wanted to be, I became involved with a series of very unfulfilling people.

VIRGINIA JOHNSON: Naomi, would you like to tell us something about yourself?

NAOMI: Well, I've been married fourteen years. I have no children. My husband and I are very close—we work together.

I've had three extramarital affairs—you might even call them foreign affairs, because one

was in India, one in France and one in Italy. And
I must say that it wasn't just being in a foreign
country or having a spree or something like that.
Each of these men is very interesting and we were
very attracted to one another, and each affair was
absolutely marvelous. The first was with a French
boy whom I met briefly in New York through
business—very attractive, very sexy. At the time
I did a great deal of foreign traveling with my
boss; and so when I went to Paris, I saw this boy
and had an affair with him. The second experience was with an Italian, whom I also met
through business—a wonderful, wonderful man.
I met the third man in India on a trip; he was an
American sculptor and we had a marvelous experience.

As Jessica said, I loved all my lovers, and I
still do. I don't make love with them now, but I
still love them.

VIRGINIA JOHNSON: How long did each relationship
last?

NAOMI: Well, when I was involved with the French
boy, I used to go to Europe two or three times a
year, and the affair lasted about two years. And
then I met the Italian, and I dropped the French
boy for him. The American sculptor that I met in
India was separated from his wife because she
was very mental. She had a mental state, and he
just couldn't live with her—she had to be taken
away. We promised in India never to see each
other in New York, and when he came here, he
never called me, I never called him. But we ran
into each other on the street, and I brought him
up to meet my husband, and the three of us became great friends.

The Frenchman and the Italian have become
best friends of my husband, too. They come to
New York two or three times a year, and we see
them whenever we're in Europe. I've met the
Italian's wife and his children. She's become a
dear friend, and whenever she's in New York she

stays with us. And we stay with them every summer. Of course, after I met her I could never sleep with him again—I guess it's just a sense of values.

Maybe it's because of my religious upbringing, but I've never had an affair in New York, because I think it would be fouling my own nest, so to speak. That's about it for my extramarital activities.

My husband and I, as I said, are very close. He would like to make love every night. He's always eager and willing and is very much in love with me. I don't think I could marry anyone else and be as happy as I am with him.

VIRGINIA JOHNSON: Did you have much sexual experience before you were married?

NAOMI: I was married at twenty-five. I had lots of premarital sex. I must also say that I came from a very large family—I'm the youngest of ten children—and I had lots of brothers, and I realize that most of my premarital affairs were with older men, because if I went to bed with somebody my own age, it was almost like going to bed with my brother, which was sort of taboo, naturally. Anyway, premarital sex was quite fun until I had a two-and-a-half-year relationship with one man, a doctor. Unfortunately, he couldn't resist anything in skirts. And when I found out, about a year after we started living together, that he was very, very sexually active, and that he was having extraneous affairs all over the place, I was destroyed. I was very young, and he was my prince on a white charger, and I was destroyed. But I loved him very much, and so even though it was a year of suffering, I stayed with him. I'm not one of those women who leave and come back and leave and come back—I can't do that—so I stayed with him until I knew I could not any longer.

For about two years after that relationship ended, I had relationships with a number of men. But I must say that I've never been promiscuous—

I'd have one lover at a time and it usually lasted over a long period. I found, though, that affairs were very unsatisfactory—not sexually, but in the sense that I was so bitter about the first relationship that I was getting even with whatever man I was with.

VIRGINIA JOHNSON: And nothing worked for you?

NAOMI: No. But as a matter of fact, I got engaged. I was engaged twice after I lived with this man, and I was engaged when I met my husband.

VIRGINIA JOHNSON: You seem to have such positive feelings about your extramarital affairs. What do you think they have done to enhance you? What have they given you?

NAOMI: I come home light as a feather, happy as a lark.

BILL MASTERS: Is your husband aware of them?

NAOMI: He never mentioned it, but I think he may have suspected the French boy. He never touched me in the presence of my husband—he just sort of mooned around. I don't know, though—I just saw more than my husband did.

VIRGINIA JOHNSON: To your knowledge, has your husband gone outside the marriage?

NAOMI: I don't think he has. And if he has, I don't want to know about it. I don't want him to know about mine either. I don't think that confession is good for the soul.

Virginia Johnson comments: Naomi is an interesting example of the individual—male or female—who breaks certain basic socially accepted rules and substitutes an almost rigid set of substitute rules. In this case, infidelity is not only justified but validated by living according to very special standards. When these arrangements are successful, they seem to create a kind of "extended family," in which the third sexual partner is somehow brought in touch with the existing marriage. To some extent, of course, this might be described as a self-imposed compartmentalization. Thus extramarital sex is made "right" by the imposition of intricate rationales on the lives of all concerned, with great emphasis based on ostensible kindness, devotion, responsibility and so forth.

Naomi's emphasis on the fact that she still "loves" the men with whom she had her affairs, even though she no longer "makes love" with them, is just one example of the kind of clichéd requirements that such people use to maintain their meticulous sense of themselves as decent human beings—or, as she puts it, a person who does not want to be guilty of "fouling the nest." Most often these individuals are genuinely talented people with a considerable capacity for creative work and they characteristically make use of whatever circumstances are at hand to enhance their total way of life, including sex. Naomi, in this case, remains true to such a philosophy as is evidenced by the fact that she would not want to know about her husband's extramarital affairs, if he were indeed having any. Again she makes clear that this kind of sexual gamboling should be as pristine as possible.

All this is based on the idea that the sexual experience can be dominated, if not dictated, by the intellect. Of course, this completely ignores one of the most important aspects of human sexuality—namely, its ability to invoke in human beings far deeper passions than they themselves might ever have dreamed they possessed. If, in order to have affairs of this civilized kind, men and women are willing to regulate their emotional responsiveness, they may succeed in doing so, paying a price that they themselves may not be aware of: a lost capacity for powerful emotions, emotions which will not listen to reason and might therefore upset the marital applecart.

BILL MASTERS: Almost everyone here seems to have a completely happy story to tell. Only two of you so far have expressed any doubts or talked about any bad experiences in terms of your infidelities. Oliver, did your extramarital affairs leave you completely happy?

OLIVER: Only after I quit drinking. I don't know what

the hell was the matter before that, but since then, yes.

BILL MASTERS: No doubts, no questions of any sort?

OLIVER: No, I think my affairs have enhanced my sexual awareness. I'm a product of the Catholic Church and the Marine Corps and a couple of other incredible disappointments, which all sort of combined to make me terribly inhibited, terribly uptight. All along, my wife and I have had mutual orgasms, orgasms all over the place, but I think I still had this vision of wife over here and girl friend over here, and, you know, the illicit aura of running around and what not. It's a hell of a lot better now—and this is only because of my experiences with these other women.

For a year and a half after I stopped drinking, I was with one woman who was separated from her husband. I had two wives, in a sense, and it involved unbelievable logistics. But it was fulfilling because this particular person was inclined to do things like camping out, things that I like but that my wife doesn't. And, of course, I held that against my wife and resented her; "Hell, you don't like to camp out." Now I'm coming to the point where I realize that my wife is what she is, and so if she doesn't want to sleep in a tent, that's fine.

I'm very, very happy about my extramarital involvements, and I don't feel guilty. I did when I was still drinking, because there was so much deceit involved. But for the last six years there's been no deceit. I point that out because it's very important. And since my wife and I have been living apart, everything has been fantastic. Eliminating phone calls and having to say when I'll be in has been wonderful. We're constantly talking, though. I'm going to be back tomorrow night, and we'll have another great weekend comparing notes. I don't know what the hell is going to happen now—whether the marriage is going to last or not. We're just starting to work on this.

VIRGINIA JOHNSON: You said the year-and-a-half relationship you had gave you perspective and helped you to realize that your wife is what she is. Did it also give you an increased appreciation of your wife and a pleasure in her?

OLIVER: Not only her but all human beings.

Bill Masters comments: Many husbands—and wives—who are engaged in extramarital sex have a great need to rationalize their behavior. It is their way of justifying what they are doing, a justification that is almost always expressed in extravagant language. In Oliver's case, he maintains that his extramarital affairs have made everything better—they have enabled him to appreciate his wife, with whom he has, as he expressed it, absolutely marvelous sex; it makes him happier with himself because he can now be open about his affairs; and it even leads him to be delighted with just about everybody in the whole world. This kind of rationalization is another instance of "protesting too much." Interest is always directed to what the other side of the coin must be—because Oliver, as any other individual will do in a similar situation, is really talking to himself, persuading himself that what he says is true. To put it another way, he probably does not believe it to be true or he would not have to go to so much trouble to insist that it is. He is trying to explain away the feelings of guilt that persist and he is simultaneously concerned with making himself appear, at least in his own eyes, to be a good man, someone who has overcome the emotional limitations that most people suffer from. The fact remains, however, that individuals like Oliver feel hollow—and sound hollow to objective observers.

CELIA: I don't think you have to experience a number of outside relationships to become happier about yourself and things in general. But after being with this one person, I've thought of nothing but sleeping with every man who appealed to me. Really, I walk down the street and look at everybody and wonder whether they are looking at me and what would they be like to sleep with. And somehow, just this one experience with this boy, which wasn't terrific and didn't make me terribly happy sexually, was enough to make me feel much more excited about being with people. It gave me a new feeling about life, which I never had with my husband because I was so dragged down and smudged.

VIRGINIA JOHNSON: Did it kind of make you feel more like yourself again and help you to enjoy sex?

CELIA: Yes. I became aware of what I was as an individual as opposed to what my husband wanted me to be. I was living exactly according to the traditional image of the female, because my husband couldn't accept anything else. And one morning I woke up and said, I hate cleaning the house and I want somebody to help me, and I'd like to sculpt in the middle of the night and paint in the middle of the night alone. And I want privacy and I want individuality and I want to be recognized for being a girl—not even so young any more!—with definite interests. I am human and individual and also female, and I don't want to be submerged in this housewife role.

VIRGINIA JOHNSON: You deferred to your husband to the point where you almost forgot who you were or what you wanted or what you thought.

CELIA: Yes, but I have to blame myself for that, because I decided that it was my role as a woman to please a man and therefore completely to submerge my own identity.

BILL MASTERS: How are you going to handle yourself now? You say you're happy to walk down the street and see what you can try on for size. Are you going to hunt for relationships or are you interested in a little quantity to make up for this lack that you described?

CELIA (firmly): I'm not interested in quantity, I'm interested in quality. I just want to be able to relate to a man because . . . (*Less surely*) I don't really know what I want. I do know that I would like to end up ultimately with one man. I don't want to run to seven different men, I don't want to have twenty affairs; that doesn't appeal to me. I don't like to have friendships like that; I like to know intimately several people at a time. I can't absorb any more than that. And I would like to be able to have a strong, solid, good, fulfilling relationship with one man, and it's really all that I want.

VIRGINIA JOHNSON: Right now you're mostly busy trying to remember all the things you wanted to feel and activate the things you wanted to do?

CELIA: Yes, that is why I had the relationship with the boy. I was desperate to have some kind of communication and know that somebody could relate to me in ways that I thought I could relate, and I found it. But the boy wasn't for me and it deteriorated. No, it didn't deteriorate. I ended it because I was bored with him.

VIRGINIA JOHNSON: It served its purpose.

CELIA: It served its purpose, yes.

Virginia Johnson comments: In contemplating every man on the street as a potential sex partner, Celia may simply be indulging herself in a Walter Mitty-type fantasy. This would be understandable under the circumstances, since she has just begun to break out of her marriage and has used sexual infidelity as a springboard. The danger lies in the possibility that this fantasy expresses a more fundamental aspect of her personality, an immaturity that is more Peter Pan than Walter Mitty—reflecting a wish not to grow up. When this is the case, a man or a woman uses extramarital affairs as a way of avoiding responsibility for the achievement of an enduring relationship. For an affair, after all, can be an opportunity for growth, a chance to experience more than simply sexual pleasure—a chance to work at a relationship so that it will sustain sexual pleasure and even intensify it. The alternative is to go from one partner to another, experiencing little beyond a temporary relief of sexual frustration.

This is certainly not Celia's intention—intellectually, at least. The danger lies in the ease with which good intentions dissolve in the face of easy opportunities to act otherwise. Marriage is, among other things, a challenge to two individuals to find their identities by meeting the responsibilities that arise in the natural course of events, but affairs have no such built-in challenges. It is all too easy to continue an affair only to the point where it requires an individual to grow up, to accept some responsibility for his or her own development and to invest attention and feeling and energy *in developing a long-range relationship* rather than concentrating it all on short-term pampering of the individual self.

JUSTIN: I feel a little ill at ease. Most of the people here seem to have really cared for the individuals they got involved with. And yet I have never really had any kind of lasting relationship outside of my marriage, even though I've maintained a friendship with many people. If a person attracts me, I feel like going after her.

CELIA: But do you also have to like her?

JUSTIN: Yes, I do. I genuinely have to like her; I have to have an interest in her. I haven't been able to make love to people whom I've only had a physical attraction to. There must be more than a physical attraction for me to have it last more than once or twice. I have never had a so-called one-night stand. Anybody that I've had any relationship with, I've been with two or three times at least.

NAOMI: I think I was attracted to each man that I met, not because I was lonely or because I needed a sexual relationship whenever I was away from my husband. I was attracted to each man because he was interesting, and because we had a lot in common.

BILL MASTERS: Naomi, you said that you had these affairs because the men were attractive and you found yourself drawn to them. What prevents you from having more frequent affairs, considering the fact that often there must be other attractive men around you?

NAOMI: Not as attractive as my husband.

BILL MASTERS: Three have been.

NAOMI: Yes, well, not as attractive as my husband— it was the place and the circumstances. When I was in India, I was stimulated by the country— it was the first time I'd been there. I had so much in common with the man I met, it was just sort of natural to go to bed with him. It's lovely having an affair in an Indian city . . .

LEAH: So what you're saying is that it was just a little bit of change and fantasy to keep you going?

NAOMI: No, I liked this man.

LEAH: So you didn't really search for a man to have an affair with.

NAOMI: No, I never have. My husband satisfies me. That's why I really don't have any desire to have affairs when I'm in New York, when I'm with him.

LEAH: From what Naomi has said, she's had a very good relationship for a long time with one man, and within that time she has met only three people whom she has felt really close to. It seems she is getting the best part of everything.

CELIA (*enviously*): I agree.

BILL MASTERS: Are you searching, Leah?

LEAH: Yes.

BILL MASTERS: Why?

LEAH: I told my husband point-blank about my last affair because I wanted him to leave. While I was in this affair, I was as determined as I can be—I wanted out of my marriage. I did not want to marry the person I was in love with, but I did feel a certain amount of safety in having someone to help me through a breakup. That's not what happened, though—a divorce really is a very, very heavy thing, especially when there are children involved. And yet I keep looking for someone else. I know I'll never experience peace or contentment as long as I keep going around, and yet I do. The only thing that makes me feel real joy and contentment isn't sex, it's ballet. I can still take a dance class and feel just great. I get sweaty and I feel good. I know my limitations and yet I enjoy that.

VIRGINIA JOHNSON: For a moment you're into yourself, and all of you is being expressed.

LEAH (*nodding*): That's right, that's the only time.

VIRGINIA JOHNSON: What did your parents want for you?

LEAH: Too much.

VIRGINIA JOHNSON: Did they tout any particular thing as you were growing up?

LEAH: I've always let them down. I'm a butterfly in their estimation. My mother said to me—one thing that I'll never get over—"You have more guts than brains." She used to marvel that when things happened to me I would always bounce back very quickly. This is my defense mechanism, I guess. When one thing didn't work out, I would immediately set my goal somewhere else. I need this goal, I really need it.

VIRGINIA JOHNSON: Do you like being told that you bounce back well? Is that a source of pride?

LEAH: It used to be, but now I'm questioning that. Maybe it means I don't care enough about any one thing.

JUSTIN: I haven't heard anybody talk about being motivated by what motivates me, and that is either boredom or lack of challenge. I found myself very, very uncomfortable with my wife during foreplay, because I knew exactly what I could expect. It provided no challenge for me, and I think that is the initial reason I started going elsewhere.

VIRGINIA JOHNSON: Did you ever think that you might be able to alter this situation by introducing creativity?

JUSTIN: There isn't a room in the house where we haven't had sex or a position that we haven't tried. It's just a matter of knowing what's in store for me.

(*Abruptly*) I have something to confess. I must say I am very, very impressed with these individuals gathered here because of their unusual frankness in revealing their intimacies. Being the first speaker, I felt very, very withdrawn, not knowing what to reveal or what not to reveal. And I'll admit that on the night preceding my wedding, I spent the night in my sister's house and I had sexual intercourse with her.

VIRGINIA JOHNSON: Was that a first time?

JUSTIN: Yes. At the time my sister was getting a divorce, and she was very disturbed emotionally because of it, and I was very scared of getting married and giving up my freedom. And in the act of consoling one another, we found ourselves releasing our frustrations in bed.

BILL MASTERS: How old was your sister?

JUSTIN: She was thirty-three or thirty-four. She is an extremely beautiful woman, a dietitian.

BILL MASTERS: How did you feel about it the next day?

JUSTIN: I really enjoyed myself the night before I got married, and when I saw my sister the next day at the wedding, it did not make me feel guilty in any way.

BILL MASTERS: No self-consciousness on your part?

JUSTIN: None whatsoever.

BILL MASTERS: Nor on her part either, I gather.

JUSTIN: No. We never have been involved since then, but we still have a great love for each other. I've never been as close to anybody in my life, my wife included, as I am to my sister.

BILL MASTERS: By the way, has she remarried?

JUSTIN: No.

JESSICA: Was your wife like your sister in any way?

JUSTIN: No. My sister is very much like me. She is a very insecure individual, who must be constantly surrounded by members of the other sex. My wife happens to be the exact opposite of myself. She is a homebody, does not wish to go out, does not wish to mingle, whereas I am out virtually every night of the week—not late but till eight or nine o'clock. I'll have a dinner date or go out on business.

DAGNY: I'd like to ask you a question. Do you consciously or maybe, if you think about it, unconsciously, look for women who remind you of your sister, who are the exact opposite of your wife?

JUSTIN: I've never even really given it much thought, but now that you bring it up, the women I get involved with must have something that is in the lines of, in the realm of something close to, what my sister represents. She is middle-class America in the purest . . .

DAGNY: Pure Italian, right?

JUSTIN: I have Italian and Jewish heritage.

JESSICA: Great, that's a good combination.

JUSTIN: But I happen to think that my sister, and I'm prejudiced in this very respect, is a perfect individual. She has compassion, she has . . .

DAGNY: She's perfect, you said that.

JUSTIN: Yes, she's perfect.

VIRGINIA JOHNSON: What attracted you to your wife?

JUSTIN: She's an extremely beautiful woman. I met her once in a nightclub in New York and, in fact, she was very much the aggressor. I was always very timid before I got married. I was afraid of being put down, of being rejected. If I got involved in a relationship, it was because I was in an atmosphere of friendliness where I knew I'd be accepted. My timidity ceased whenever I found that a girl was genuinely interested in me. Then I became very much the aggressor because I knew then I wasn't going to be rejected or put down.

DAGNY: May I say something that may have nothing to do with this, but because of something Justin said. It has been on my mind. Very recently a man whom I loved, who has never lived with his daughter and had seen her only a couple of times while she was growing up, had his daughter move in with him because she had no other place to stay. She is twenty-two, he is forty-six. She became very seductive, and he fought it. But to make a long story short, it did happen. He said to her, "Okay, this is what you want, this is what you're going to get," and they went to bed. He insists he does not feel guilty about it.

At first I was in a little bit of shock. Then I examined my thinking and asked myself, but how do I really feel inside? And the only thing I could come up with is, it's conditioned. It's conditioning plus the fear of creating a line of bleeders or idiots. I am searching for a taboo other than conditioning, and I cannot find one.

BILL MASTERS: The great taboo is a very real one that is based on the possibility of genetic distortion. Beyond that, I guess the next greatest taboo has to do with "conditioning," but that isn't the word that appeals to me.

VIRGINIA JOHNSON: May I ask you something, Dagny. What difference did it make to you?

DAGNY: It hasn't really made any difference.

BILL MASTERS: Is it now a continuing relationship or did it last only one night?

DAGNY: It was a one night thing.

JESSICA: Does she live with him anymore?

DAGNY: No, she moved in with a friend.

Bill Masters comments: The less traumatic kinds of incest involve, first, brother and sister; and second, father and daughter. By far the most traumatic type of incest is mother-son. The last type may be the least frequent of all, as far as overt sexual expression is concerned. But a domineering, smothering type of mother is responsible for what can with some fairness be described as a psychosocial incest relationship. Males can be crippled in this situation without ever having been to bed with their mothers. As adults, they suffer from sexual dysfunction, particularly primary or secondary impotence.

In terms of explicit sexual expression of incest, it is important to distinguish between single incidents and continuing relationships. The two references during the symposium to incest were of single incidents and these are either readily forgotten or relegated to the past with a minimum of distress. On the other hand, incestuous relationships that have been maintained for long periods of time and that have not been psychosocially released when physical activity is terminated, cause the greatest difficulty in later life.

One other factor ought to be mentioned here. When infidelity has been absorbed into a pattern of life and when the individual has the freedom to act in accordance with private needs, it is not at all unusual to have an incestuous opportunity utilized in response to the impulse of the moment. The instance given of the man with his sister, seeking solace and support in terms of his own personal insecurities and his fears of his wedding night, is quite understandable and probably not particularly traumatic for either brother or sister.

BILL MASTERS: Getting back to extramarital relationships, I'd like to ask a question. Have any of you ever had to cope with feelings of regret, remorse or guilt because of your extramarital affairs? When you tell lies to your husband or wife about your involvements, do you feel you are protecting him or her?

VIRGINIA JOHNSON: Or the marriage?

NAOMI: I never told a lie. I wouldn't do anything to jeopardize my marriage, and I don't think I have.

ALEC: I think that's where it's at. First of all, you have to be somewhat optimistic that life is basically going to work out. In other words, you don't start an affair with the idea of being discovered. Sure, there's this fear that it might result in injury. I don't believe my wife would leave me if she found out—I think it would be much worse than that. I think she would stay—

DAGNY: And make your life miserable?

ALEC: . . . And try and find some other ways to get back at me. But my desire to have more relationships with other people is stronger than my fear of being found out. The thought of spending forty-three years married to one lovely woman and never knowing anybody else is something I just can't envision.

I find when I get to know somebody at great depth, it seems like the most natural thing in the world to go to bed with her. The truth of the matter is, if a woman calls me at the office or I call her, and we get together and have lunch—if I'm being unfaithful at all, that's where I'm being unfaithful, because I am relating to another woman. Whether it becomes a sexual act or not is almost immaterial. So I feel that the idea that someday it may come out, which I would sincerely regret, is outweighed by other considerations, probably selfish ones.

CELIA: Really, where can a happy medium be achieved if you want to be around people and want to know them well—people that are very talented, very cosmopolitan? How can you have them in your life and still be married? You just can't run around being intimate with everyone.

VIRGINIA JOHNSON: Well, having friends like that doesn't necessarily involve being intimate with them, too.

CELIA: But according to what everyone here says, it seems that it does. I think what Naomi is saying is that if the opportunity comes along and you relate to it or respond to it, you shouldn't turn it down.

VIRGINIA JOHNSON: Let's try to clarify this a little. Although there are significant differences, Naomi's and Alec's value systems are similar in many ways. Both of them seem to have a very firm sense of their own identity and a real belief in themselves. They're very comfortable being the people they are. Naomi, I hear you as saying that your relationships, highly selective as they have been and appropriate to the time, place and circumstance, are experienced as a natural extension of your life experience. They're not for the sake of sex, they're not to put down or to destroy, they're not seeking anything other than themselves. In fact, it sounds as if you could be saying, "We saw a lovely painting together," or "We wove a beautiful tapestry together." In other words, your relationships are a way of expressing yourself at the time and in the place and under the circumstance. It may never happen again in your life or it may happen many times—at least I gather that is the way you feel about it. And it sounds to me that for you, the sexual act represents the ultimate in human interaction. It's just kind of a lovely thing to cap feelings that are being exchanged by people.

NAOMI: Yes.

ALEC: That's really where it's at. What I find is that after having some kind of sexual encounter with a woman, our relationship on every other level, our ability to talk about meaningful things to each other has increased. As a result, with all but one of the women I've been involved with, there remains to this day a much broader, deeper relationship than I think would have been possible otherwise.

BILL MASTERS: Certainly sexual functioning which is, after all, a means or form of communication is handled in different ways depending on one's maturity and one's security. It may be a form of sport or a form of expression or a form of barter. Justin describes himself getting lost in quantity at this stage of his life. So the thing that is of interest is when will it be important enough to him to express himself in a quality relationship? When will sexual functioning become sexual communication?

JUSTIN (*defensively*): What I said may have led you to the wrong conclusion. Really, I am very particular about whom I have a sexual relationship with.

BILL MASTERS: That wasn't my point. I'm talking about some continuity within a relationship. You don't describe this yet.

VIRGINIA JOHNSON: Some investment of yourself.

BILL MASTERS: That's it, investment in a relationship.

JUSTIN: I think I'm very fearful of that.

BILL MASTERS: Right, so time alone will reveal the course you intend to follow.

Virginia Johnson comments: Among the women who participated in this symposium, two motivations for infidelity come through quite clearly. One is a desire to settle a score with their husbands, to square accounts—a way of getting back at their partners for what they see as injustice or inadequacy. Perhaps the men are saying the same thing but they have additional culturally stereotyped attitudes to express, such as their right as males to engage in sex as a diversion or, again as an extension of the double standard, their right to seek the company of women who are more innovative or entertaining or compliant than their wives.

Sex is, of course, only one area in which a sense of "arrested development of self" is experienced by a man or a woman after they have been married for a while. They become aware that they have not had a chance to try their wings and they belatedly feel the urge to discover how far and how well they can fly. This awareness becomes focused on sex, chiefly because society has made it such a charged aspect of life. It is certainly reasonable for someone to wish to catch up with himself, to experience the feelings that he— or she—feels are legitimately his and which he feels capable of achieving. But this search for identity is a much wider problem than can be encompassed by sex alone.

It is just that when sex is not good, when sexual

deprivation or sexual distress of any kind is occurring, it tends to dominate the individual's feelings. Under those circumstances, many people see sex as the only really important thing in their lives—they feel deprived, even cheated, of one of life's great satisfactions. Consequently they often become overly dramatic, indulging themselves in emotional baths, losing perspective on the totality of their lives. It is this preoccupation with sex-for-the-sake-of-sex that makes so much extramarital sex ultimately self-defeating because in time it is the *totality* of an individual's life that determines whether sex will continue to be a fulfilling experience or will become a demoralizing one. It would be just as reasonable, and more logical, for a man or a woman who lacks a sense of self-esteem and who feels cheated of sexual satisfaction to begin the search for greater happiness by undertaking achievements in other aspects of their lives—whether in a career or by cooperating in some community project or by turning to education for the achievement of new skills and greater knowledge. Out of such efforts, a sense of self materializes that may very well lead either to the improvement of existing emotional relationships or to the beginning of new ones that promise more enduring satisfaction—including sexual pleasure.

Infidelity is a very chancy and unreliable means to use in searching for one's identity, in exploring one's true emotions, in struggling not only to find out what one's deepest feelings and beliefs and responses may be, but also communicating them to someone else. This is true for many reasons, including the fact that a man and a woman who are involved in an affair generally have different investments in their relationship, and these affairs are most often conducted under less than encouraging conditions. In addition, social attitudes—including those internalized by the man and woman—make it certain that in a good number of cases, the individuals will have to cope with feelings of guilt, one way or another. Either the guilt will intrude on their ability to accomplish their goals—to discover dimensions of their own personality—or it will require them to deny that the feelings exist, and in doing so, to sweep other feelings under the rug along with the discomfort of guilt.

Undeniably, even so little a thing as a few kind words, and certainly a sense of companionship or—even more importantly—the first achievement of orgasm, carries with it a significant strengthening of motivation for change and may nurture self-esteem to a point where a man or a woman have that much more confidence in their ability to develop more rewarding patterns of behavior. But it is very difficult to depend on a single happening, or a series of happenings, to sustain the energy, interest, courage, and zest required by a "lost" individual who is trying to develop in the important ways that he or she feels are necessary if life is to have more meaning. Real and lasting achievement of goals which require a significant change of emotions, attitudes and habitual conduct must be carried out across a broad spectrum of one's life, if they are to become real and lasting achievements.

It is true that when one partner finds satisfaction in extramarital relationships, this may turn a potentially destructive marital relationship into a cautious friendship, at best, or a supportive "acquaintanceship," and in that sense it is better than open marital warfare with all its attendant bitterness and destructiveness. But this is *not marriage in the sense of two human beings with full regard for each other,* sharing the wish to negotiate differences between them and developing mutual pleasures to the fullest extent possible. Making do in marriage is not fulfillment through marriage. Even if infidelity represents the first step in a positive direction—toward making do instead of making war—it is still a long distance away from the goal of becoming committed: true to oneself and loyal and vulnerable to one's partner.

7

Swinging Sex
Is There a Price to Pay?

This symposium, held in Chicago in June, 1971, brought together a small group of men and women whose lives at the time were governed by a code of sexual behavior that can best be described as "permissive." They shared several basic convictions. One was that sexual intercourse, like verbal intercourse, should in no way be limited by the fact that a couple are married or live together. Second, all sexual relationships must be acknowledged; the secrecy and deception commonly associated with infidelity are unacceptable. Third, sexual pleasure is to be taken whenever, wherever, and however it is found—as part of a game in which any number can play. Colloquially, these individuals were sexual swingers.

If newspapers, books and magazines are to be believed, swingers can be found in every major city in the United States and in a great many suburban communities as well. This may be true; there is no reliable statistical information to prove or disprove the contention. But on the basis of the effort involved in finding participants for this symposium, one factual bit of evidence is noteworthy: in one of the most cosmopolitan of all American cities, it proved extraordinarily difficult to find swingers and even more difficult to reach those men and women who were comfortable enough with what they were doing to be willing to sit around a table and discuss the subject.

The following symposium involved four couples and one trio. Gary and Jill Dorler had been practicing group sex for more than a year. She was twenty-eight years old and an interior decorator; her husband was twenty-nine, a college instructor in the mathematics department of a major university. They had been married for five years but had no children. Simon and Dee Maxwell, who had also been married for several years and had lived together before that, resided in a suburb of Chicago. Dee, twenty-nine, was a social worker; her husband, thirty-one, was a lawyer. They had two children. Tina Brooks, twenty-six, and Rick Brooks, thirty, had been married for four years, and during half that time they engaged in swinging. He was a writer and his wife was a magazine illustrator. They had no children. The Sanders, Joan and Kyle, were in their mid-forties. This was the second marriage for both of them; they had three teenaged children. Joan was a college instructor in social science; Kyle, a businessman. The trio included two men and a woman—Bruce, Quentin and Debbie. Bruce and Debbie had been living together for almost three years and Quentin, who had his own apartment, was absorbed into their "family" more or less as a constant companion. Bruce, a sculptor, was twenty-six; Debbie, a neophyte ballet dancer, was twenty-five, and Quentin, a stage designer, was in his early thirties.

VIRGINIA JOHNSON: Gary, would you tell us how it all began for you?

GARY DORLER: Going outside our marriage and having sex with other people really came rather easily to us, probably because it came very slowly. It was a process that took about a year and a half or two years. First Jill and I had a friend make a film of us making love. Not a porno movie or anything like that—more along abstract lines, something like the film called *Geography of the Body*. Anyway, that introduced someone else into the room, and from there on it was a matter of evolution—getting involved in the arts and having the sketches shown publicly and so forth. So it became something that could be discussed with other people, people we thought this could never be mentioned to, and who turned out to be thinking the same things. And having done it, slept with others, we sort of realized how unimportant it is. I feel it's unimportant if I sleep with women other than Jill. But it *is* important to have done it, if only to discover it's unimportant. Then the hard part comes: how to introduce other people into our lives in a full and meaningful way. Having people is only one small start. I mean you have people over, or you go out with them, and you have sex with them, but what about washing dishes and having children and the 99.99 percent of other things you do in your life? We haven't managed to achieve it yet but what we want to do next is to somehow live with other people in a meaningful way. We don't happen to be interested in living in a commune, but we do want to try to develop some type of social structure where we spend a lot more time with other people, sharing in all functions.

VIRGINIA JOHNSON: About swinging, in what was its importance invested? The turn-on? The give and take of just basic human exchange? The fun of being close to other people?

SIMON MAXWELL: I think there was some of that, but I think in the process we lied to ourselves a little, too. We sometimes just ball other people casually, balling for the sake of balling.

GARY DORLER: You don't find that erosive, balling with people without having a fuller, more human relationship with them?

SIMON MAXWELL (*sighing*): Do you mean erosive of us, or erosive of our relationship with them?

GARY DORLER: Both.

SIMON MAXWELL: Well, we're not into it that often. You know, it's kind of like if you want to go out and play bridge once a month. Or you can get into—well, ten couples swinging; we had that at our place three weeks ago, and it happened to be one of those things where everything went right. All the emotions went well, and nobody got hassled. Of course, there was some selection to make sure that it would go well . . .

GARY DORLER: How long did it take you to identify ten couples you thought would go well together? We tried that once and it was quite a project. (*Laughter.*)

SIMON MAXWELL: We happened to be very lucky. There is a couple we know whom we've swung with a couple of times, but with whom we also have some emotional ties though the intellectual thing is just not very much there. And their talent for finding other people is just incredible, and they provided about half the party—people we'd never seen before, but who were beautiful people, and we found about four couples ourselves; all in all, the selection was fine.

RICK BROOKS: How long did this last, how long did it go on? It's not a communal situation, is it?

SIMON MAXWELL: No, no. I was responding to the question, how can you just ball—just enjoy it as a sex thing? And I was saying it *can* happen; we do it, and it's good.

VIRGINIA JOHNSON: I have a question. You have said, in effect, we did it, and now we don't *have* to do it; we're almost at a point where it's optional. Are you saying that it's now an option having to do with the time, the place and the mood?

DEE MAXWELL: I'd like to speak to that. First of all, there is a difference between swinging with people with whom you've developed a relationship and swinging for fun on a spontaneous basis with a very large group of people you don't know and can't get terribly close to because there isn't very much time. Besides, there is too much stimulation in a large group. It isn't erosive of your closer relationships, and to do it with a large group can be just a grand amount of fun. I think *fun* expresses it, rather than saying there's nothing happening there.

VIRGINIA JOHNSON: Like going to a picnic?

DEE MAXWELL: Yes. But who wants to be on a picnic all of their lives? I think back to the question you asked in the beginning, how did we get ourselves into this unique business of swinging? Fun was part of it, but a big part of starting to swing back in 1968 was the notion of doing something unique. . .

BILL MASTERS: Why were you looking for something unique?

DEE MAXWELL: Well, it has to do with our own ego needs, and our own strengths and weaknesses, with wanting to do something . . .

VIRGINIA JOHNSON: Special?

DEE MAXWELL: Special, yes.

VIRGINIA JOHNSON: Or to be special people?

DEE MAXWELL: Yes, or to think about ourselves in a special way, to find out what this strange new thing is. You find that it's not really something you *have* to do, but on the other hand, it's fun. Also in the beginning we found it was a stimulating thought and a stimulating thing to act on; and bringing more people into both of our sex lives eliminated the conflicts of jealousy and the insecurities of each of us going outside our marriage separately. We were doing something together that was enhancing our own sexual relationship.

GARY DORLER (*to Dee*): Specifically, how did you actually get into it the first time? What was the process from the idea to the actuality?

DEE MAXWELL: The process was, look at these funny magazines where these people are advertising all these funny things! Gee, wouldn't it be a lark to write to them and exchange photographs? Then, a few weeks later, Oh, my God, that's illegal, and it's really not *that* worthwhile. But here was an ad from somebody saying, we'd like to meet and talk with you. Okay, we said to ourselves—but they really want to do something more than talk! And after investigating in our own minds for a couple of days, we told them we were willing. But we never heard from them again. Then we said to ourselves, well, look what we've got here, friends of our own, and we started with some people that we'd gotten very close with, we started working it out . . .

GARY DORLER: Specifically, how did it get brought up?

DEE MAXWELL: We brought it up.

SIMON MAXWELL: We all talked about it, among ourselves, and decided that we wanted to . . .

GARY DORLER: That didn't come as any shock to them at all? Had they been thinking of it also?

DEE MAXWELL: Oh, it was a shock. There was a little anxiety, but . . .

SIMON MAXWELL: When we started, we picked some very uptight people. We picked a narrow type— white-shirted, cocktail-party people . . .

VIRGINIA JOHNSON: Deliberately?

SIMON MAXWELL: No. They were just some people we knew.

DEE MAXWELL: They were just around and we were the closest to them.

GARY DORLER: We had a funny experience with picking. For about a year or so we were saying, who could we possibly ask among the people we know? And we thought we could never ask them. And it wasn't until it was sort of exposed through other things we were doing that we discovered that everybody was thinking the same things. We didn't ask people, you see, it just came out in a conversation.

JILL DORLER: I think our approach was quite a bit different. Sleeping with other people is very much integrated into our lives. I personally got into it because I didn't think marriage meant sexual exclusivity. I felt that I was a person, and there were all kinds of other people I could get to know, and I knew that having sex with them wouldn't harm our marriage. That went for both of us. But people we're excited about are in our lives anyway, they're not strangers. For instance, Gary is sleeping with the wife of the head of his department and his secretary and one of his students, and you know, it's completely integrated into our lives, and we've never sought people just for sex; we even avoid that.

DEE MAXWELL (*to Jill*): This conversation is interesting because we're talking about our needs and trying to identify the tensions and the interplay of our needs. Unlike the morals of so many swingers, we're talking about getting closer and getting emotionally involved with other people, allowing that to happen. So we're very much where you're at, we're working very hard to find people, and we're breaking a lot of the ethics of swinging which say you won't get emotionally attached.

BRUCE: We've been together, Debbie and I, for about five years. We're not married by preference. And I don't know if you would call our life "swinging." About two years ago we became very close with Quentin, and we've gotten increasingly closer. The situation just evolved. There were no ideas, no program about it—it just occurred. Quentin lives in a separate place, though the three of us are together constantly, and, for instance, we're going to South America this summer. With this kind of life, in a certain way I feel that I'm not part of society. The feeling is of someone living outside of society although they perhaps link up with society occasionally. It's not a desire to be iconoclastic, you know; it's the idea of being free, of being a man in the world and knowing what's there, and what's usable, and what's possible . . .

BILL MASTERS: For you?

BRUCE: Yes.

BILL MASTERS (*to Quentin*): How about you?

QUENTIN: Well, I'm attached to Bruce and Debbie. I feel I am part of a true love relationship. I feel about sex and marriage the way I do about the other institutions. I think they tend to be too structured, overused and in a sense corrupt.

DEBBIE: Stifling . . .

QUENTIN: I feel that in relationships with other people, I want mutuality. If I'm attracted to or interested in a person, I want that person to be accessible to me. And, naturally, I want to be accessible, too—it's based on mutuality.

BILL MASTERS: Accessible sexually only, or how?

QUENTIN: Not only sexually, no. I think I'm not a promiscuous person. My best relationships are with people with whom there are emotional attachments, not just haphazard sort of meetings, though I have those, too, and probably will continue to have them, so I don't exclude that. But my most satisfying relationships and sexual experiences are with people I care about, and those people generally tend to be involved with other people.

VIRGINIA JOHNSON: I have a stuffy question to ask. When you like to be accessible to someone, and have that person be accessible to you, does this also carry with it responsibility for one another? By responsibility, I don't mean financial and so forth. I mean responsibility in the sense that your presence in the lives of others will enhance them as well as you—that kind of responsibility. I'm very much interested in knowing how this works for the three of you as you interact together.

BRUCE: Well, Quentin poses absolutely no threat to me. I mean I'm not in any sense jealous. I have no negative feelings at all about a relationship between Quentin and Debbie. It's not a relationship in which I would consider Debbie my possession, so my rights are not being violated. What I feel is this: whatever Debbie would have with another person in no way changes what we've had together, and the other person is actually an addition to what we have had together. You know what I mean? It's not taking anything from what Debbie and I have.

VIRGINIA JOHNSON (*turning to Debbie*): Does your relationship with two men, seeing yourself mirrored in two people, provide you with a delightful sense of security—security in yourself as a person and as a woman?

DEBBIE: I feel very secure only because I feel extremely loved. But I feel threatened by a lot of things, too.

VIRGINIA JOHNSON: You mean by things in the big world out there?

DEBBIE: Yes, but in that sense I feel protected by Bruce and Quentin. There *are* a few areas of conflict that concern the three of us, though. I find it necessary to get involved emotionally if I have sex with a person. That's the only way I can really enjoy the experience. And though I think maybe it's a general thing with men, too, I don't think that Bruce and Quentin have it as much as I have. So that's sort of a bit of a conflict. But otherwise it's a beautiful thing, the relationship among the three of us; it is really something that gives me complete security, in the sense of love.

BRUCE: I guess in a sense it's like we have a kind of family unit, but one in which everyone is equal, as opposed to my first experience with a family unit; that was pretty disastrous.

KYLE SANDERS: So you just sort of construct a world that suits your needs as opposed to one that's handed to you, right? Or the one that you come into.

BRUCE: Certainly what I'm doing with my life makes a very comfortable operating base for me. It's a good thing to start from when I have to go out in the world, and it's good to return to.

BILL MASTERS (*to Kyle*): And what about you?

KYLE SANDERS: Well, Joan and I have been married seven years. Both of us were previously married, but there was a long interim between the marriages, and by the time we met we didn't have many sexual taboos. Joan slept with any boyfriend of her choice, and I slept with anybody I wanted to sleep with. When we got married, we didn't consider that the taboo against sex outside of marriage went with our union. So if Joan needs someone else, and develops a sexual relationship with that person, that's all it is, a sexual relationship, and I don't feel threatened by it. We don't put a heavy emphasis on sex. It's just like going to dinner with someone, no more. We've tried a few of the group-sex things, too, but that was just sort of to see what they're like, as an experience. But primarily our marriage allows us both the freedom to have sex with individuals we feel like having it with, as each of us wishes. Most of the people where I work know what we're into and so do most of our friends and people in the neighborhood.

GARY DORLER: Do you conceive of the possibility that Joan might have dinner with someone, become incredibly excited by him, and you'd get a telephone call from California the next day with Joan saying, we've gone off together?

KYLE SANDERS (*shaking his head*): Well, living with Joan every day, that chance seems very remote. Joan is not the type who is going to run off with someone.

JOAN SANDERS: When Kyle and I first met, we had been living our own lives. I had been married before, I'd had three children, I was involved with many people. The involvements kept on, I didn't suddenly cut everything off because I had met Kyle. I think this has a philosophical basis for me. I want to be as happy and as able to pursue happiness in this world as I can. There are certain restrictions, of course; I'm restricted by economics, for one thing, or maybe by health, but I don't want to have any restrictions inside of me; I want to be able to go out and pursue happiness . . .

VIRGINIA JOHNSON: You don't want guilt-producing restrictions.

JOAN SANDERS: Right, right.

BILL MASTERS: Does that mean "don't want" or "have none"?

JOAN SANDERS (*firmly*): Well, I hope I have none but I certainly don't want any.

SIMON MAXWELL: The way people are talking, I must
be the least healthy person in the room. I've been
jealous at times.

JOAN SANDERS: All right. I've never been jealous but
I've played the jealous game at times.

VIRGINIA JOHNSON: What do you mean?

JOAN SANDERS: It was just something that was expected
of me, like dressing to go out into the street. You
have to wear clothes; you're supposed to be jealous
—that's all. But in the deepest way, I've never
felt jealousy. You see, what I want for myself, I
also want for those I love. That includes my children, my husband, my friends. I want the same
kind of free relationships for them that I want for
myself. And if you're talking about mere sex,
neither Kyle nor I care for subterfuge; you know,
the kind of thing that goes on in what people consider an open marriage. If I ask Kyle what he's
done during the day, and if, among other things,
he's had a sexual relationship with another woman,
that's an important part of the day, too, and I don't
want that held back. And I want to be as open and
honest with as many human beings as possible,
too. Unfortunately, in this world honesty is restricted for people like me and Kyle. Most people
that I meet deserve nothing more from me than a
smile.

VIRGINIA JOHNSON: The open honesty between you, has
that had any pitfalls? In other words, has one of
you failed to live up to this honesty on occasion?

JOAN SANDERS: No.

KYLE SANDERS: The thing is, both of us have this great
fear of subterfuge. It's subterfuge that leads to undesirable emotions. We feel that subterfuge would
be a sure sign of a marriage heading for destruc-
tion. It's all very well to say that everybody can
have complete freedom, and to say, "I don't care
what my spouse does so long as I don't hear about
it." But with this secrecy you've already driven a
wedge into the marriage, right? Say that among
two couples there's a subject that's not to be dis-

cussed, or that one or the other of the people can't take. Well, that hurts the way everybody relates to everybody else. That's the second wedge that goes in there. Any little thing can start pushing a wedge into the relationship.

VIRGINIA JOHNSON: What spot is the weakest?

KYLE SANDERS: Whatever it is that even momentarily may pull one of you back, or startle you, or cause you a little pain, or something. To hide anything would be much more destructive than doing it openly. We have faith in each other, and faith in ourselves. We consider that we can take anything that comes up—and we consider our relationship so strong that nothing is going to crack it. But the thing we hate most is deception and subterfuge and dishonesty. That's the most destructive thing. We see it in other people and it destroys many relationships.

JOAN SANDERS: I also believe that if you are honest, it becomes easier and easier, and not harder and harder. That's the only way that you can go. I wouldn't want another kind of relationship.

VIRGINIA JOHNSON: Did this attract you to one another in the first place? Was this something you sensed, or checked out? And was it this that brought you together?

JOAN SANDERS: It might have. You see, I was very happy before I met Kyle, and I think he was very happy before he met me. We didn't marry out of *need*. It was out of *want*, and that's the only way I want to stay with anyone.

VIRGINIA JOHNSON: Did the absence of this kind of freedom drive either one of you out of your previous marriage? Was it a longing for this kind of relationship?

JOAN SANDERS: Well, what drove me out of the previous marriage—and I was the one who terminated it —was that there were so many things that couldn't be discussed. As Kyle put it, there were so many wedges in the relationship that after a while there *was* no real relationship. It became extremely superficial. We could only focus on what I did in the house today, what the children did, and so on and so forth; there was nothing else.

VIRGINIA JOHNSON: No depth of living.

JOAN SANDERS: That's it.

BILL MASTERS (*to Tina*): You've been trying to get a word in edgewise for some time, haven't you?

TINA BROOKS: Well, we *fell* into sexual freedom. One night after a party, Rick slept with this really cool friend of ours, Gail, and didn't tell me, and her husband Kirk wanted to sleep with me, but I passed out, so that was that. And six months later they came to New York and they were divorced but didn't want to tell us. They felt it might ruin our weekend together. Anyway, Gail and I went shopping, and she finally let it out that they were divorced. I wasn't supposed to tell Rick because we were sure if he knew he would be upset. So we all met for drinks and I looked at Rick and I thought, he doesn't know. And later, we were just sitting on mattresses (that's the way we lived then) and Rick sort of asked me calmly, what would you think about sleeping with Kirk? And I said, Rick, you can't think about that because I don't think Kirk and Gail are getting along too well. (*Laughter.*) Then Kirk and Gail had a little conference of their own and began to laugh and laugh because it turned out that we all knew about the divorce. (*Laughter.*) Rick hadn't wanted to tell me because he thought it would hurt me, and I hadn't wanted to tell Rick because it would hurt him. And then everything was out in the open, and we were just sitting around naked, and everything seemed to flow from that . . .

RICK BROOKS: We just screwed like mad, and it was all fine. (*Laughter.*) That's the truth, it really is.

TINA BROOKS: It was incredible! Because I had a "thing" about Kirk, he's fantastic! I used to have dreams about him before I married Rick and it all came out; we got to be really good friends. So in a way it does relate to what Jill and Gary have been say-

ing, that you have to, well, be involved with a
person, and not just screwing for screwing's sake,
you know. But after that weekend we didn't do it
again for a year.

DEBBIE: How did you feel about your relationship with
Rick afterward?

TINA BROOKS: It made me feel better because I had
thought I was very dull in bed, and afterward I
was surer of myself.

KYLE SANDERS (*with an edge of anger*): I'd like to ask,
has anybody here made an examination of society
and the structured way we live? You're told, "This
is the way to do this," and, "You can't do that,"
and so on. I'm not just talking about the sexual
attitudes of society and what your behavior is supposed to be, but all sorts of things. I've started
questioning—where the hell did all those rules
come from? Who says so? And who says, "You
can't do that," when your own head is asking,
"What's wrong with it? It's good!" You feel like
just smashing the rule, whether it has to do with
sex or the way you should dress, or greet someone,
or whatever.

BRUCE: Well, I grew up in Ohio and there's a lot of that
there. All through my childhood I felt I was growing up with strangers, and I spent my childhood,
like, digging in the attic for adoption papers because I felt these people can't really be related to
me. (*Laughter.*) So I was really glad to find out
there are real people in the world. For instance,
here's something I was interested in, the idea of
jealousy. I still think about that. I mean, I find it
strange that one should be more threatened if your
girl or your wife has sex with someone else—after
all, that's only organs functioning—than if she has
a real heart-to-heart six-hour talk with someone.
Why should the sex act be considered an infidelity
and the other be all right? It's totally crazy. It
seems to me we put a terribly heavy emphasis on
the physical side. Why should we value the sex
act as something more than it is?

JOAN SANDERS: I don't want to push the Women's Liberation thing, in which I happen to be very much involved, but I think male attitudes as far as their wives are concerned generally have been something like this: "Go out and get as emotionally involved as you want, but just don't screw around." And women's attitudes have been, "You can go out and screw around but just don't get emotionally involved," which is just the opposite. That's crazy. What everybody should be striving for is greater freedom for everyone. In this society, if I have four children, I'm supposed to love them all equally and love them all at the same time. If I'm married to one man, I'm supposed to love only him. Well, you know, there's something wrong with that. I'm capable of loving a great many people. Obviously if I can love four children at once, that's a start right there.

SIMON MAXWELL: I'm in total agreement with what you're saying. But like Bruce, I grew up in the Middle West, and I've ended up with some real emotional hang-ups. The goals we're all talking about are easy to state and easy to believe in, but in working them out—well, Dee and I have had some failures because of my getting unhappy when Dee was balling somebody else. Unless I'm into somebody, too, unless there's at least that kind of mechanical equity, I do have jealousies, and they're very real. And, you know, I wish I didn't have those hang-ups. They've been disastrous to me personally because of my desire to live with the kind of goals we've all been stating here today. My jealousy was much stronger than what, in my good judgment, I thought it should be. I've had some bad emotional reactions.

VIRGINIA JOHNSON: A quick question: when you're involved and she's not, do you ever feel sorry for her?

SIMON MAXWELL: The thing is, one of my sicknesses— or what I think is a sickness—is that I don't let that happen. I play safe, emotionally safe, by saying, I'm not going to get emotionally involved, not unless Dee is emotionally involved with somebody else.

BILL MASTERS (*to Dee*): How do you live with his bad moments?

DEE MAXWELL (*slowly*): I feel guilty. And as it has developed, I've gotten very angry at him sometimes for making me feel constrained. But I hope for evolution. I have to believe that things will develop in such a way that we will both be able to have relationships with other people as we choose.

QUENTIN: Something puzzles me. Simon is perfectly willing to say to himself, there's something wrong with me because I feel jealous when Dee is balling someone else, and I'd better cure myself of it. And Dee simply accepts it on that level. I keep wondering, where is the feeling for the other person? Where is the commitment to the other person, the commitment that says you're aware of the other person's feelings, and you want to work at your marriage so that *both* of you are equally happy with the arrangement?

SIMON MAXWELL: The commitment is there. Maybe we can come to it if we talk about the process that we're going through.

DEE MAXWELL: The process at this point comes down to a very serious question: what is the degree of commitment to our relationship? Simon and I have the feeling that to have a worthwhile relationship, and we're committed to that, we have to go through the process of becoming strong individuals, and then bringing ourselves, as individuals, into a very strong relationship together. I think that is why most of us here are strongly involved in Women's Lib. Most of us at this table consider ourselves far too influenced by society and its rules, and that's why, first of all, we feel that the only way we can have a strong relationship is to be two, strong, free individuals.

SIMON MAXWELL: You see, I think it would be nice if we were free and comfortable in our freedom. If

I were comfortable, I wouldn't be making Dee feel guilty and constrained. And I wouldn't impose constraints on myself in order to minimize the swinging relationship, to say nothing of the pain I sometimes feel.

BILL MASTERS: What is your reservation, Tina, about this discussion? You've been sitting there, not like a Doubting Thomas, but obviously with a reservation. What is it?

TINA BROOKS: Oh, I don't quite know what to say. It's something personal about myself. I don't know what Rick thinks when we get together with other couples, but I always think that definitely one couple is having a better time than another. And it's really freaking me out.

BILL MASTERS: How do you know this?

TINA BROOKS: I know this because Rick hasn't really had a good time except twice—that is, with two particular girls—while I've had a good time . . .

BILL MASTERS: Most of the time?

TINA BROOKS: Every time.

BILL MASTERS: Every time?

TINA BROOKS: Oh, except once or twice. (*Laughter*.) But it's probably mostly in my head, you see.

BILL MASTERS (*to Rick*): Is this true for you or is this just what she tells you it is?

RICK BROOKS (*defensively*): For me? It's like there are good days and bad days. It doesn't have to be explained. I don't know why things are good or bad, but if it feels good, it's good, and I don't have to talk about it if it isn't good.

BILL MASTERS: But obviously you have not relieved her concern in the area. Why? If you accept it as just a good or a bad day, and she can't accept it this way, what do you suppose it means?

RICK BROOKS: To be frank with you, I don't understand your question.

BILL MASTERS: Why haven't you tried to reassure her? She's raised an issue. "I'm uncomfortable," she's saying—at least as she comes through to me.

RICK BROOKS: Right. She says at times it's an uncomfortable situation, and I say if it's an uncomfortable situation, it's past, it's done with; let's not do it anymore. It's as simple as that.

VIRGINIA JOHNSON: It's a bigger issue than that.

RICK BROOKS: It might be. But my particular frame of mind has never permitted me to think about it that way, because I don't approach sex in that way, I approach it as fun, and if it's not fun . . . Let me put it this way: I'm no more concerned about her uneasiness over sex than if she has had a bad day shopping. I'll say, "I'm very sorry, dear, that it was a bad day," and I'll kiss her, and then we'll go on and have dinner; and that's it. It's not a big enough issue to make a fuss about.

TINA BROOKS: Well, I can tell when he's uptight and I try to understand the situation. But if I'm having a good time and I know he's not, I can't go over and help him.

JILL DORLER *(to Rick)* You know, Gary and I have been together with Tina and you, and I want to contradict you. I think you're not admitting the extent to which you care when Tina doesn't have a good time. I remember that time when we were with you, and Tina didn't feel that Gary was really responding to her as a person while you and I had a great time. And that affected you. I know because when we wanted to take drugs, you felt it wouldn't work because Tina and Gary really didn't hit it off. And now we want to go away on a weekend with you and Tina, but you feel you need other people to insulate her in case she gets off with Gary, and it doesn't work again. So, it really *does* affect you. I think you're just not facing it, you're not admitting it.

RICK BROOKS: I would like to defend my position, but I can't. I guess I may have been giving you a lot of jive, even though I really didn't know it myself. Because I obviously do care, now that I think about it; I'm a bit more concerned than I thought I was. You see?

KYLE SANDERS *(to Rick)*: I understand how you feel

when you're afraid that things haven't been going well for Tina but, speaking for myself, I would want to say that it's important to keep these things in perspective. In our marriage, Joan's activities enrich my life. That's my attitude toward her. Whatever she does—whether she sees a good movie and gets turned on by it and comes and tells me—she enriches my life, see? And because I am so close to her, I enrich *her* life. In this way we both increase our lives, enrich each other by the experiences we have, and sex is just part of the whole thing. You see, our marriage does not stand or fall on the basis of a good or bad sex experience. Our interest is in *experiences,* they could be good or they could be bad, depending on the situation. If she's had a bad experience, that means she's had a bad few hours, she's gone to see a bad movie and it bombed. (*Laughter.*) That's all it is. So you just don't go to that one again.

JOAN SANDERS: That's exactly what I wanted to say to you, Tina. I wanted to give you a different perspective on your feelings when you enjoy yourself and, say, Rick doesn't enjoy himself. I know that if I enjoy myself and Kyle doesn't at that particular time, he's still getting something out of it because I am enjoying myself. When one of us has a good time, you know, that's shared between both of us.

BILL MASTERS: There's an aspect of this discussion growing out of what Kyle and Joan were saying that is a little difficult to understand. Instead of talking about sex, we'll stick with Kyle's example of a movie. After all, a movie is about as impersonal as a thing can be . . . Now if a man goes to a movie with his wife and he enjoys it but she doesn't, he certainly has the pleasure of his own enjoyment. But there probably is a part of him that is sorry she isn't enjoying it, and if he had it to do over again, perhaps he would hope to find a movie they both would enjoy. And as I listen to you, I'm looking for that kind of mutual awareness and involvement.

JOAN SANDERS: You can't set life up in such a way that everybody enjoys everything, and everybody goes off into the sunset happy.

GARY DORLER: I haven't gotten the impression that all of these couples here are unresponsive to each other just because they haven't dwelled on problems. I remember going on this fantastic canoe trip once and for ten days it rained; it rained the whole time. I was miserable, but looking back, you know, you remember the good parts. Now we could sit here and tell you about everything that ever went wrong, and how we tried to bolster each other up, but it just isn't the way we see things, and it isn't the way we experience them. (*To Bill Masters*) Why do you have to imply that things have been bad?

BILL MASTERS: I don't imply that. I'm suggesting that life is rarely without pain as well as pleasure, unhappiness as well as happiness, and that this is particularly true in any deep emotional relationship. We remember both the pain *and* the pleasure, and we don't have to deny the fact that both can exist at the same time. Because there is no appreciating the good times without remembering and understanding the hard times, remembering how you got to the good times.

SIMON MAXWELL: What you are saying is that we ought to talk about the bad side as well as the good side of things, that we ought to bring out our painful experiences, too, in order to understand what it's all about.

JOAN SANDERS: Well, outside of an out-and-out tragedy which has no comic relief, I can almost always find something good in an experience. I mean I can have a sexual encounter with some guy and it can be really lousy, and then when I look back on it, I can say, "That was a funny thing he did!"

VIRGINIA JOHNSON: That's a measure of your personality and the way you see things as an individual. As an individual, you tend to put things in a positive perspective.

JOAN SANDERS: If you're interested in investigating life, you want to know all of life. You don't want to know just the good times, and just the happy people; you don't want to make yourself blind to part of the total experience.

BILL MASTERS: Yes—but a good many of you haven't wanted to look on both sides of experience. These three nice people on my left [Bruce, Quentin, Debbie] have described a very warm, comfortable situation but they haven't described the whole situation at all. While these two nice people on my right [the Maxwells] have been far and away the most specific of the group. They have said what their areas of concern are. Now this is what has come through to me as I've been listening.

GARY DORLER: Naturally, you have to expect some ups and downs in anything you do. But it's the ups that you remember after it's all over. Like . . . Jill and I had been talking about having sex with other people for a long time. In fact, we had been talking about it so much we got to a point where we just couldn't conceive of there being any problem with it. So I asked this girl I knew to come home with me, and I made love to both of them— Jill and this girl. They didn't really get very involved with each other, but the next morning I was walking about four feet off the ground. I remember going into a supermarket and it had never looked so great in my life. It was like being in love with the world, you know. And Jill had to go out to work, and later I picked her up, and both of us felt fantastic about it. Yet I've felt jealous when Jill's been out with other people, say, if she had a date, and I was trying to arrange a date for myself because now I had a free evening before me. Sometimes I wasn't able to make a date or I didn't bother. But I was less jealous when I could make a date. I also remember feeling jealous when we'd go to a cocktail party and she'd be talking to some guy for two hours. I would get a little annoyed about that though I don't think of it as an issue.

JILL DORLER: I think we went through a lot of different stages in the beginning. We wanted to explore different areas of ourselves. For instance, I might have wanted to get to know a man who was interested in poetry, or who had a level of sensitivity that Gary didn't have. So we kind of developed along the lines of seeing people separately.

BILL MASTERS: Was sex involved?

JILL DORLER: Yes. And it was like having separate feelings and relationships. At the same time we were seeing couples, swinging, but we found that to be more of an artificial situation and more purely sex oriented, than when we saw someone individually and that person was adding something to both of us. It's like what Joan and Kyle are talking about; when we could more fully develop ourselves as people, it sort of enriched both of our lives. Just the same, there were things that I missed sharing with Gary and I found myself wanting to do less and less without him, and I wanted more and more to spend my time with him. Now it's as if the two of us are above it all; we really work beautifully together, and we're supportive as well. We've always been sexually compatible but, you know, we allow all the other areas of expression to exist—to enjoy, to glory in. Now we're always interested in expanding our world to include other people, but we, the two of us, are the center of it.

BILL MASTERS (*to Jill*): Are you more interested in casual exchanges or would you prefer to have, say, a semipermanent arrangement?

JILL DORLER: The more permanent thing.

VIRGINIA JOHNSON: Does the word "family" have meaning in what you're saying?

JILL DORLER: Well, we're going to have children in a couple of years and that's changing our whole approach.

BILL MASTERS: In what way?

JILL DORLER: I don't think we should raise children in a nuclear family. I don't think it would be fair to lock them up with us, to make ourselves the only two people through whom they experience the world. I think if we have four or five couples and their children, there would be variety, a richness of personality which would be better for the children. And if all the adults are having sex together, it's just that much more natural and loving.

BILL MASTERS: Do all you people feel the same way about that?

TINA BROOKS: Yes.

RICK BROOKS: Yes, to a large degree.

TINA BROOKS: In fact, we were going to go into a building together with some other people and the people we were going with want babies, too. We all want them at the same time.

RICK BROOKS: But the arrangement is proving that it's not as communal as it could be—which is a disappointment.

BILL MASTERS: Why do you want babies?

TINA BROOKS: I want them for a lot of reasons. One: I want little Ricks. Two: I was pregnant once and it was fantastic; I mean you really feel like a woman, and I know just from that short experience that it's supposed to be a fantastic thing to have a baby. I just don't want to miss it. Then, too, I'm going by the people I know, my sister, my mother, friends, and I feel this is something I'd be crazy to miss. I want our own children, but I also want to allow them to have other parents. If they prefer Gary to Rick, or Jill to me, that's okay.

DEE MAXWELL: Really?

TINA BROOKS: Absolutely.

BILL MASTERS: Of course, you realize that at this stage of the game, it's theory.

DEE MAXWELL: You think that now, you decide how you *should* feel about a situation, but when it comes about, you may not feel that way.

VIRGINIA JOHNSON: Rick, how do you feel about having babies?

RICK BROOKS: Well, I don't know quite what to say about that, I really don't, but I do think that I want to have them. In fact, I *know* I want to have them. As for the reasons, I'm not analytic. I'm just accepting the fact that I think it'll be fun to watch something grow and develop . . .

VIRGINIA JOHNSON: Get a plant. (*Laughter.*)

KYLE SANDERS: Joan and I have discussed this—the commune—but we both work and we both dig each other, so that's really the nucleus of our marriage. In other words, we're just as happy to be with each other as with other people. In fact, we get the most fun out of each other, and with friends dropping over. And sometimes we just want to be by ourselves; we don't even want our best friends to drop in, especially when the way we live, and with our attitudes toward people, our house is a goddamned commune whether we like it or not. The door is open. The kids have friends and they have friends. And we have friends, too . . .

DEE MAXWELL: I don't see why, in an extended situation, privacy wouldn't be possible. Or, if you don't have a large group, why couldn't one extend what we have in a base relationship of two, to two units, and relate on that basis?

KYLE SANDERS: It's not the physical layout that is an obstacle. You could have private rooms. What I'm talking about is this: when you care for people, and you are relating to them, it's an expenditure of energy, and I have just so much energy. I have only so much for work, so much for a relationship with this person, so much for that person. What energy I have is already spread out to my wife, my children, the people that come to visit, and so forth. I feel that all my energy is already absorbed.

DEE MAXWELL (*to Joan*): I'm curious—do your children know that you swing?

JOAN SANDERS: They certainly know our attitudes.

SIMON MAXWELL: Our children are too young, but I think they will know when they get older.

JOAN SANDERS: We have three teenagers and they're certainly aware of our attitudes about sex. However, if we've gone to an orgy, we certainly don't come home and say, "Gee, kids, it was a great orgy." But were they to ask us, we wouldn't hide anything and I know they could understand.

GARY DORLER: Do you think your youngsters may be doing it?

JOAN SANDERS: I'm sure for a fact that our two boys, who are fifteen and seventeen, are having emotional trips.

GARY DORLER: Do you think they might be doing it in other than pairs?

JOAN SANDERS: They might. We've never really sat down, you know, and said, we're going to have a sex discussion tonight, and what are you into? But I don't feel that any of them would be shocked; that's because we haven't presented one set of ideas to them while maintaining or living another.

RICK BROOKS: May I ask you a question about that? You said before that you love Kyle the way you love your children, right? It's kind of a personal thing. If you two discuss things openly at the end of the day, why don't you carry that through to your children and talk about sex with them the way you do anything else? I'm just curious about how I'm going to react in terms of this with my children, when they come along.

JOAN SANDERS: We do discuss things openly with the children but it depends on what comes up. For instance, communicating with Eddie is generally about things like his guitar, his friends or school. Now were he to ask me how I felt about other things, I would give him my opinion. But what may interest Kyle and me does not interest Eddie at this time.

RICK BROOKS: Then it's not a reservation about talking about sex?

JOAN SANDERS: Not at all.

TINA BROOKS: But if you brought up the subject, would

that perhaps bring your son out? Maybe he really wants to talk about sex but doesn't dare.

JOAN SANDERS: Oh, no, that's not the case.

BILL MASTERS: May I point out something that those of you who don't have children haven't had the opportunity to realize? And that is, when kids are in the home, you don't talk about what interests Mom and Pop because they couldn't care less. You talk with the children about what interests them.

KYLE SANDERS: That's right. All you can do is to keep the atmosphere open so that the children don't feel that sex is a taboo subject, and when they're ready, then you discuss it, whatever they're into. For instance, we've had a fifteen-year-old going through a heartbreaking love affair. He has gone from the heights to despair and, you know, we felt like we had a potential suicide on our hands. At fifteen, you can be terribly depressed. We tried to draw him out, to find out what was wrong, but the affair had been over for two weeks before he would even admit that this was what was wrong with him. He's heartbroken. Now we know what heartbreak is—we've all experienced it, but there's nothing we can say to him. The point is, if he wants to talk about it, fine, and if he doesn't want to talk about it, all we can do to help him is to stand by and sympathize, and maybe tell him, yeah, we've had heartbreaks, too.

JOAN SANDERS: Here's another thing: when our oldest was about sixteen, he had some friends staying over at the house. We didn't tell anyone where to sleep, there were enough places for them to flop down. When I got up in the morning, there was Tommy, my son, with this young girl sleeping on the couch, and as I walked by, he said, "Hi, Mom." Well, obviously he never asked me whether he should sleep with her, but he felt relaxed enough —knowing that I was going to walk by in the morning—to say, "Hi, Mom." Now the only discussion I felt I *should* have with him at that point was a discussion on birth control. What I know I shouldn't do is to ask him how groovy his relationships are.

VIRGINIA JOHNSON: What about the girl's mother? Does she know her daughter . . .

JOAN SANDERS: No, no. The child's mother assumed that we have the same values she has and she trusted her daughter to sleep over. I was talking to Kyle and I expressed some concern about that, and he said, "My God, you hypocrite," and he was absolutely right. I do not have to take on the morals of other parents, or their responsibilities. If they're very religious people, for instance, and I am not, I don't have to pretend to go to church on Sunday. So I do not have to pretend that I am shocked, or that I am against this sort of thing, when actually I am not.

VIRGINIA JOHNSON: I completely concur. You don't have to pretend to be shocked. And I'm with you on the matter of church. But there is a pitfall here. There is your responsibility toward the parent who presumes that because you're a parent, you are going to be a protector of her child, and there you've got to face her and say, "Look, this is who I am" —you know? You have to forewarn the other parent.

SIMON MAXWELL: You've got to show your hand.

VIRGINIA JOHNSON: Precisely.

BILL MASTERS: I think this is terribly important. If the daughter is going to sleep over, what that means to me might be entirely different from what it means to the girl's family. At this stage of the game, we don't have to agree, but we do have to be responsible, to be aware of the fact that people presume that your feeling is essentially the same as theirs, whatever theirs is. And if they are presuming wrong, you ought to let them know.

VIRGINIA JOHNSON: You cannot duck the responsibility. But there are kinds of sidestepping things you can do. For example, you can say to the girl, "Look, it's fine with me, but it's up to you to clear it with your family."

JOAN SANDERS: Then my responsibility would have been to tell the child this. The other thing would be to make absolutely sure that Tommy knew everything there was to know about contraception.

VIRGINIA JOHNSON: Yes, to extend the protection.

JOAN SANDERS: It is my responsibility because my son is not going to come directly and ask me about it.

BRUCE: What about your daughter? You said you also have a daughter.

JOAN SANDERS: It is absolutely no different. I do not have different values for my sons than I have for my daughter. My daughter is thirteen and she knows whatever she wishes to know about sex, birth control and so on.

BRUCE (to Bill Masters): What we've been describing here, about swinging, seems to me very normal. To me it's the attitude of a cross-section of people I know in Chicago—or maybe I just know a lot of strange people. But from your experience, people you've interviewed or worked with, would you consider it abnormal, or unusual?

BILL MASTERS: If you're talking about a cross-section of the population, yes, it's unusual.

VIRGINIA JOHNSON: That's a statistical statement, not a judgmental one.

DEBBIE: Do you think ours is a healthier attitude?

BRUCE: Yes, let's have a judgmental answer; we want to know your opinion.

BILL MASTERS: That's a fair question. And yet I'm going to have to dodge it—for very good reasons. We have an absolute philosophy; we must be nonjudgmental. And unless we know, or we are reasonably sure of an answer, we don't give one. In this case I'm not reasonably sure of an answer so I'll say my personal opinion matters not a damn. There's so much personal opinion, and so much theory, and so little fact in the field of sexual behavior that we never present a personal opinion. If we can get to the facts, or if our concept of the facts is reasonably secure, then we talk. Otherwise we don't. So, you see, that's why I'm dodging the questions.

VIRGINIA JOHNSON: To learn—that's why we're here, you know; and that's why we asked you to be here —to learn what works for you. In our work we see a lot of the things that happen to people as a result of repression. Needless to say, we're not a cheering section for that, but for us to go out and say that something else is ideal—well, that raises other considerations that do not belong in this discussion.

Bill Masters and Virginia Johnson comment: If in truth swinging is enjoyable for both members of a committed unit, one can only say: how fortunate! But there are a number of important ifs—*if* the extramarital activity (whether it occurs with both partners in the same social situation or with each functioning individually in outside affairs), actually is stimulating to both of them in such a way that it reinforces their desire for each other; *if* it is an activity that each unequivocally supports for the other, with no doubts and no reservations; and *if* the extramarital sexual pattern proves over a period of time to strengthen the relationship between the husband and wife, then and only then would this kind of behavior be understandable. These are very special conditions and they are not likely to be met by many couples who engage in this experimental kind of lifestyle.

One important observation is worth making: husbands and wives, who have been quoted on the basis of their participation in swinging, consistently maintain that this sort of extramarital sexual activity makes them appreciate each other more than ever and, indeed, that they find each other "better" than anyone else with whom they have sex. To any objective observer, such remarks are surely suspect. It is another case of individuals who are "protesting too much." It is against logic, if not against any understanding of human nature, to believe that in such an explosive and powerful a situation as this, many husbands and wives do not in fact find other partners superior to their married partners. But for them to admit this would be to end the swinging then and there; the only way this diversion can continue is if both partners reassure each other that they are, of course, the "best."

As soon as the issue of jealousy is raised, it becomes apparent that the surface expression of the joys of swinging conceals fears that trouble one partner, if not both. Who is jealous? What creates the sense of jealousy? There is something incredibly naive in the belief that when one partner is having extramarital sex, the other partner's jealousy is of the sexual activity itself—and therefore as long as both of them are engaged in this practice, there will be no occasion for jealousy. This foolish notion completely ignores the true sources of jealousy, which include, among others, a fear of being displaced in someone's affections as a result of encounters between men and women whose only concern is the intensification of sexual sensation.

Under these circumstances, jealousy goes underground. Once the insecure partner has been persuaded or cajoled into participating in swinging, so that nominally jealousy is no longer reasonable, true feelings can no longer be expressed and so they simmer, building pressure to a point where it must ultimately explode. This does not augur well for the future of the marriage; it is safe to say that under these circumstances the dissolution of the marriage would not be unexpected.

What always exists as a problem in a swinging situation is the surfacing of a fear of sexual inability. This is found more commonly among men, for obvious reasons. No matter how Simon Maxwell rationalizes his feelings, the truth is that his jealousy stems from his insecurity about sexual performance. Whether he is aware of it or not, he is afraid that he will come off second best, compared to the male who is at the time having intercourse with his wife. The problem is then complicated by the fact that not only must the male deal with his own doubts concerning his sexual prowess but he must also try to persuade himself that his jealousy is groundless. Thus his self-esteem is eroded even further; he cannot perform and he cannot control his only-too-natural emotional reaction to the situation. Under these circumstances, his effectiveness as a functioning male is undercut so severely that it would be remarkable if he were able to perform in spite of it.

It may be instructive to glance briefly at three cases, totally unrelated to the symposium, in which sexual pathology came into existence after the couples concerned had been involved in episodes of swinging. These couples came to the Reproductive Biology Research Foundation clinic for treatment of sexual dysfunction.

One man was in his late twenties; he and his wife had been together with two other couples, with the understanding that each partner was free to have sexual relations with any other member of the opposite sex. The younger man had had a good deal to drink and then discovered that he was unable to achieve or maintain an erection with any of the women, including his wife. Since the other men had had as much to drink as the younger man, they all felt free to make fun of him and thus created a fear of performance which had not existed before then. Consequently he found himself unable to function effectively with his wife; on those occasions when he did manage to achieve penetration, he lost his erection almost immediately. Only after therapy was this dysfunction remedied.

Another case involved a man in his mid-forties. He and his wife had been one of four couples who spent a weekend together with the understanding that everyone would be sexually available to everyone else. The older man was able to have intercourse the first night with two of the four women and by the second afternoon had had intercourse with the remaining two women. But for the rest of the weekend he found himself unable to achieve and maintain erections, for reasons that could not be conclusively determined but that no doubt included tension and possibly sexual satiation. Like the younger man in the first case, he was teased for his inability to perform. Although he was only in his forties, as were two of the other three men, the fourth man being in his mid-fifties, he was singled out to be made fun of and to be teased for becoming too old too fast. Obviously the teasing stimulated performance fears which had not previously been present. As a consequence, long after the swinging episode was over, he found himself unable to function effectively with his wife. And on three different occasions when he tried to reassert his prowess with other women, he found himself confronted by failure.

In the third case, a woman had been talked into swinging by her husband. Through the twelve years of their marriage, sex had been satisfactory for both of them, although of late they had found themselves restless and willing to consider extramarital affairs. After she discovered that her husband had participated in a few one-night stands, she in turn became involved in two incidents herself. When her husband then suggested that they swing together, she felt that this might be preferable to having private extramarital affairs which had to be concealed.

They went to one swinging session—he eagerly, she nervously—and found that almost everyone present was younger than they were. Moreover the wife felt that the women were more attractive and had better figures and she became completely turned off sexually. She did accept two men during the course of the evening but considered herself a consolation prize. Although she had gone along with the idea, reluctantly but with some degree of willingness and curiosity, she subsequently viewed the whole incident as one in which she had been "forced" by her husband to participate, a feeling that freed her to be sufficiently angry at him to remain sexually unavailable for almost three years. During that time, she secretly made one effort to return to each of the two men with whom she had previously had sexual relations, only to discover that with them, too, she was unable to respond.

Many couples who engage in swinging do so because they find the presence of other people exciting. It is not unusual for couples to desire some kind of additional erotic stimulation. In itself there is nothing wrong with this; on the contrary, whatever means a couple finds mutually acceptable—whether reading books or looking at movies or anything of the kind—which succeeds in arousing them so that sexual exchange becomes heightened, fulfills a useful function. Even so, two points must be noted. First, if such contrived means must be resorted to frequently or consistently, this indicates a possible problem in the couple's intimate relationship and heralds ultimate onset of sexual dysfunction. Second, the need to resort to essentially artificial methods of arousal is evidence that one of the partners, or both, are unable or unwilling to improve the quality of their sexual relationship by improving the quality of their emotional relationship, and it may also indicate that they have failed to find the ways that will heighten sexual pleasure purely through the efforts that each one makes to please the other.

For Jill and Gary Dorler, it seems probable that the pleasure of sex as an intimate exchange and expression of spontaneous feelings had faded. They needed some kind of artificial stimulation. Inviting the friend to film them during intercourse provided one of them, or both, with the extraneous excitement that comes from being watched. It is not entirely unlike children who show off in order to prove to their friends—and, of course, to themselves as well—how "special" they are. In addition, they then possessed films that they could use to generate excitement at other times, whether viewing it themselves or showing it to other people and being stimulated by the audience reaction.

Fantasy is, of course, one of the most commonly used means of bringing extra stimulation into sexual functioning. There is nothing inherently wrong if a man or a woman, while engaged in sex with a partner, imagines the scene or the partner or the sexual exchange itself to be quite different from the reality.

(It is to be hoped, however, that such fantasies are not always required for sexual satisfaction to be achieved.)

But acting out a fantasy—which is the case here—is another matter. It suggests exhibitionism more than anything else. There can be little doubt that anyone's performance, in any activity, may be heightened by the presence of spectators—as athletes and musicians, for example, know very well. A single "performance" or perhaps one that is repeated a few times as an expression of a wish to experiment or, as is more likely, to do the forbidden, childish though this may be, need not be considered too serious a matter. Immaturity is not a cause for grievous concern; in time and with experience, escapades of this order can be recognized for what they are, even by participants—as reenactments of adolescent fantasies.

Immaturity of another order is evident in the actions of the trio who participated in the symposium. Although they were not really what the French call a *ménage à trois*—literally, a family unit of three—since Quentin had his own apartment, they nevertheless did reflect some of the forces that are often present in such arrangements. Popular opinion tends to exaggerate the sexual component in any unorthodox arrangement for living. In fact, the motivating force that unites individuals this way is less the search for sexual novelty than the need for emotional security. The young—and the not-so-young—band together to draw warmth, comfort and strength from each other. Sex, when it is not on a one-to-one basis, is frequently an expression of genuine feeling, rather than the sort of experimentation that characterizes much of the activity of other men and women who live by permissive sexual codes. (It should be noted, incidentally, that in the case of this particular trio, the sexual relationships linked each of the two men with Debbie but not, as far as could be determined, with each other.)

By nature, such arrangements are delicately balanced and not likely to endure for long periods, especially if those involved are on the immature side. For them, living communally represents a stage of develop-ment, a kind of halfway house between their parental homes and the homes they will ultimately establish for themselves as fully responsible adults.

Some communal living arrangements, however, in-volve mature, intelligent individuals who are genuinely seeking a way of life that will be superior to that of the isolated nuclear family, and their efforts should not be confused with those of young people who still have not found themselves with any sense of personal se-curity in what they see as a frightening world.

A similar distinction should be made in relation to swinging. An unorthodox sexual code is not neces-sarily a sign of immaturity and may be adopted, even if only for a particular phase of life, by responsible men and women, as in the case of Joan and Kyle Sanders. If their remarks are accepted at face value —and nothing that they said during the course of this symposium would indicate otherwise—they emerge as a couple who are not only older and more experienced than the other participants but who have, in addition, lived through enough emotional conflicts to have evolved a philosophy of life that serves them well. They seem to have a sense of security in their relationship and they seem to share a value system that sustains them as individuals and as a married unit.

There is a vast difference between people who have had an extensive sexual life prior to marriage— or prior to a second marriage, too—and people who have not yet lived full enough lives to distinguish be-tween the adolescent search for sensation for its own sake and the adult search for those experiences that contribute to personal growth. For the Sanders, sex is neither an all-consuming passion nor a matter of sec-ondary importance. As Joan has expressed it, neither partner is willing to put up with subterfuge and, while their involvement with swinging was apparently a brief phase motivated more by curiosity than anything else, they cannot and will not arbitrarily live by a monoga-mous standard. Each apparently finds no threat in the other's extramarital activity; both are fundamentally convinced that intercourse is to be expected within the context of a social relationship that has some warmth and meaning in itself and both partners apparently have sufficient confidence in each other and in themselves individually so that the extraneous sexual relationship poses no threat to their marriage.

It is, of course, impossible to tell whether these views reflect logic or self-deception; only a long-term follow-up of such a marital commitment could answer this question. If they are self-deceived, their commitment will falter; if they are acting according to a genuine emotional logic that applies in their particular case, their commitment will survive and prosper—and in all likelihood the need or the desire for other partners will diminish over time. (This tendency toward increasing personal commitment as a relationship matures will be considered in more detail in the following chapter.) Their case is clearly not one in which either partner, or both, is using this unorthodox way of life as a means of achieving status by bragging about it to friends or neighbors—unlike a couple who use their sexual lives as a means of calling attention to themselves and achieving a notoriety purely on the basis of their sensational disclosures concerning their private sexual experiences.

The idea of using sexual intercourse as a means of achieving friendship and emotional intimacy outside of marriage is indeed a seductive one. And it is certainly true that sexual functioning is a potentially effective means of communication between two partners—regardless of whether they are married or not. To be perfectly logical, it would almost seem that sex, considered as just another way of communicating, should make it possible for any two people to achieve friendship and to become emotionally involved with each other.

Unless there are emotional bonds which link a man and woman and which exist entirely apart from the pure physical relationship, unless they share interests and values which exist outside the bedroom, sexual functioning is not sufficient in itself to establish enduring friendships. In fact, although it would seem that if a man and a woman are sexually intimate they must also be emotionally intimate, this very often proves to be not true; sex, as any prostitute will testify, can take place any number of times with no emotional involvement whatsoever. Intimacy must be nourished by a mutuality between a man and a woman that may include but must go beyond the physical fact of intercourse. Intimacy, like any other emotion, must either grow and become deeper or it must wither and die.

Certainly sexual consciousness—that is, a pleasurable awareness on the part of two people of their complementary sexuality—is an additional factor in friendship between a man and a woman, but it certainly would be foolish to confuse sexual consciousness with sexual intimacy. In fact, what the individuals in the symposium were suggesting is a false similarity—a physical interchange is not an emotional interchange, and physical intimacy is not the same as emotional intimacy. Neither physical interchange nor physical intimacy is a sound basis for a continuing relationship. Anyone who suggests that intercourse is in itself a good foundation for friendship proves, with that single statement, an ignorance of two different relationships; such a person knows nothing of the meaning of sex in the context of an emotional involvement—and such a person knows nothing of the meaning of friendship, neither of its origins nor how it is developed nor the part that it can play in the lives of any two individuals.

At the start of the symposium, the participants were emphasizing the positive side of their activities and virtually ignoring any possible negative considerations. This is understandable; they were, after all, in an unfamiliar situation and it required some time before they could be comfortable enough not to be defensive. But as the discussion proceeded, it became fairly evident that whatever their original motivations may have been, impelling them to experiment in various fashion with sexual exchanges, they experienced an evolution in approach which culminated in arrangements that stressed the interpersonal relationship rather than the sexual exchange *per se*. The general picture might be likened to any orgy: all the individuals scramble around for a while, until eventually they become more selective and limit their sexual exchanges to a smaller and smaller number of individuals—and it would not be surprising if, in the end, they discover themselves happier to restrict their sexual involvement to just one partner.

Postscript: One year after the original symposium took place, the same group was invited to meet for breakfast with Dr. and Mrs. Masters, who happened to be in Chicago. Tina and Rick Brooks did not respond to the invitation and all efforts to determine whether they were still married met with failure. Of the trio, Bruce and Quentin were present but, as Bruce explained, Debbie had gone off several months earlier to search for her own identity as a person. All the other original participants were present at the breakfast meeting. Without exception, they all indicated that the pace of their sexual activity had slowed considerably; several of them had stopped swinging altogether; and two of the men indicated that they were having potency problems. One further note: it was subsequently learned that the Maxwells, one of the couples present at the breakfast, were divorced not long afterward. Obviously the symposium participants can in no way be taken as representative of the swinging population and no conclusions can be drawn concerning the dynamics of this particular subculture. Suffice it to say that all but two of the participants—the Sanders couple —emerged from their experiences seeking an improved sense of personal security. Only Joan and Kyle Sanders seemed to have a relationship in which each partner felt safe with the other. It may be worth noting that at the breakfast meeting they said they were no longer swinging because they didn't have time for it. "There are too many other things we want to do," Joan Sanders said, "and we need time to be alone together."

8

What Sexual Fidelity Means in a Marriage

LEAH: I've lost a good job because of my affair. I made it very blatant, and now I can see I was asking to be caught. So here I am at thirty-three, and I really don't know where to go or what to do.

OLIVER: I had my first extramarital activity two or three years into the marriage. . . . I fancied myself some sort of gay blade. So I decided, I'm going to get laid somewhere. And I did. And I kept on doing this for probably eight years.

CELIA: I don't think you have to experience a number of outside relationships to become happier . . . But after being with this one person, I've thought of nothing but sleeping with every man who appealed to me.

SIMON MAXWELL: We sometimes just ball other people casually, balling for the sake of balling.

JILL DORLER: Sleeping with others is very much integrated into our lives. I personally got into it because I didn't think marriage meant sexual exclusivity.

In recent years, the value and meaning of marriage has become a matter of considerable controversy. Some critics, for example, maintain that monogamy—with its emphasis on mutual commitment as the basis for an exclusive union of one man and one woman—is no longer a realistic way of life. They view conventional marriage as more of a hindrance than a help to men and women struggling to develop their individual potentialities while coping with the stresses of contemporary society.

Such an outlook would certainly be affirmed by all the men and women who participated in the two preceding symposiums. Apparently unable to find the full and enduring satisfactions they want and need in a sexual relationship with the one person they married, they feel compelled to search elsewhere for the pleasures they lack. Without passing judgment on them— indeed, with full appreciation of their courage and, in some cases, their desperation in reaching out for what they desire—it seems worthwhile to try to put the subject of extramarital sex in perspective, to examine briefly the nature of sexual commitment and its relevance to marriage.

When a man and woman first commit themselves to each other sexually, they do so for reasons that have been impressed upon them by society since childhood. They have been told to believe that on the basis of their union, they will find physical, emotional and social fulfillment—and some people would include spiritual fulfillment as well. These are dimensions of human needs that have been intricately woven into "patterns" for commitment; woven and rewoven by successive generations from concepts of love and sex, which reflected prevailing religious and cultural philosophies.

Unfortunately the sexual concepts reflected even today in these patterns for commitment continue to embody ideas from the past that are demonstrably inaccurate or false or that are now completely unrealistic and incompatible with contemporary concepts of love. Sex as a conjugal duty, for example, or as an economic barter is not as palatable as it once may have been. Out of this unfortunate heritage of erroneous notions about the nature and function of sex arise a number of the difficulties that plague many married couples. Personal discomfort and anxiety, or hostility between partners, often can be traced to such depressingly familiar beliefs as that sex is the price that must be paid for love or that sex is separate from love.

But what can be said with any validity about love and sex? There now exist a few significant scientific facts which might possibly serve as the basis for a tentative reassessment of sexual expression in relation to love and other values as the basis of the man-woman bond. To do so, however, would require a reasonable definition of love. Having observed that love is interpreted in many ways—according to the values, perceptions and circumstances of those individuals who attempt to define the word—we choose to accept as an unalterable fact that love in its infinite variability is and always will be subject to individual interpretation.

It seems futile, for example, to define love as passion—that is, some subtle combination of emotional, romantic and spiritual feeling—for someone to whom love means, with equal justness, authentic and sustained kindness or emotional and economic sustenance or protection from harm. To attempt to revise either definition so that it will better accord with the values prized by some other person would mean diminishing equally cherished values. To do so would be not only fruitless but potentially destructive.

Therefore the emotional components of love, in any of its forms of expression, are implied in this discussion and throughout the book—but there will be no attempt at defining the concept and no specific references to it. When it seems appropriate or necessary, we ask the reader to apply his or her personal interpretation as it has developed out of a lifetime of beliefs, feelings and experiences.

Since love, sex and commitment, however, tend to be inextricably woven together in our society's pattern for man-woman relationships, it should be noted that the combination is arbitrary. Society, past and present, has chosen to assign sex and love to the marriage covenant. But the linking of sex and love reflects a tacit assumption that this is how it *must* be in spite of the fact that from an objective standpoint love need not necessarily be a condition of sex for a person to function sexually and sex need not necessarily be a condition of love for a person to be emotionally fulfilled.

Sex and love are separate life forces, each capable of being sustained without the other. Sex, like any natural function, theoretically can be integrated with any psychologically valued stimuli and will then produce effective physical response, and love certainly has a recorded history of being able to sustain itself admirably in the face of overwhelming physical handicaps or even when the lovers choose to live celibate lives.

Against this background, the question implicitly raised in the two preceding symposiums can be seen more clearly. Should sex no longer be assigned as part of the covenant of marriage?

The question is being asked by a number of young people. Having observed too many disillusioning examples of sexual disharmony in marriage, they are unwilling to commit themselves in any traditional sense, but prefer to live together only for as long as they please. They choose to practice sexual freedom or sexual exclusivity within their relationships on the basis of personal preference. If and when they decide to have children, they may marry—although for some individuals, even then wedlock may not be considered mandatory. Unwed motherhood, a status previously accepted out of unhappy necessity, is the deliberate choice of a small but not inconsequential number of women, and the legal right of a single person to adopt a child has been established in some states.

On the basis of this and other such evidence, some observers suggest that the institution of marriage, which has necessarily been changing over the centuries to accommodate the needs of a changing society, now faces a future in which it may gradually become obsolete. In their judgment, marriage will ultimately manifest itself not as a religious sacrament nor a legal certification but simply as a sociological fact. Thus, when a man and woman—or two individuals of the same sex—decide to live together both socially and sexually, they will be considered "married," and when they decide to stop living together they will be "unmarried." Society, no longer claiming the right to approve or disapprove, will merely register all such unions as a matter of civil record.

Social critics who contend that monogamy is losing its institutional viability have no difficulty shoring up their argument with numbers. At present, of all couples who marry for the first time, approximately one out of three will sooner or later seek a divorce; and the nation's divorce rate has been on the rise since 1960. This is not, however, a steady upward trend. Historically, the divorce rate has fluctuated over periods of time, and on one occasion, from 1945 to 1947, it was almost as high as it is at present.

In addition, a national divorce rate statistic is, by itself, virtually meaningless. It is the by-product of social and historical developments, and any intelligent understanding of its significance depends on analyzing the underlying influences.

To take a single example, for illustrative purposes —divorce occurs far more frequently among people who marry young, who have little education and little money. Once the point has been stated that way, it can be seen as simply common sense. There is a limited chance of success for a marriage—*or any other joint enterprise*—if the two individuals become partners before they are experienced enough to choose each other on any sound basis, if they lack the education that prepares them to communicate with each other effectively and to meet the social challenges and complexities they must face, and if they have so little capital, and so little hope of gaining more, that any pleasure they might find in their association is sapped by the struggle to stay financially solvent. Obviously the odds against such a pair are disproportionately high. When such unions are dissolved, the explanation has less to do with the inadequacies of marriage per se than with inadequacies inherent in immaturity when combined with little education and income. Placed in this perspective, the national divorce rate says less about the questionable state of marriage than about the questionable amount of guidance and emotional support society gives to its marriageable population.

It is as foolish to try to gauge the value and meaning of marriage by examining divorce statistics as it would be to gauge the value and meaning of life by studying mortality rates. If a moment of fantasy be permitted, it could be argued that the only sure way of evaluating the desirability of life would be to find out how many among those who have left life would take the opportunity to return.

This is, in fact, the most important way to look at divorce statistics—by checking the statistics on remarriage. The evidence is striking. According to Paul C. Glick and Arthur J. Norton of the U.S. Bureau of the Census, acknowledged authorities on the subject, the accelerated divorce rate has been accompanied by an accelerated remarriage rate. An estimated eighty out of every one hundred divorced persons remarry—and at least sixty of those eighty marriages prove permanent. Thus the very individuals who theoretically have had the experience needed to evaluate monogamy, choose to find another partner rather than live alone, and most of them do their best to make that marriage last a lifetime.

This makes no sense at all if marriage is, as some critics insist, a booby trap. Were that true, a divorced person, having savored the freedom of being single again, would hardly be lured back into matrimonial harness or, at the very least, would surely be less tolerant of constraint and more likely to slip the traces by getting a second divorce. But this pattern is the exception rather than the rule.

Contrary to popular belief, therefore, it seems clear that divorced men and women do not ride on a marital merry-go-round. Evidently experience has taught them that some important and rewarding satisfactions, which cannot be obtained otherwise, are possibilities inherent in a stable sexual relationship. Consequently even after one failure, they consider marriage a major goal in life.

This is not the case for everyone, of course, and there is much to be said in favor of a society that permits individuals sufficient choice so that those who are ill-suited to marriage can remain single all their lives with no loss of social approval. But they are a small minority of the population, and indications are that for some time to come they will so remain. For everyone else, however, what was true in the past is no less true at present and gives promise of being true in the future: the search for happiness and personal fulfillment, for the pleasures of a life that has meaning, sooner or later leads to marriage.

Some social critics who recognize this fact contend that while marriage will remain the fundamental building block of society, spontaneously chosen as a way of life by most men and women, the marital commitment will no longer include sexual exclusivity. They argue that the concept of fidelity is outmoded and must yield to a flexible arrangement which permits both husband and wife to engage in extramarital sex. More radical proposals call for this freedom to include not just the traditional heterosexual affair, but the full range of male-female combinations, including casual encounters, domestic trios, mate exchanges, group marriage, plus acceptance of bisexual relationships within these varying arrangements.

This kind of conjecturing, which totally repudiates the established principles of sexual commitment, owes less to disciplined observation of what most people require in order to live sexually effective lives than it owes to wishful fantasies about how they ought to live. When such ideas are imaginatively conceived, as they were in novels like *The Harrad Experiment* and *Stranger in a Strange Land*, in addition to being enjoyable escapist reading, they may even succeed in shaking up a reader's preconceived notions. Of course, they may also create apprehension in thoughtful readers who do not find the concepts abhorrent but do find them inconsistent with other cherished and reliable values.

These writers, and numerous nonfiction authors as well, place the pleasures of intercourse entirely in the service of self-gratification, with perhaps a moment's polite attention to a partner's request for release in one fashion or other. They reject the idea that sex might have something to do with such considerations as privacy, discretion or esthetic sensibility. And what they consider to be emancipation from Victorian prudery more closely resembles exhibitionism, on a level not much different from that of adolescents who enjoy "mooning"—dropping their pants and baring their buttocks to discomfort some unsuspecting stranger. Small wonder, then, that they consider the bond of a sexual commitment between a man and woman to be as antiquated as a chastity belt.

They are free, and should remain so, of course, to behave according to whatever standards they choose and to believe in whatever rationalizations they may need to justify that behavior. The problem lies in the fact that when a few individuals with a professional background—including such sensitive fields as psychiatry, psychology, and the ministry—act out their particular erotic fantasies and write about their experiences, they are passing along advice which implicitly urges the reader to "go and do thou likewise." This amounts to irresponsibly encouraging people to jump into a deep river with dangerous undercurrents, ignoring the fact that they may not know how to swim.

The success of these books, some of which have sold millions of copies, cannot—and should not—be attributed solely to their undeniable capacity to titillate the imagination. It also signals the existence of a widespread need for information, an understandable and almost insatiable public curiosity about the varieties of sexual expression, a subject that until recently had been kept in a shroud by censorship.

Social freedom to express this curiosity is accompanied by an attitude of dissatisfaction with the rigid

behavior codes of the past. This questioning of old
strictures is part of a healthy skepticism about sexual
values. It is characterized by a pragmatic approach to
sexual experience which may fill life with more excitement and opportunity for pleasure—but which also fills
it with greater danger and the possibility of pain.

With the abandonment of prescribed rules based
on a theological concept of virtue and sin, each individual is now forced to fashion a private set of moral
and ethical values which, it is hoped, will sustain him
over the years. Unable to achieve an effectively functional sex life by basing his conduct on the commandments of the Word, he must sift through words by
the millions in newspapers, magazines and books,
seeking some insight into his own particular nature. He
must learn to distinguish fact from fiction, blueprint
from daydream, reason from rationalization.

This is difficult to do when the subject is extramarital sex because the question calls into play a fundamental human paradox. A person feels most fully alive
when he can be stimulated by the challenge of the
unknown and yet have the security of the known to
give him the confidence he needs to try something
different than he has attempted in the past. The pleasure of being alive depends to a considerable degree
on an individual's ability to include both elements in
his life and to have as much control as possible over
the extent to which, at any given period of time, one
of these polar extremes is dominant.

For many people, however, a monogamous marriage means putting an end to this alternation between
the new and the old, the challenging and the reassuring, at least as far as sex is concerned. They lack the
imagination or the motivation to revitalize sexual interest in their own marriage, and the only variety to
suggest itself to them is having a variety of partners.
Since they find this morally unacceptable, or simply too
risky, they settle for security and, no matter how reluctantly, accept as a fact that monogamy inevitably
becomes monotony.

But the wish that it could be otherwise remains

strong. And so it is only to be expected that a great many men and women today, who until now have believed that sexual fidelity was an ideal to uphold, even if they themselves could not hold to it, are fascinated by arguments that make a case for the acceptance of extramarital sex. They half want to be persuaded that having one married partner need not mean having just one sexual partner, that any modern couple should be able to enjoy the challenge of extramarital affairs and still maintain the security of their marriage. Looked at one way, it amounts to offering husbands and wives the opportunity to have their cake and eat it, too. Looked at another way, it amounts to a magic cure for marital doldrums. Either way, the lure is powerful.

But for sexual swinger and sexual conservative alike, at the heart of the wish for sexual newness or change is a stereotyped concept of sex which omits any idea of sex as a medium for creativity. For sex can be a living medium where the feelings and the needs of two individuals take on the mood of time, place and circumstance and are communicated clearly and without exploitation of either partner by the other. The idea that sex functions naturally when it is "lived" instead of "performed" seems to escape many people. That sex can be "lived" in marriage or in a deep and continuing commitment seems to have escaped almost everyone.

The opposition to sexual commitment expressed by some young people is essentially political in nature. It is an attack on the Establishment—which, freely translated—means simply that they feel compelled to reject any standard their parents might possibly approve. Feminists who approve extramarital sex because it takes them another step away from the sexual double standard, are also using the sexual code of behavior as a political weapon. Their chief purpose is to assert that they have equal rights to any freedom that men claim—without attempting to determine whether that freedom necessarily contributes to the well-being of any individual, male or female. A different, and nonpolitical, rationale is offered by feminists who see affairs outside marriage as a means of enabling certain wives to throw off their culturally induced inhibitions and to awaken their long-dormant capacity to respond to sexual stimulation.

There can be no argument with any of these positions as long as they are not rationalized as the foundation for a general structure of sexual values. But it is important to understand that this is the pleading of special cases. If some young people must reject their parents' social-sexual values before they can be free to have the experiences they need as the basis for validating other values—or reaffirming those that were originally rejected—they are acting no differently than young people have for centuries. If some women must first establish their right to indulge in extramarital sex, as a way of regaining their self-esteem and their sense of being independent and equal human beings, so that as equals with men they can get on with the important tasks of learning to live well together, their tactics are certainly understandable. If other women must go outside their marriages in search of affirmation of themselves as sexual human beings, their actions deserve compassion and support.

But this is not the same as saying that the sexual commitment in marriage is dispensable. It says only that in some cases, under certain circumstances, the sexual commitment may warrant being compromised. *And even stating the matter on such general terms is so misleading that it almost amounts to being a deception.* For it omits several crucial qualifications, such as the fact that extramarital sex is a step to be accepted as a last resort, and that it carries with it the potential of a cure that is as unsatisfactory as the problem to be cured; what begins as an isolated act or two may become a premeditated and repeated pattern of action —which is generally as destructive to the emotional fabric of a marriage as anything can possibly be. Thus, compromising the sexual commitment as a means of patching up a marriage may succeed only in tearing it further apart.

Turning from abstract language to an illustrative example may put the problem more clearly. After reading that an extramarital relationship may help revitalize her sexual energies, a sexually distressed wife has an affair. Immediately there are questions that cannot be ignored. Has she openly communicated with her husband about her dissatisfaction? If so, why have they been unsuccessful in finding a remedy? Or getting help? And if she has not communicated with him, why not? If it is because they are emotionally incompatible, or if they cannot communicate about anything that really matters to her, what kind of a marriage does she have? If the marriage is that emotionally impoverished, why make the issue seem to be the rightness of extramarital sex—when the issue is really the inadequacy of the marriage?

Nor do the questions stop there. Even if the affair turns out well and the wife becomes sexually charged, what does she do with her drive? How can she cope with the powerful feelings that dominate her but cannot be shared with her husband? Or, trying to share them, how can she help comparing one man to another —and if her sexually unsophisticated or incompetent husband suffers by the comparison, what does she do then with her feelings? Bury them and bury too her newly kindled sexual responsivity? Or respecting her natural right to those feelings, does she embark on a succession of affairs? Or does she divorce her husband?

The questions are, in truth, endless. The few that have been raised are intended only to illuminate the virtual meaninglessness of all special pleading in favor of extramarital sex. Generalized principles are useless guides to human sexual behavior; what may apply to one person will not apply to another—and, in fact, what is true for one person at a particular moment in life may not be true for that same person at a later moment. Thus, without knowing in great detail the nature of the marriage and the psychological histories, past and present, of both a husband and wife, there is no possible way for anyone to offer a secure word of advice about the consequences that may follow if either partner, or both, decide to put an end to their sexual commitment.

Of all those who offer such advice, and who stress their conviction that extramarital sex often proves beneficial to a marriage, perhaps the most disconcerting are a few highly principled individuals, some of whom are affiliated with the ministry or religious institutions. It would be unjust, however, to place their judgment in question without first giving credit to those in their ranks who led the way in the early 1960s. Their goal was urgent and praiseworthy: to relieve the needless suffering of guilt-ridden men and women, the victims of repressive religious indoctrination.

A pamphlet issued in London in 1963, *Towards a Quaker View of Sex,* was the first major contemporary effort to turn the ethical and moral force of fundamental religious principles into a defense of the very behavior that until then had been condemned by those principles. The pamphlet, coauthored by a group of eminent Quakers, used compassionate Christianity as the reference point for what came to be called "the new morality." Although its primary purpose was to create a less hostile social climate for homosexuality, it also expressed the view that married individuals whose emotional needs led them to establish extramarital sexual relationships could be defended, at least in some cases, on moral grounds. It should be stressed, however, that the emphasis was on the personal relationships, that sexual need played a secondary role, and that the actions of all individuals involved were always presumed to be contingent upon the need to spare pain to innocent persons.

This new Christian approach to sexuality was long overdue, and from a scientific point of view merited support then and still does now. It begins to bring religious attitudes toward sex into the twentieth century. Dogmatism is being forced to yield to humanism, no matter how slowly and grudgingly, and the idea that sexual intercourse is intended for pleasure as well as procreation seems beyond contradiction.

Unfortunately, new ideas have a tendency to swing far in proverbial pendulum fashion. As attitudes change, they pick up momentum and move toward extreme positions. Language itself reflects this fact. *Adultery* became an old-fashioned word and was replaced by a more clinical one, *infidelity;* this gave way to the nonjudgmental term, *extramarital sex,* with its implication that sexual affairs occur outside marriage but are not in opposition to it; and the most recent expression is *comarital* sex, which implicitly makes any and all sexual relationships possible and acceptable in marriage.

This change in the general climate of published opinion has not been without its effect upon religious writers who, out of genuine compassion for their fellow man, originally intended only to correct the punitive, harshly judgmental, double-standard values of religious orthodoxy. In the decade since the Quaker report appeared, one book has followed another on the subject of religion and sex, attacking moral injunctions as the standard of sexual behavior. In place of such commandments, they wanted to establish responsibility as the frame of reference for evaluating any sexual encounter. The ethics of each act were to be judged in relation to the total situation, of which the sexual encounter was but a part. Consequently extramarital sex, for example, might not only be pardonable but commendable, depending on the circumstances.

Whether deeds or rules should be the basis of a moral code is a thorny theological issue and completely outside the scope of this inquiry. A different question must be considered here. Certain theologically oriented writers have rightly reacted against the old moral rigidities and have rejected automatic condemnation of fallible men and women for sexual behavior disapproved by the church. But have they presently overreached themselves and therefore inadvertently undermined the concept of voluntary sexual commitment? Is it possible that they have lost sight of a human need for the security of reasonable limits in sexual relationships, a need that exists independently of religious doctrine?

Extramarital sex is a case in point, and one pronouncement on the subject can be singled out both because it summarizes the issue and because it has been commended for its wisdom by a Catholic priest, Robert T. Francoeur. It originally appeared in 1968 in *Honest Sex,* a book with the subtitle, "A Revolutionary Sex Ethic by and for Concerned Christians," written by a husband and wife, Rustum and Della Roy. They are described as "active Christian lay people involved in church, community and educational organizations and concerned with mental health." The sentences quoted below are referred to with unequivocal approval by Dr. Francoeur in his recent book, *Eve's New Rib*.

The Roys write: "We find that sexual relations with persons other than a spouse are becoming more common. When other criteria of appropriateness are fulfilled, such relations do not necessarily destroy or hurt a marriage, nor do they inflict an unbearable hurt on the partner not involved. Indeed, when human need is paramount, such relationships can serve as the vehicle of faithfulness to God."

These are not three sentences taken out of context; they express the core of a particular philosophy, which is why they were chosen by Dr. Francoeur as a summation of his own beliefs. Their meaning, however, is something less than precise. For example, what is the purpose in noting that extramarital sex is "becoming more common"? Is the frequency with which something happens a reliable indication of its value? Besides, by what objective measure have the Roys been able to confirm as a fact that such behavior *is* more common? Compared to when?

Who sets the "criteria for appropriateness" by which extramarital intercourse is to be judged, the partner who participates or the partner who does not —or do they decide together, and if so, who has the final decision? Whose "human need" is being considered—that of the involved partner, the noninvolved partner or the third party? Moreover who is to define these needs, sexual or otherwise, and then weigh them to determine which deserve to be labeled "paramount"? Such a fantasy conjures up an image of passionless creatures who expect that their rational minds, like computers that have been fed all the available data, can be trusted to make the right decision, uninfluenced by such a natural emotion, for example, as physical desire.

To encourage such a belief is to encourage the dangerous and self-serving malady of megalomania. The Roys verge on doing this with their assurance that having extramarital relationships may "serve as the vehicle of faithfulness to God." But since they are aware that men and women caught in sexual triangles are imperfect and vulnerable human beings, they must acknowledge that there are risks. They do so, however, in evasive terms. Extramarital sex, they say, does not "necessarily" harm or destroy a marriage, nor does it inflict "an unbearable hurt" on the uninvolved partner. Not necessarily—but possibly? Even probably? And who decides whether this real risk of harming or destroying the marriage is worth taking—the partner who will enjoy having an affair in which the act of intercourse is conceptualized as an act of Christian charity? Or the uninvolved partner, who has little, if anything to gain, and a lot to lose?

As for being hurt, what does "unbearable" mean? Must the hurt partner commit suicide to prove that it was beyond endurance? Or suffer an emotional collapse? Or does asking for a divorce suffice to make the point?

It is one thing to repudiate the idea that every instance of extramarital sex is an anathema to God; it is something else to advance the idea that in certain cases extramarital sex is a way of being faithful to God. Such a suggestion, coming from authorities who are concerned with the ethics of sex, is doubly dangerous. Not only does it lend itself to the most seductive of rationalizations but it undermines the value of sexual commitment by subordinating the exclusive physical bond between husband and wife to the apparent needs of a third person.

What is the basis of such counsel? On what ground does it stand, other than conjecture? When and where and by whom has this approach to human relationships been observed and how have the effects been measured? Who has ever attempted to follow up the consequences after a lapse of time? If answers to these questions, based on even the simplest of research designs, have not yet been produced, a reasonable person would do well to remain skeptical. It is inadvisable to write with assumed authority in a field where so little is known and there is real and serious risk of harming any number of people who read and blindly follow.

The purpose of raising this issue is not to take sides in a debate over extramarital sex but to suggest that the theological approach to the problem be more carefully constructed. The emancipation of sexuality from the one-dimensional judgments imposed in the past by religious dogma represents a major advance in man's efforts to understand and accept his biological nature. This in turn has led critics, in both the clergy and the laity, to press still harder for more sweeping changes in the teachings of the church. But as a nineteenth-century British statesman, William Ewart Gladstone, once remarked: "To be engaged in opposing wrong affords, under the condition of our mental constitution, but a slender guarantee of being right."

That "slender guarantee" rests, in large part, on exercising rigorous intellectual discipline in weighing alternatives and their possible effects. This holds true for moralists as well as politicians. If the church is to continue to make progress away from a negative philosophy of sex and toward a positive one, liberal religious leaders must have strong support. But that support does not relieve them of the obligation to learn everything they can about the physiological and psychological realities of human sexual experience before they recommend changes in ethical standards, particularly those relating to sexual commitment. Otherwise the "new" morality, like the old, will amount to little more than empty pontification, an unreliable guide for the millions of confused men and women who are searching for emotional principles that they can trust in structuring their sexual relationships.

These are the men and women who constitute the overwhelming majority; when they are single they know they will eventually marry, and when they get married, they do their best to stay married. But any confidence they may have in achieving their goals cannot avoid being undermined by a society in which most of what is published in books and magazines on the subject of sex and marriage promotes the idea that, to paraphrase Ralph Waldo Emerson, a foolish fidelity is the hobgoblin of little minds.

In such a climate of opinion, discussions of commitment are not likely to flourish. An entire vocabulary shrinks; among educated people who consider themselves sophisticated, such words as loyalty and faithfulness, honor and trust, are avoided because somehow they seem suitable only for sermons. Yet all human association depends on these and other such values, and they cannot be ignored in relation to marriage. They certainly cannot be ignored by those men and women who, while welcoming their new freedom to enjoy sex openly, hope to use that freedom not just for novelty in sexual relations but to intensify a sexual relationship.

As couples, the question they want answered is not what makes extramarital sex right or wrong—but what makes it unnecessary? And the answer they need is not one that preaches the moral virtues of commitment and fidelity but one that translates these values into functional terms, that examines how and why the sense of being mutually committed may contribute to the sexual responsiveness of both partners and to the durability of their exclusive relationship.

THREE

THE MARRIAGE
THEME RESTATED

9

Second Marriages
When Communication Really Counts

Seven couples from the Philadelphia area met in June, 1971, to talk about their marriages; with the exception of four people—one couple, the Balls, and two husbands—all the participants had been married for the second time. (Enid and Hugh Ball had been invited specifically to vary the composition of the group, on the chance that they might see matters in a somewhat different light than the other participants.) Gail and George Stein were married for thirteen years, both for the second time. They were both forty-eight years old and had two adopted children. George was an electrical engineer and Gail was formerly a public schoolteacher. Don and Lois White had been married for five years; it was her second marriage, his first. Her two teenaged children lived with them. It was a second marriage for both Donna and Tony Ross, who had been married for nine years. Their family included five teenagers— three were hers, two were his. Donna was an executive in a textbook publishing concern and Tony was a clinical psychologist. Lil and Larry Lockwood had been married for four years, and for both it was a second marriage. Lil was pregnant with their first child, and her two children from her previous marriage lived with them. Larry's two teenaged children visited them on vacations. Lil, thirty-two, was a registered nurse; Larry, forty, was the president of a printing company. Pat and John Quill, twenty-nine and thirty-three, respectively, had been married for three years and had a three-year-old son. It was the second marriage for both. John was an executive with a public relations firm; his wife, formerly a secretary, was not employed at the time. The Bradleys, Debbie and Mike, married for twelve years, had a ten-year-old son, and Debbie Bradley's daughter by her first husband lived with them. Mike was forty-five and a computer specialist; Debbie was forty-six and a college administrator. Enid Ball was twenty-seven; her husband Hugh was thirty; and they had a three-year-old child. Hugh Ball was a stockbroker; Enid did not work outside the home.

VIRGINIA JOHNSON: May we begin by going around the table and having each of you tell us a little bit about yourselves and perhaps give us, if you can, a one-sentence summary of what you believe to be special about your marriage? Gail?

GAIL STEIN: George and I have been married thirteen and one-half years. We have two adopted children, a girl of ten and a boy of eight. What is unique about our marriage? I guess it's compatibility. I think we're basically similar in our outlook on kids, politics, religion . . . whatever. We have real differences but we usually work things out together.

GEORGE STEIN: I go along with Gail's description.

DON WHITE: Well, it's my first marriage and the second for Lois. We've been married now for four and a half years. We have—I have two splendid stepchildren: a boy, nearly eighteen, and a girl who will be sixteen on Monday. I find it hard to single out a way in which our marriage could be described as being unique. Perhaps Lois can. (*Lois White just smiles and shakes her head.*)

VIRGINIA JOHNSON (*turning to Tony*): Will you continue?

TONY ROSS: We're married nine years, I think. (*To his wife, Donna*) Am I right? Nine years. It's a second marriage for each of us. We have five children, none of them of our combined manufacture. I had two boys by a previous marriage, Donna had two girls and a boy, and we have all five living with us. I would say we have had, and are still having, difficult times, not so much in terms of the marriage but as a family complex. What describes our marriage best is the word "exciting." It's not necessarily always pleasurable but it's very, very exciting for me.

DONNA ROSS: I can't add anything to that.

LARRY LOCKWOOD: This is our second marriage, Lil's and mine, and we each have two children from a previous marriage. Lil's children are with us, my children come to visit. They come for longer and longer periods of time; they seem to enjoy it. And Lil is pregnant, so we are having our first child together. We will have been married four years in August, and the baby is expected in October. I guess all I want to say about this marriage is that it's a great deal better than my first.

LIL LOCKWOOD: One thing about this marriage—compared to my first—is that we're really aware of each other and concerned about each other. I'm terribly conscious of how Larry might react to things. One of our problems has to do with the children. We're a new family, and I think it takes time to get the feeling of *familyness*. Another thing I've had to cope with is my feeling (*a long pause*) I guess "competitive" is the word. I can't keep myself from feeling that I'm competing with something that might have been in Larry's life at another time.

VIRGINIA JOHNSON: You mean your husband's other marriage?

LIL LOCKWOOD: Yes. I should be able to accept things as they are because for the most part everything has been great, even though we've had ups and downs. But I realize that subconsciously I have been competing with my husband's past.

VIRGINIA JOHNSON: That's a common pitfall. (*She turns to Pat.*)

PAT QUILL: This is a second marriage for John and me. And we have a three-year-old son, which is perhaps the biggest problem in our marriage at this point.

VIRGINIA JOHNSON: You mean the child's intrusion into the relationship?

PAT QUILL (*she nods*): It's strange—you sort of know ahead of time that your life's not going to be the same with a child, but when you're faced with the hard reality, you find out how difficult it really is.

VIRGINIA JOHNSON: Did you enjoy your life tremendously before the child came along?

PAT QUILL: Very much. But I was pregnant before we got married—we did it on purpose. We'd been together for about a year and a half, off and on, before I finally got my divorce, and as soon as I got back from Mexico and knew that I was no longer attached to this other man, I immediately got pregnant. And, you know, that seemed fine at the time, except looking back, I think it wasn't the wisest thing to do. We didn't have enough time together as married people before our son came along. But Victor's a great kid, and I feel it wouldn't have been Victor if we'd had a child a couple of years later. And I guess maybe the best thing about our marriage is that it's a good working partnership. We've had our big hassles, just like everybody else, but our marriage is something we work at together, as a partnership.

JOHN QUILL: I can describe it in a one-liner: it's real, it's a living reality, not a dream.

MIKE BRADLEY: Debbie and I have been married for twelve years. We have a child by this marriage, which is my first marriage, and Debbie has a child by her previous marriage. I'm very happy that we're here at this point in time because something unusual has happened. Just now—within days, almost—we've reached some kind of peace and ease with each other which we had never had before. I think it is the result of hard work on the part of some therapists (*with an uncertain laugh*) and a lot of hard work on Debbie's part, because I think Debbie is certainly the one who has solidified things and (*to his wife*) I thank you.

VIRGINIA JOHNSON: Did an event mark the change? Or are you saying that you suddenly realized a few days ago that this change had occurred?

DEBBIE BRADLEY: Well, we've been going to a new marriage counselor for a year. Before that we worked with another counselor, and we have both had a lot of individual therapy. So what solidified the marriage is really a combination of the therapy and our mutual desire to change things. And it's been more than a few days; it's more like six months . . .

MIKE BRADLEY: (*teasing*): How dare you disagree with me? (*Laughter.*)

DEBBIE BRADLEY: What's happening is that it's all starting to work. Individual therapy didn't seem to be changing our marriage, although maybe it was changing *us*. But this year the marriage has been affected for the first time; I mean, we could see solid evidence of change. We've always been happy even while we were *un*happy, which is different from my first marriage where we were *un*happy while we were unhappy. That's why Mike and I have stayed together all these years—and this is the first time we've been happy while we're happy! (*Laughter.*)

ENID BALL: This is my first marriage—Hugh's, too— and all I can say is that I hope getting divorced isn't catching! (*Laughter.*) We've been married for four, almost five, years and we have a three-year-old daughter, and I really don't know what else to say about us except that my parents were divorced, so perhaps that qualifies us. (*More laughter.*)

VIRGINIA JOHNSON: If you're married, you're qualified,

all right. All we hope to learn from all of you is what it is that you think contributes to the making of a satisfactory relationship.

HUGH BALL: Since our marriage has had its share of ups and downs, we're certainly aware that we have a lot to learn, and that's one of the reasons we're glad to be here today.

BILL MASTERS: Now that you've all introduced yourselves, there is a question I want to ask Lil. You spoke of competition with your husband's first marriage. What initiated the competition? Was it all your doing?

LIL LOCKWOOD: I think I put myself into competition.

VIRGINIA JOHNSON: Was it that you had a sense of failure because your first marriage didn't work and now you wanted to prove that you could be half of a totally successful, shining new marriage?

LIL LOCKWOOD: Not that so much as my refusal to accept the fact that Larry, even for a small moment of his life, could ever have been truly happy with somebody else. The idea of womanhood entered into it, too—trying to be sexually better for him than anyone else could be.

VIRGINIA JOHNSON: Oh, heavens! (*Laughter.*) Tell me, Lil, how much of a need to be a really special person, a whole person, entered into this?

LIL LOCKWOOD: I think I became more aware of my own identity once I realized what I was doing. I was knocking myself as a person and that made me feel I was in some kind of competition. Larry didn't do anything to start it; it was my own doing.

BILL MASTERS: Did you ever think that Larry might be feeling the need to compete, too, and for exactly the same reasons? Would there be any possibility of his thinking: "Well, gee, I want to be darn sure she realizes that I'm the best man that's ever bedded her"?

LIL LOCKWOOD (*apparently confused*): For a long time it was a kind of jealousy with me. I didn't use the term, jealousy, at the beginning because I think jealousy is different from competition. But I consider myself a more jealous individual than Larry.

BILL MASTERS: You haven't answered my question. Did it worry you that he might be feeling competition too? Did that ever occur to you?

LIL LOCKWOOD: (*shakes her head no.*)

BILL MASTERS: Larry, did you ever have any such concerns?

LARRY LOCKWOOD: There was always some concern but I treated matters differently. I just made the assumption, early on, that if she didn't care for her first husband and they were divorced, then that was that. Our marriage was a totally new thing. Besides, I'm not as intense as Lil in either competitiveness or jealousy.

DONNA ROSS: I wonder if it's a male-female kind of thing?

VIRGINIA JOHNSON: I wonder, too. In our culture women have been made so basically insecure about the man-woman relationship that they often compete for reasons they themselves do not understand. Lil's competitiveness may reflect this culturally induced sense of insecurity. It may simply be more difficult for her, as a female, to make the perfectly rational assumptions that Larry made—that, after all, "if Lil divorced him and chose me, that's that; it's fine!" Perhaps if the women's equality movement achieves its potential for social change, women will be relieved of some of this insecurity.

JOHN QUILL: It seems to me that Women's Lib takes the whole concept of women's place in society and turns it upside down. A lot of the roles which are called into question are biological roles. But a lot of others are strictly social roles. These are questions that a man has to deal with when he is married to a woman who is attempting to find her own real identity—her true self and not her sociological self. It's extremely difficult for both of us.

VIRGINIA JOHNSON: Of course. We're in transition and

that's always hard on the people who are caught up in it. Can you relate this a little more concretely to your marriage?

JOHN QUILL: The problems lie, to a great degree, in attitudes. Like, sometimes I've caught myself putting Pat down without realizing it, by thinking along the same old lines. I'll make assumptions like: she's a woman and so naturally she thinks *that* way. Or: she's a woman and naturally she acts *that* way. Well, it's just not so! She's a human being and she will have certain individual responses just as a man will have certain responses. It's the old problem, I think, of men putting women in a certain light—like the old belief that women think irrationally. (*Laughter.*) I question that, and yet sometimes I catch myself thinking, "Oh, she's being irrational about it . . ."

VIRGINIA JOHNSON: As a woman?

JOHN QUILL: Sure. You know, just like a woman. But I should be thinking of her as a *person*.

BILL MASTERS: I get the impression that something about Women's Lib threatens you?

JOHN QUILL (*slowly*): I think it has the potential for breaking up a marriage, in that Pat might come to see that marriage is essentially a false relationship between a man and a woman. Sometimes I think it might come to that, that it might possibly get in the way of our having a really working thing. Or she might decide she has to do something on her own.

BILL MASTERS: Does the women's movement necessarily mean that marriage concepts are false?

JOHN QUILL: I don't believe so. But it does mean that there's got to be a greater sense of reality between the two people in the marriage.

VIRGINIA JOHNSON: In other words, they have to make more of a marriage than just leaning on the legality of it.

PAT QUILL: I'm not a militant feminist but in the past year or so, I've come to realize a lot about how I was brought up and why I feel the way I now do about my life—about the relationship I want with my husband and with my child. I'm not lashing out and screaming that I'm oppressed but I know that there are certain things I can no longer accept, things I was perfectly willing to go along with until now.

BILL MASTERS: Can you be specific?

PAT QUILL: Here's one example. I have always been terribly protective of John, in all kinds of ways to try to make up for deficiencies in his past life. And in this protectiveness, I have suppressed things that *I* cared about or that I wanted to do. It was always the wish to "make it nice for John." For instance, I might have a problem or be upset about something, but if he was upset, I would put my needs aside. And that pattern really doesn't work because after extended periods of putting my own needs aside, I begin to feel bothered. "What am *I* getting out of it?" All I'm really doing is saving *his* soul, you know? But I'm not getting any satisfactions myself.

VIRGINIA JOHNSON: Have you ever thought that with your habit of putting yourself last, you are depriving John of the opportunity to do the same for you? If you always get there first, he doesn't have a chance! I'm talking now about people who *always* have a pressing need to do the giving and thereby cheat themselves of the pleasure of receiving—and cheat others of their chance to experience the pleasure of giving. Culturally this translates into the sexual stereotype of the woman giving pleasure to the man. Do any of you have thoughts about this?

DEBBIE BRADLEY: Can we first go back and talk a bit more about competition? Mike and I were given a psychological test to measure how competitive we are—to see how well we could cooperate. Well, we got a zero prognosis for marriage as a result of it! This happened while we were getting counseling; in fact, our counselor had suggested that we take the test. But the thing I found out as a

result of the test made a difference for the better
in our marriage. I learned that my husband was
in competition with me, something I had never
realized.

When I discovered this, it was very painful,
but it brought something home to me. I used to
think that the things he said about me were true,
that I was a worthless person, but as a result of
the test, I understood that my husband was really
fearful of me, that he felt inadequate. That was
why he competed.

This knowledge was the pivot on which
things began to turn for the better in our marriage. Because once I realized that my husband
was fearful of me rather than hateful, *I* became
less fearful and hateful. It enhanced my entire
feeling about myself, and I became much kinder
to Mike because I finally realized that we are both
terribly afraid of being close.

Mike speaks about the fact that in the last
six months, things between us have been pretty
good. Well, that's because we realized that the
negative things between us were not directed
against each other but were coming from our own
particular fears and problems. This realization
opened me up sexually to Mike, which I hadn't
been for years. In fact, last week—for the first
time—I complained to my therapist that Mike
hadn't tried to make love to me. My therapist
almost fell on the floor. He couldn't believe the
statement was coming from me. But it's interesting
that Mike, right now, is withdrawing from me as
I'm getting closer to him.

MIKE BRADLEY: I don't agree. (*Laughter.*) Well, I
agree *somewhat*. I agree with the main portions
of what Debbie has said but not with her last
comments. It's true that I've hit a low physical
period but that's very rare. Something else is on
my mind right now, though. Perhaps I'm being too
critical and you can tell me if I am, but my feeling
is that Debbie is focusing attention on herself in-

stead of on the discussion. She certainly didn't answer your question about sex.

DEBBIE BRADLEY (*calmly*): May I speak on what he is doing now? In the past, even last year, I would have flushed and gotten terribly angry. Now I sit back and say to myself: "This is Mike's problem, and maybe what he's saying is right. I must listen because he has often been right." This is the gain I've made in recent months. It's much more important for me to hear what he's saying than to respond as I did in the past.

BILL MASTERS: All of us have a tendency to think that we must be responsible for our emotions. *Nothing is further from the truth.* How we feel is how we feel and no one, least of all our marriage partners, has the right to make us accountable for those feelings. We are accountable only *for what we do* as a result of those feelings.

VIRGINIA JOHNSON: You're entitled to your feelings.

BILL MASTERS: You're entitled and your partner does not have the right to interpret or evaluate or judge your feelings. On the other hand, it is your responsibility to express your feelings and thoughts as clearly as you can. Making your partner guess is asking for trouble. And the more comfortable you are in expressing those feelings and the more comfortable your partner becomes in accepting the feelings as an honest reflection of where you stand at that moment, the easier it is to communicate.

MIKE BRADLEY (*sheepishly*): I'm afraid my tendency is to wear a mask.

BILL MASTERS: Masking your feelings?

MIKE BRADLEY: Well, somewhat, somewhat.

DON WHITE: Dr. Masters, what you were saying spoke to me very directly. In fact (*glancing at his wife*), it spoke to both of us.

LOIS WHITE (*nods in agreement.*)

DON WHITE: It's wild. I've been in therapy for over a year and I haven't learned that lesson yet, even though I've been told often enough about the danger of masking feelings. I grew up in a good

Protestant achievement-conscious family, and what I was taught was to hide my feelings—even from myself. I was told many times, "You don't really feel that way!" And: "You must control your feelings," or "Just don't let anybody know that you feel that way." I was taught to pretend. "Don't let the other kids know that you're scared." And then because I was always rather big, I'd be told: "You're bigger than they are so you have no reason to be scared of the other kids." And I'd be told: "Don't cry!"

VIRGINIA JOHNSON: Boys don't cry.

DON WHITE: That's right—boys don't cry! Oh, man! What it has come to is that now I have a terrible problem getting in touch with my own feelings. I don't know *what* I'm feeling, much less why I'm feeling as I do. I'm often quite angry but I know that the anger is irrational so I say to myself, "There's no reason to be angry; you shouldn't be angry." And then I find myself pretending not to be angry. So I sit there and radiate anger—infrared. (*Laughter.*) So Lois gets uptight and stops talking. Having been married for almost five years now, each of us is sensitive to what is going on with the other one. Maybe Lois will say, "Look, are you mad about something? Has anything happened?" And I'll say, "Of course, I'm not mad!" But I want to snap her head off for suggesting that I might be angry.

LOIS WHITE: I want to speak to the question of being two separate people . . . (*Her voice fades; then she recovers herself.*) In my first marriage we were successful in a way, but we were so terribly close that neither of us could function as an individual. We enjoyed our two great kids and in lots of ways we lived a comfortable and rewarding life. But there was a limit on our personal growth; we were stifling each other. This led to the marriage breaking up. I entered the second marriage with a feeling that Don and I had a lot more going for us. I expected things to be just great. And then suddenly I was lost. Nothing that had worked for me in my first marriage was working in the second. The lesson of learning independence, the ability to be two separate but united people, is really a rough problem. And I found myself floundering as I tried to learn how to be independent myself and to accept Don's independence without feeling that we were splitting apart.

BILL MASTERS: It's a hard ideal to achieve—to be two separate people with total respect for each other as individuals and still manage to function *together,* both partners holding to the basic concept that as a unit . . . *we* have more to gain by being together than either of us can gain being alone.

VIRGINIA JOHNSON: But both people have to communicate, they have to know each other and let themselves be known. Don has depicted a pattern that is all too familiar in this society, a value system about men and their feelings that has been rigidly built into him but which doesn't represent him as a human being. And Lois has explained why she could not stay in a marriage that seemed stagnating, that gave her no opportunity, as she saw it, to be creative. Now how are they going to reach out to each other? Bridges are built most easily through very simple kinds of negotiation. He is a man who has had no opportunity to express himself or to discover his own dimensions as a person because of the rigid value systems instilled when he was a little boy. All right, if he is angry for whatever reason, rational or not, he can let his wife share that anger. He can force himself for a while to say: "I'm angry and I don't know why but this is how I feel," and he can let her share his feelings. That helps her to avoid shadowboxing or pretending that all is well when she knows it is not and it gives her the opportunity to be the creative, growing kind of person she feels herself capable of becoming.

DON WHITE: You're quite right. Sometimes we fight

and feel better afterward. And sometimes we talk and have very painful conversations and feel better about that, too.

DONNA ROSS: Oh, I understand that so well! My second marriage has been a most satisfying one, and I think it is because we communicate. I had a very unhappy first marriage, which seemed fine to a lot of people, but was really unrewarding. We just didn't talk to each other. I came into this second marriage thinking "I'll be damned if I want to fail again." You think about the other person more; your perceptions are sharper. Instead of being hung up with all sorts of angers and other concealed feelings, you're busy trying to figure out what's really bugging *him?* And I think Tony does the same for me. I work; Tony works; we're very independent people. Yet we have a tremendous feeling of family and we work hard at it. We spend a lot of time talking about our feelings, about what we hope for and what we need of each other. In this marriage I feel that I am a totally free human being. I am me all the way. In my first marriage I felt as though I were an appendage of something. I didn't really know myself and I couldn't even express my feelings.

VIRGINIA JOHNSON: A few years ago when the New York newspapers were on strike, a *New York Times* columnist was asked his opinion of something and he said, "How do I know what I think unless I can read what I've written?" It was an amusing way to express the fact that we often do not know what we think or how we really feel until we have a chance to express ourselves and to hear ourselves and then to decide whether that is actually what we believe. Sometimes just saying something aloud to another person is enough to make us realize that we don't fully believe what we've said—which frees us to change our minds. It's obvious that if a husband and wife don't talk to each other, neither one can know what the other thinks, but it may also be true that they are not certain of what they themselves think!

TONY ROSS: Speaking your mind is important but it helps if you don't try to make every disagreement into a federal case. I know that Donna and I make a great effort to separate the wheat from the chaff. We try not to get hung up on incidental crap. Donna has helped and encouraged me and I hope I have helped and encouraged her to be independent. We both understand that we don't have to agree on everything. What we're saying to each other, I suppose, is: "I'm going to fight like hell to get my point across to you but if, in the final analysis, you don't agree—well, okay, I love you anyway." The argument fades away and in the end I think we have a better understanding of each other. Sometimes I'm not so positive, but deep down I believe I understand this woman and, likewise, I feel that she understands me. And this may be the one thing that makes our marriage what it is.

MIKE BRADLEY: It's funny but sometimes I think it's easier to understand someone else than it is to understand yourself.

LARRY LOCKWOOD: Well, you always *think* you understand yourself and you always *think* you're being honest with yourself and then later, after something happens and you see yourself differently, you can see how wrong you were. If the something that happens is a divorce, you can see a hell of a lot, and there's a lot of pain involved. You only learn about yourself through pain, I think. I don't know many people who learn about themselves by reading books. That certainly hasn't been my experience. You can kid yourself about how you feel until it hurts too much to go on pretending. Like you might walk a while with a tack in your shoe but sooner or later it would hurt too much and you'd have to stop walking and get rid of it.

DONNA ROSS: There's also the pain of not feeling anything at all, just a kind of deadness. That can hurt, too.

LARRY LOCKWOOD: Absolutely. That can be the worst of all. It's definitely true for me on the sexual level. In my first marriage I thought that having sex and having sexual pleasure were the same thing, and I didn't understand that there is a huge difference between being tolerated and being wanted. So when I found there was no sense of excitement in our sexual relationship, I assumed that that was life, and all the rest was just talk by people who were lying to each other. I could never make *that* mistake again. I could never stay married if my wife and I didn't experience physical pleasure in being together.

GEORGE STEIN (*frowning*): I get the impression that you think that if the sexual relationship isn't going right, then you just have to admit ipso facto that the whole relationship is wrong. I don't agree with that. (*To Bill Masters*) I've read your book and I guess I'm down in it as a man with secondary impotence—a person who faces anxiety and a problem in a marriage relationship by withdrawing sexually. This was the symptom that occurred in my first marriage when I was quite young. I began going to therapists and continued for many years, trying to get at the underlying causes and to get rid of that particular symptom. Well, I learned a lot from the therapy and my life improved in certain ways, but the symptom had a life of its own. It didn't go away and my marriage finally broke up.

I was so terrified of going through that whole painful experience a second time that when I met Gail and fell in love with her, I didn't want us to get legally married—even though we had a good relationship going, including a good sexual relationship. I was afraid that the secondary impotence would come back and I'd have to go through the terrible business of another marriage breakup.

Well, Gail and I worked that out by living together until I felt secure enough, and I've always been grateful to her for helping me get past that fear—even though, soon after we adopted our two children, the secondary impotence came back. But by then I had developed a different point of view. Gail and I had so many things in common, and we had such strong feelings of love and respect for each other, that I felt the relationship had a lot more going for it than just how we made out in bed. And I think that Gail, too, felt that way—that ours was a happy marriage and a fulfilled marriage, whether or not we ever had sex.

Finding out that your clinic [Reproductive Biology Research Foundation] could do something about secondary impotence gave me a new lease on life. All I have to do is get down to St. Louis for two weeks of treatment (*laughter*) and I suppose I better not put it off too long because if I don't solve this problem now, I'm dead anyway! (*More laughter.*) Well, I guess I have until I'm seventy—but seriously, I feel I just have to disagree that a good sexual relationship is essential to a good marriage. It would be lovely to have a good sexual relationship and I'm certainly not quitting in my attempt to have one. But I feel it is not the mainspring of a good marriage.

VIRGINIA JOHNSON: Perhaps we better go back one step. If I heard Larry correctly, he was only reporting something that was true *for him.* In the process of ending one marriage and starting another, he learned certain things about himself. He discovered certain needs that he has and he knows now that it matters a great deal to him to have those needs met in his marriage. As I heard him, he was not telling anyone else that this is how it *should be* for them. (*Larry nods.*)

BILL MASTERS (*to George*): In your marriage, there are two sets of value systems—yours and your wife's. We've heard something of yours; we haven't heard hers yet. Keep in mind that all of us construct our systems on the basis of our unique experiences and that *those systems change as our experiences change.* Correction: they *can* change —depending on the individual. Some people are open to change—they grow and mature. Other people just get older.

Your present sexual value system is colored by a specific marital situation. This is natural and inevitable. As it comes across to me, it sounds like a static concept. But it doesn't have to be. The nice thing is that situations such as you described, which reduce many marriages to utter chaos, are actually reversible in a high percentage of cases. There's no question about it.

But we learned long ago that the only way to do it is to educate *both* partners. I might add that you yourself illustrated that principle when you referred to the fact that Gail had been so supportive during your early years together, and how effective her support had been. It isn't too surprising, incidentally, that a dysfunction that evolved in a first marriage should recur, later on, in a second marriage. One partner assuring another simply isn't enough; two partners reassuring each other, on the basis of new information, can lead to a rapid reversal of the problem.

I must point out that if you ever came to St. Louis, we would not treat your impotence. It doesn't have to be treated. We treat the marital relationship and this is a matter of education, not medical treatment. You see, there is no such thing as an impotent male—or a nonorgasmic female—on the basis of I-me-myself. If you were able to observe a man during his sleep, a man who could not achieve or maintain an erection while awake, you would see that he has any number of erections during the night. Having an erection is a natural function. No man learns to have one; he is born with that facility. As a one-time obstetrician, I can tell you that there's many a baby I've seen with a full erection before his umbilical cord was tied and long before he got around to nursing.

VIRGINIA JOHNSON (*smiling*): That's inspiring, isn't it?

BILL MASTERS: And there's not a woman in this room who didn't lubricate in the first twenty-four hours of life. It isn't something she had to learn. It's simply that sex is a natural function like breathing or eating. Now the minute we can accept this concept at gut level, the minute the man understands that his erection will take care of itself and the woman understands that her lubrication will take care of itself, their fears of performance—which every man and woman has to some degree —are eased, and as a couple, the two partners are considerably ahead of the game. (*To George*) We constantly assure people that sex need not be the be-all and end-all of life—but, as you yourself said, it surely is a lovely thing to have.

LIL LOCKWOOD (*hesitantly*): There is something I've recently become aware of, a certain distinction— I wish there was some marvelous, correct term I could use but . . .

BILL MASTERS: Try it.

LIL LOCKWOOD: I've become aware of sex-sex and love-sex.

BILL MASTERS: That's fair enough.

LIL LOCKWOOD: Well, frankly, there are evenings when it's not that I love my husband any less, but the tension, the buildup is different and I have a different kind of enjoyment in the sexual act than during a night when I feel very cuddly and loving and totally relaxed.

VIRGINIA JOHNSON: Sometimes it helps to make an analogy with food and sometimes it doesn't. I think it may help here. A certain amount of food is essential to life, but beyond that, what is food consumption? It's a medium of sociability, and it varies in nature, depending on the particular circumstances of the moment. You acquire certain preferences—an elegant restaurant, perhaps, or intimate conversations or a special preparation of a favorite dish, whatever—and these preferences enhance the pleasure of eating. Then you have to take your mood into account. You may feel sad but you are still going to eat, and that sadness inevitably affects the experience of eating. Or you may be very happy and the meal is a celebration, and as you eat to satisfy your hunger, you are experiencing everything at that moment in an entirely different way. *But these aren't two different kinds of eating.* In both cases, you are you, satisfying your natural hunger in a natural way, but the subjective experience is different.

(*To Lil*) I know that you didn't mean that there were two different kinds of sex but I wanted to be sure that no one here received the wrong impression. There is a tendency for some people to think of sexual expression as something to be kept in a little silver box with a ribbon around it, to be taken out only on special occasions, instead of recognizing the fact that sex is the expression of human need, as natural as the hunger for food.

Perhaps I misinterpreted your hesitancy but it seemed to indicate a little doubt on your part, as though you were saying, "Gee, maybe it shouldn't be this way but sex for us isn't always 'love' and if it isn't 'love,' if it isn't the peak and the ultimate and all-loving, then it's 'less than' it should be." And I wanted to assure you that there is no "should be" about it, not for you or anyone. Your sexuality is a dimension of your personality and whenever you are sexually active, you are expressing yourself—the self that you are at that moment, the mood that you're in, the needs that you have. You act in accord with your feelings and without explanation or justification or apol-

ogy, not to anyone else and certainly not to
yourself!

PAT QUILL: In my first marriage the sexual thing was
physically satisfying but emotionally it was totally
unsatisfying to me, and I went to other people for
emotional satisfaction.

VIRGINIA JOHNSON: Dividing up your self-expression?

PAT QUILL: Oh, very much. There were always one or
two other men in my life during my first marriage,
and I needed them because I was not getting any
reaction other than the purely physical from my
first husband. The mechanics were dandy.

VIRGINIA JOHNSON: Two bodies.

PAT QUILL: Two bodies doing all the right things. But
nothing else went on, so I went to other men just
to be held and loved in a different way, you know?
Or for the feeling they could give me that I was a
person. In this marriage it's not that way at all.
The whole thing goes together.

BILL MASTERS (*to Donna Ross*): How is your second
marriage different, sexually, from your first?

DONNA ROSS: Sexually my first marriage was not really
satisfying. I was very inexperienced. I was married for about ten years, to a boy I had always
gone out with, and even though sex wasn't satisfying, I didn't know anything else was possible. Or
I just felt that maybe it was me, that I was inadequate. But our marriage (*she flashes a smile
to her husband*) is a whole new different kind of
thing. I guess it has to do with the freedom to be
an individual, to give, to receive, to fail, to succeed. Which makes it okay if our sex life is sometimes not so marvelous because most of the time
it *is* marvelous. I'm much less inhibited than I
was because I'm much more trustful of Tony. And
when things go wrong, when problems interfere
with our sex life, we manage to deal with the
situation.

BILL MASTERS: What kind of problems?

DONNA ROSS: Oh, "children" problems and financial
problems.

BILL MASTERS: How do they interfere?

DONNA ROSS: When we're tired or tense, we certainly don't respond to one another totally.

BILL MASTERS: Do you avoid the issue?

DONNA ROSS: No, that's one thing we *don't* do. That's the nice part of our marriage. Whatever is happening, we talk about it.

BILL MASTERS: Do your problems diminish the frequency of your sexual interaction?

DONNA ROSS: Sometimes. Sometimes, if we're tired or upset, that happens. But we discuss it, we don't try to pretend it's not happening. Talking doesn't always resolve a problem instantly—I'm not saying that. But it does relieve a lot of pressure. At least each of us knows how the other one feels.

VIRGINIA JOHNSON: You're saying that two people are at least always represented in the action.

DONNA ROSS: Absolutely.

TONY ROSS: We've gone through terrible emotional crises together, and sometimes—maybe because we felt the need to be close or to reassure each other—it leads to sex.

DONNA ROSS: A comforting, a closeness, an intimacy kind of thing.

DON WHITE (*emptying his pipe*): Everyone has been talking about sex as communication, and although I enjoy sex—I love sex—I don't use it as a form of communication. When I hear other people talk about using sex as a way of relating to each other, it makes me feel like someone on the outside, looking in.

VIRGINIA JOHNSON: Is it something that you would like to work at?

DON WHITE: I would. I'd like very much to have the kind of relationship that I hear about from some of you. I think you get an awful lot out of it that I'm missing.

BILL MASTERS: Let's look at this matter of sex and communication a little more closely. Coitus is itself an act of communicating, an intimate exchange of feelings between a man and woman.

Obviously there are two kinds of communication, verbal and nonverbal, and messages are constantly being exchanged, quite apart from specific sexual interaction. In fact, communication can be, and often is, a kind of foreplay, and it is usually nonverbal.

VIRGINIA JOHNSON: I'd like to ask everyone here, do you use touch to express things that you'd be reticent to express otherwise? Would you use a physical movement to get your message across, where you might be shy to verbalize it?

DONNA ROSS: Yes, I love to be touched. In fact, lots of times Tony will come home, and I'll be in the kitchen getting dinner—it's a very small kitchen, and I'll have the kids around me—and he'll come in and greet all the kids and walk by me and kiss me on the cheek and grab me by my rear. And it's just marvelous and I love it, because it says he's home, and it's a reassuring restatement that he loves me and finds me sexually appealing. In bed I love all the exchanges. We sleep sort of all tied up—and then I do use touch rather than speaking.

TONY ROSS: I'm kind of a compulsive toucher. I talk with my hands all the time. Even when I'm with a business associate I'll reach over and touch him to make a point. The only time I'm ever self-conscious about doing this is when the person stiffens right up. I guess all of it is because of the way that I was brought up. In my family, we were always very open about our feelings and emotions—nobody ever held back in terms of yelling or grabbing or touching or things like that.

VIRGINIA JOHNSON: Touching was a legitimate form of saying where you were emotionally.

BILL MASTERS: Is anyone uncomfortable with being touched, in any way?

LOIS WHITE: When I talk to people, I want to touch them, and I always loved to touch my husband, in public and everything, and it would just drive him crazy. He used to say, "You're being an extrovert, doing that in front of other people." I wanted to kiss and hug and touch him all the time, but he just couldn't take it. At least, that's the feedback I got from him. So as a result, I now feel that of all the people I *can't* touch, it's him!

My husband turned me off from wanting to touch him, especially in public, because he feels if you touch him you've got to have sex, and obviously sitting around the table with people is the wrong place. I don't always want to have sex— and there's nothing wrong with not always wanting to have it. I would love to have the touching all the time, and the touching-sex sometimes.

DON WHITE: I love to be touched, but for a long time I was very much afraid of it. In my family we almost never touched, never kissed; there was very rare physical contact. When we got married, Lois was always demonstrative and affectionate in public. This would generally tend to get me excited, and I would find it very difficult to cope with. So what I would do was try to prevent it by saying, "Hey, look. Cut it out."

In recent years—the last year or two—I've become a lot more comfortable about touching, not only with Lois but other people, too. It's a lot easier for me now to feel warm and close to other people, and to touch people that I feel warm and close to—especially if I feel that they're not going to react negatively. I think I've become much more comfortable about both touching and being touched by Lois, whether in private or in public.

BILL MASTERS: You don't consider touching to be an immediate invitation to intercourse or you're more comfortable with an erection in public? (*Laughter.*)

DON WHITE: I think I'm less uncomfortable. I understand the dynamics of the situation and that helps me.

BILL MASTERS: Are you saying that you have a better understanding of Lois's need?

DON WHITE: I think I understand her better, too, but mostly I think I understand my own reaction.

VIRGINIA JOHNSON: You mean on the basis of early deprivation of touch, you found it—from a practical standpoint—overstimulating. But now, since you don't have to be afraid you're going to embarrass yourself, you get pleasure from it.

Early on, though, when you would tell Lois to cease and desist because of the chain reaction, did you explain why?

DON WHITE: Yes. I'd say, "Hey—we're starting to make out in public, and we can't do anything about it. So cut it out till we get home." We'd talk like that, and she'd say, "Well, I'm not 'making out.' I just wanted to touch you." And there was the conflict because I would feel: when you touch me it means we *have* to make out. Recently we've had a lot of discussions about that, and I think we both understand each other a lot better.

BILL MASTERS: I could ask this question of almost anybody, but I'd like to ask Mike—when you are actually making love, how much or to what degree is being touched important? Or is it not part of your lovemaking?

MIKE BRADLEY: I always felt that I was doing a lot more stroking and touching than I was being stroked and touched, and I always wanted more touching. I never got enough of stroking and touching.

BILL MASTERS: What about the other men here?

TONY ROSS: It's absolutely essential.

JOHN QUILL: Without that as a prelude, making love is not satisfying.

HUGH BALL: I find it quite exciting. But like Don, I think I tend to have mixed feelings about it in certain respects. In my family, touching seemed to be used as a show of affection, a measure of comfort —that type of thing. As a result, I feel very uneasy about touching in public—sort of a hang-up, I guess. Whenever Enid and I have a problem, my initial reaction is to get closer to her, to hug her.

But always in private. To answer your question, as a part of sexual activity, I find that it's essential.

VIRGINIA JOHNSON: Back to the formative aspects of your statement—you said that in your family touch was a comfort, a righting of wrong. But did you also learn in a subtle kind of way, through your parents, that a certain kind of touch is sexual? In other words, you touch certain people when you wish to comfort them or give them solace, and if you touch them under other circumstances, it becomes sexual and therefore you must be very careful?

HUGH BALL: I guess the answer is yes, although I really haven't thought about it.

BILL MASTERS: Would you like to muse a little bit on your discomfort with touch in public?

HUGH BALL: It's something, even today, that I can't really figure out. I guess I must have grown up with the attitude that touching was something that was done within the home or within the family. Maybe I put the wrong emphasis on it—I was *aware* of it much more in a crisis situation, but that's not the only time it was done. Still, I always recall it being done in private.

VIRGINIA JOHNSON: Larry?

LARRY LOCKWOOD: I find myself freer about touching in public. It's funny, with my first wife I can't remember a single time where there was any stroking or touching—either giving or taking or both. It's completely different now with Lil: she's good to me, in this stroking and touching.

VIRGINIA JOHNSON: I'd like the women to talk about this, too. Would you say that, between you and your husband, touching is a very important form of communication, an expression of who you are and where you are and how you feel?

DONNA ROSS: An interesting thing just dawned on me. My dad was a very tense guy, and one thing that he used to enjoy was having his back tickled. Now, it wasn't the tickling that you do to make somebody laugh—it was a very gentle stroking. And we sort of had this unwritten agreement that sometimes he'd do it to my back and sometimes I'd do it to his back. This went on for years and years, and it used to make my mother almost become unglued, because she thought it was a very sexual thing to be doing.

I'm perfectly aware that I had plenty of sexual feelings for my father, but I never felt as though I was going to have a climax if he was rubbing my arm or my back. Now I find myself, against my mother's objections, rubbing my children's arms or backs or foreheads, and she's convinced that I'm going to raise sick children. I keep telling her that I'm making my own mistakes.

It's very interesting, because I can never remember my mother touching me, except for washing my face or brushing my hair. And I remember a particular period of being an untouchable—when I was gangly—from thirteen to eighteen, and if she had washed my face I would have died of embarrassment, because I was old enough to do it myself. I brushed my own hair. There was no physical contact at all. I'd kiss her good-night, but it was just sort of a nothing.

BILL MASTERS: Debbie?

DEBBIE BRADLEY: There was very little touching in my family. I remember that I was told to kiss my father every night before I went to bed, and I found it very difficult. I would have to get a mental set and stand for a few minutes before I could get up the feeling that "okay, now it's time to kiss Dad good-night." It was a very formal procedure. He would be behind his paper and would sort of look up and say, "Good-night, dear." He touched me once in a while, but there was no real warmth. So when I married Mike—Mike is very outgoing, very warm—and he would touch me in public, I just wouldn't know how to handle it. I always associated touching with sex, and within the privacy of our room, we enjoy it—*I* enjoy it. But if it's in public, I still have problems.

BILL MASTERS: Enid?

ENID BALL: I can say the same about being raised in a family that didn't touch or kiss. It was always a kind of sexual thing, and therefore taboo, and I became overly demonstrative in public—maybe because I was trying to prove that I could do it as other people do. It means a great deal to me— probably too much, because I feel deprived. I probably touch Hugh and caress him more, because I always feel that I should give him more than he gives me.

VIRGINIA JOHNSON: Do you feel as though you're making up for lost time?

ENID BALL: I guess so.

VIRGINIA JOHNSON: For what it's worth, I'll give you another theory about why you might do it in public. When you do things in front of people, and you see it reflected back to you, then it becomes real.

BILL MASTERS: Since most of you have been married before or have had sexual relationships before you were married, can you in any way evaluate the quality of a sexual relationship with someone who likes to touch and someone who doesn't? Have you found yourself more responsive in ways you didn't even realize, when touch is an important part of your sexual relationship?

PAT QUILL: I am inclined to touch, but only with people I'm close to. I like touch—I love it—but I'm very uptight about it with strangers. With John, I'm not at all. And I'm not at all uptight with anyone that I'm very close to. With my first husband I was giving much more touching than I was getting, and he was not the kind of person who could appreciate this. Touching, I really agree, is a kind of communication, and if you're not getting something back, it's like sitting and talking when nobody is listening, or nobody is answering. With John, I find just the opposite—it doesn't even matter whether he touches back, I just know that it's being appreciated. This makes a very big difference.

JOHN QUILL: I think it's a very important part in our relationship. In my first marriage, I found the same thing as Pat—I was doing all of the touching and didn't seem to be getting any of it back. But Pat and I seem to be about equal. I think we're both slightly repressed about touching each other in public. But other people seem to know we care for each other, so our feelings must show somewhat.

VIRGINIA JOHNSON: Are the signals pretty clear between you?

PAT QUILL: Yes, they're pretty clear. It takes a while to work them all out, but after a while they're clear.

VIRGINIA JOHNSON: When a signal goes awry, do you verbalize in order to set it straight?

PAT QUILL: Very seldom. I would have to say that in bed we very seldom talk about sex. Most of the time it's worked out through activity rather than words.

BILL MASTERS: Did any of you have to overcome inhibitions about variations in making love—by that I mean the positions you use, the places where you want to make love, the kinds of what is called foreplay? Did you find yourself going through any sort of evolution such that you could enjoy something you hadn't enjoyed before, or do you find in your present marriage that each of you is tuned to the other and that you have no difficulties in that area at all?

ENID BALL: Well, I had had very little sexual experience before we were married. I guess you could say I was frigid—I never really enjoyed sex and would rather do anything than get in bed and have intercourse. It's very difficult to say how we finally worked it out. We never would actually confront each other. Talking was probably what really worked it out.

VIRGINIA JOHNSON: What would trigger the talking?

ENID BALL: Complete frustration. I just never thought that I was ever going to feel fulfilled sexually, and many times we thought of leaving each other. At the same time, I was very stubborn about admitting that I was frigid, that I couldn't feel anything. I think now that we have worked on it, I can accept a lot more than my background ever allowed me to.

HUGH BALL: Touching was a very large part of it. In the beginning, it was very constrained.

VIRGINIA JOHNSON: Enid, you said earlier that you really loved touching and that it was kind of an overkill to make up for the deprivation. Was this from the beginning of your relationship with Hugh, or did it come later?

ENID BALL: I always felt a desire and a need to touch, but when it actually came to the final act . . .

VIRGINIA JOHNSON: You didn't really do it? You got close, but you didn't really do it?

ENID BALL: Yes, and it can only go back to my relationships with other men, because I was brought up to believe that a girl ought to be a virgin when she got married. So with another person, it was always, "We can only go this far."

VIRGINIA JOHNSON: In other words, the very strengths you built up to protect the things you held dear were backfiring on you when you got into marriage?

ENID BALL: Yes, definitely. Hugh and I traveled together before we were married and stayed in the same room, yet we never really made love. I think maybe that was the biggest stumbling block in our whole marriage, because I had played with him to such a degree that I was unable really to have intercourse. Everything that led up to it was all right, but not the real thing.

VIRGINIA JOHNSON: When you used the term "frigid" did you mean that you couldn't involve your feelings in a sexual encounter with your husband? That you were almost an observer?

ENID BALL: Yes—and then my inability to feel anything pleasurable.

VIRGINIA JOHNSON: Or feel anything, period? I don't mean emotions, I just mean feel anything physical.

ENID BALL: Yes—but sometimes it was negative.

VIRGINIA JOHNSON: Negative because you did want to feel and you resented not feeling?

ENID BALL: Because I felt that I was being cheated. I was angry at myself, and I was angry at my husband because he couldn't make me feel anything.

VIRGINIA JOHNSON: In retrospect, deep down inside, did you think this was something your husband could make happen for you? Something a man is supposed to produce?

ENID BALL: Yes.

BILL MASTERS: This brings up a point I would like everyone to comment on. To what degree are you free in communicating while making love?

LIL LOCKWOOD: When Larry touches me, it's so great, but sometimes it's just a little bit in the wrong place. Now I don't hesitate to tell him. (*Laughter.*) At first, I wouldn't. I would just feel so happy to be touched. And now—I'm still happy to be touched, and it still feels good. But if it's a little off-center, I don't hesitate to say to Larry, "That feels great, but *this* might feel even greater." (*Laughter.*)

It's so nice just to be able to feel relaxed enough to speak up, to let him know when I'm enjoying something. Sometimes I have the feeling, "Gee, he's doing so much for me, I wish there were more that I could do for him." I keep picking up these books or articles on sex, and the emphasis is always on satisfying the woman. I keep hoping that someday someone's going to write a book that says, "Here are some marvelous things you gals can do to your husbands that will really turn *them* on." (*Laughter.*) It sounds crazy but it seems to me sometimes that I have more parts than he does.

VIRGINIA JOHNSON: Let's go to John and Pat next.

PAT QUILL: Well, if it's wrong, I move.

JOHN QUILL: Any small corrections or adjustments in any of our lovemaking is usually done by touch or movement, not by words.

PAT QUILL: I find it much easier to touch John's hand,

or move it, than to say, "Would you please move three degrees to the left."

JOHN QUILL: I do think we communicate more now, and more directly, than we did several years ago. I think we always did communicate to some extent, and we were also moderately verbal—we used both touch or moving the body and hands and so on, as well as saying things verbally. My own feeling is that now perhaps I am a little more free to be verbal, and I make a greater effort along those lines. I think this is probably part of my whole attempt to try and bring more of my feelings to the surface, to try and bring them out where I can deal with them.

BILL MASTERS: Would you say that your sexual relationship has evolved? If you looked back and you look at where you are now, do you and Pat feel that it has changed?

JOHN QUILL: I think the major change in our sexual relationship during the course of our marriage has been that we understand each other's needs a lot better, and we tend to be much more sensitive about when to have sex. There used to be times when I would want sex and Pat would feel, "Well, he wants it, I've got to give it." And I would put a lot of pressure on her to respond. Now I've come to realize that that's very unfair. We talk a lot more about this when the situation arises— when I need it and she doesn't, or vice versa—and I think we're able to deal with it a lot better now.

We still haven't resolved all of our problems in this area, but that's the direction we're moving in. I think the sex we have has been very good and very stimulating. And I think we've probably built in a lot more variety during the last few years, as Pat has overcome some of her inhibitions. My own feeling is that I don't think I ever had many inhibitions about what we do in bed.

VIRGINIA JOHNSON: Pat, what would you add to that?

PAT QUILL: The first time John and I went to bed, I immediately felt that he was the most tender man I had ever slept with. It really made the whole difference. That's when I decided I could consider getting involved in a long-term relationship. So that was my reaction to his initial tenderness.

VIRGINIA JOHNSON: Could I just ask: How would lack of tenderness have reflected itself?

PAT QUILL: Bing, bang, boom. See? John wasn't on top of me—or whatever position we were using for lovemaking—he was always *with* me. I felt his concern for my entire body, wherever it was. It was never, "You take care of your side and I'll take care of mine." When a man is on top of you, and his hand is under your head, it's totally different. So that was one very important signal a long, long time ago. John exposed to me a lot of great things about sex that I didn't know about before, but that are very stimulating. For some reason, in our society the men get to know about all the great pornographic things and women don't. And if you're going to be married for twenty-five or thirty years, you'd better learn them. I really believe that. So he introduced a lot of those kinds of things —the whole anal bit and all the rest that is totally alien to a lot of us. John was more educated in that way. And he wouldn't let me get away with any pretending.

VIRGINIA JOHNSON: Pretending?

PAT QUILL: Faking orgasm. He stopped that fast—he said I didn't have to fake anything with him. I realized that it was a bad habit I had gotten into. It was part of that old attitude I spoke about before. Call it protectiveness or whatever, it was the old idea of making it nice for the man. But John wouldn't have any of that.

BILL MASTERS: John, Pat has told us what she has learned from you over the years. Have you learned anything from her? Do you find that she has taught you anything about yourself, or about women?

JOHN QUILL: As I tried to say before, I think the most important thing I've learned is that there has to be an appreciation of the other person's needs. Just because I'm turned on at a particular time, it doesn't mean that we will or can have sex right then. If we don't, it's not a tragedy—there's always tomorrow. It has to be a dual kind of wanting, if sex is to be any good. One of the things I'm still learning about is what Pat's feelings and reactions are when she doesn't really feel turned on.

BILL MASTERS: What I'm interested in are some of the ways in which any of you have changed and developed in your relationships with each other as men and women in the sexual dimension.

HUGH BALL: I can expand on what Enid has already said. Our relationship started out with my being very aggressive and she being very inhibited—to the degree that she had almost no response. I found this very frustrating, but I kept pushing, pushing. And then came the period where we had almost a complete break—weeks and months of separation. Finally, I guess, Enid became comfortable with touching and being touched, and from that point I would honestly say that our sexual relationship swung somewhat the other way. She gave more, and I became somewhat passive.

I think today it still is evolving. I wouldn't say, by any stretch of the imagination, that we're there—and both of us know it. But it has evolved. Now the question is how can we together go from here and make it even more gratifying?

ENID BALL: It sounds like such a simple thing, but I think the change in our relationship came when Hugh finally said, "Okay, I'm not going to force myself on you anymore. If you don't want me, fine." He never said, "If you don't want me, I'll find someone else." Rather, he said, "I'll be patient with you." I finally realized that what I had was so beautiful and so wonderful with this man because he accepted my shortcomings and said, "Okay, we'll work on them." But it took two years for him to say that, and for me to accept the fact that I really was frigid.

HUGH BALL: At no point during that time did I ever consider, seriously, leaving her. There were many other things which we enjoyed together. Initially, Enid was tremendously upset, because everything she had read and heard had made her believe that a marriage is nothing if it wasn't sexually satisfying. To some degree, I guess, we both believed that, but I believed it far less than she.

ENID BALL: But he said, "Okay, if it can't be sexually satisfying, I'll make it good in other ways."

HUGH BALL: Well, that was my only other tack. I had reached the end. So I did stick with it. But there were other strengths that came into the whole relationship. Some people get carried away and say that there aren't other aspects. I find that hard to accept, myself. Fortunately—I don't know how that would have evolved—I never had to test it.

BILL MASTERS (*to Tony*): how important is the sexual dimension in your marriage?

TONY ROSS: The sexual aspect of marriage is the basis for everything else. Speaking for myself, I can't imagine a relationship without very good sex. My feelings and motives and drives about the whole thing are very strong. Trying to picture a situation like that—I wouldn't *stay* with such a situation; I'd get out of it. (*Turning to Donna, who nods*) I think our sexual life has improved with age because we've learned to talk about it. We didn't talk about it in the early years when we were first married. It was an understanding that we had, or I guess we thought we had. Being able to talk about things that ten years ago I wouldn't say, or was taught not to say, or felt constrained not to say— whatever the conditions might be that caused me to be less verbal—has really improved things. Now I feel free to say, "Listen, are you ever going to stop doing the dishes and come to bed?" Frankly, I get very angry. I don't want the dishes as my competition. One day I broke every one of them! I apparently couldn't get the message across otherwise.

What I find puzzling is why people can't

talk more. I'm probably more compulsive about being verbal than most people are. I'm really extreme this way. I can't think of a single thought or problem or question that comes to my head about a person, that I can't discuss with him. In some ways I'm very naive about it, because I find that even in business I'm sitting there talking to somebody across the table, and if a question comes to my mind, I ask it. Sometimes it has a devastating effect. Sometimes I create a lot of anxieties in other people that way. *I've* never felt hung up about it.

In my relationship with Donna, and even with the children, I'm almost overly dependent on just talking. In fact, I even shake the kids up because I'll ask them something and they'll look at me and say, "Do you really want to talk about that?" And I'll say, "Yes, let's talk about it." And what's great about it is that they've become a lot more comfortable about telling us what's on their minds.

And when it comes to sexual things, I think the biggest difficulty is that Donna is many times afraid to tell me how she really feels. Instead, she'll try to second-guess how I want her to feel. Sometimes when you talk about things, it can be hurtful to yourself and to other people, but I don't know of an easier solution to any problem. And when I say touching—touching to me is just like talking. I find it hard to separate them. And many times, for example, if we're making love, I'll ask Donna twenty-one questions and say, "Now, honey, answer one of those questions!" And I'm a little astounded sometimes when I hear people saying that they can't discuss things. Am I oversimplifying?

VIRGINIA JOHNSON: A little bit, perhaps. Remember, it is hard for those of us who are comfortable about talking to realize how difficult it can be for people who are not comfortable, who feel that they are incapable of finding the right words to say what they mean. Besides, words are certainly the original double-edged sword! Sometimes things that are said with no intention of hurting the other person or shaming that person prove terribly harmful—and surely there is no one in this room who does not know firsthand how easy it is to use words deliberately to hurt another person.

No, Tony, I think it is vital to understand that the most important thing is to *communicate,* with or without words. And all that communicating really means, when it takes place between two people who have reason to trust each other, is that each will make every possible effort to reveal how he or she feels or what he or she thinks at any given moment. If words are used—and let us grant that in most of our waking hours, words and not gestures or touching are required for communication—then it is important *how* thoughts are expressed. We are responsible for being thoughtful —and thoughtfulness is two things: thinking carefully about what we want to say so that we can say it the clearest way possible *and* thinking carefully about how to say it so that the other person knows that you are taking his or her feelings into account, that you are being thoughtful. And we have to remember that so much is said by tone of voice or facial expression or a look in the eyes, that the words are often secondary. Just consider the world of difference in meaning that happens by just changing how we say two words: *I* think . . . and I *think*.

If one theme seems to repeat itself today, it seems to me to be that each of you understands the importance of communicating, of keeping in touch, of constantly making the effort to reach out to your partner. And you seem to realize that this is not a goal that you will eventually reach or an achievement of some kind. It's a process—the circulatory system of marriage. As long as it continues, a marriage stays very much alive.

10

Touching
How Intimacy Is Born

DON WHITE: I love to be touched, but for a long time I was very much afraid of it. In my family we almost never touched, never kissed; there was very rare physical contact. When we got married, Lois was always demonstrative and affectionate in public. This would generally tend to get me excited, and I would find it very difficult to cope with.

HUGH BALL: Like Don, I think I tend to have mixed feelings about [touching] in certain respects. . . . I feel very uneasy about touching in public—sort of a hang-up, I guess.

DEBBIE BRADLEY: There was very little touching in my family. I remember that I was told to kiss my father every night before I went to bed, and I found it very difficult. . . . It was a very formal procedure. . . . He touched me once in a while, but there was no real warmth.

ENID BALL: I can say the same about being raised in a family that didn't touch or kiss. It was always a kind of sexual thing, and therefore taboo. . . .

Long before sexual attraction exists as anything more than natural curiosity about anatomical differences, little boys and girls know that the mysterious feelings drawing them into the adventure of mutual exploration are excitingly, frighteningly wrong. The degree of discomfort may vary—embarrassment for some, shame for others, guilt for the rest—but the children have absorbed from the adult world the idea that the human body is indecent. To be naked is to be avoided at any cost. And while looking or being looked at is bad enough, worse by far is touching or being touched.

The lesson is taught early in life and remains deeply ingrained. "Don't touch!" is a childhood litany. Don't touch yourself, it's naughty; don't touch her, that's nasty; don't touch him, nice girls don't do such things— the specific prohibitions may vary, depending on the situation, the age of the children and a family's values, but the message is clear. Whether clothed or unclothed, boys and girls must be discouraged from touching one another. In some cases, particularly where a sense of sinfulness is invoked with very young children, parental prohibitions are like stains applied to soft, raw wood: they penetrate so deeply, they can never be fully eradicated.

Often, however, the message is transmitted silently. The parents set clear examples of the injunction against touching. Apart from an occasional perfunctory embrace, they do not so much as hold hands with each other. They are scarcely more comfortable having physical contact with their children. Characteristically the father, for example, will decide that his little son or daughter is too old to be permitted to nestle in his lap or to be kissed, except as a formality, although the child longs for these signs of affection. Or the mother will stop giving baths to a child who is still very young, when the question of propriety is of no possible concern. Such parents cannot permit the spontaneous physical expression of feelings—the stroking, snuggling and enfolding movements with which almost all living creatures seek the warmth and reassurance that, particularly for the very young, is virtually indistinguishable from life itself.

There is reliable evidence, in fact, that for newborn babies, touch can literally make the difference between life and death. This truth came to light less than thirty years ago as a result of the medical detective work of Dr. Rene Spitz, presently Professor of Psychiatry at the University of Colorado Medical School. His task was to discover why babies in a foundling home, despite receiving good food and adequate medical care, were wasting away and dying. He learned that the infants had been breastfed by their mothers or wet nurses for three months. Then, however, after weaning them, the mothers gave up their babies. They were well cared for by the overburdened foundling-home nurses. The infants lay in clean cribs, separated by partitions, and stayed there day after day without being handled. By the end of the first year, one out of every three babies was dead. They had been unable to survive the lack of stimulation.

The complete cause-and-effect relationship has never been medically determined but experiments with animals suggest that the stimulation of the body sends messages that stimulate the brain which in turn activates critical responses throughout the organism. In any event, the relevant point is that tactile stimulation is an essential element in a baby's development. To deprive him of it is to jeopardize his chances of becoming the healthy human being that he would otherwise be.

No one has measured the effect of minimizing the stimulation of touch for the older child, the preschooler. It seems safe to hypothesize, however, that a penalty is paid, if only in the child's later need to overcome feelings of shame and guilt over the pleasure he finds in touching and being touched. Meanwhile he obeys parental injunctions. Still too young to understand why he must do so, he learns to restrain the impulse to reach out to someone of the opposite sex—or, at a later age, even the same sex. Self-consciousness spoils the natural hug, the casual walking hand in hand or arms around waists, with which friends manifest their bond. Innocence is lost.

As children grow older, the impulse to touch is transformed into the impulse to tease. This leads to scuffling and wrestling, ostensible conflicts which in fact give boys and girls a chance to experience the stimulation of close physical contact. By the time they are in junior high school, or sooner for the more precocious, they realize that parental prohibitions are merely temporary restraining orders issued by judges who are losing their jurisdiction. Most adolescents then begin experimenting with kissing games, initiated either by boys or girls. Generally, however, it is at the boys' insistence that this escalates into necking and, eventually, petting.

At this point young people might appear to be breaking out of parental orbit. This is an illusion. They are, it is true, one step removed from their parents' direct sphere of influence. Yet the basic pattern of their behavior is determined by the same beliefs that dominated their childhood. Now, however, the girls in effect become parent-surrogates. They are the ones who say, "Don't touch," thus echoing their parents and tacitly conceding what society at large has maintained all along: that sex is indeed dirty and touching means sex —so it's hands off.

But there is one significant difference between the restrictions of childhood and those of adolescence. The double standard has been added, smuggled into still another generation. Girls expect boys to be sexually aggressive, and boys expect girls to resist. In fact, it is commonly believed that something is wrong if a boy doesn't try to be aggressive—and if a girl doesn't resist. Obviously male sexual vitality is honorable, female sexual vitality is not.

This double standard pits male against female. Each regards the other, certainly during early encounters, with wariness or mistrust. Sex seems to be a contest of wills—if the boy wins, the girl loses. In this curious game, duplicity is accepted as part of the fun and the phrase, "I love you," often proves as magically effective as Ali Baba's "Open, sesame," the words that unlocked the door to the cave containing the hidden treasure.

Not only does the word "love" depreciate in value but so does the sense of touch. Reaching out, which has already been sharply limited as a spontaneous way of expressing affection and solidarity, is now stripped of all significance except that of sexual provocation. It becomes utilitarian, a specific means to accomplish sexually specific goals. Since the two sexes generally have different goals in view, since boys concentrate on having intercourse while girls, at this stage of development at least, prefer avoiding it if possible, they invest touch with different powers and use it in different ways.

Girls are more inclined, for several reasons, to let themselves be touched than to do the touching. This is partly a result of cultural conditioning, passivity as the proper female role. By waiting for the boy to reach out for her, she simultaneously affirms the male as the initiator or aggressor who must therefore bear full responsibility for his actions—and she proves to herself that she is a desirable female. In adopting this attitude, the young girl is yielding to pressures of which she is only dimly aware. She has grown up believing that if one person does something wrong to another, that person is to be blamed for what he did. She has grown up also believing that sex—"doing it"—is wrong and the boy "does it" to the girl, so that it naturally follows that he must do the touching. It naturally follows, too, that whatever happens, he is culpable.

Such evasion of responsibility, however, has more to do with a need for self-deception than with the desire to avoid blame—especially since girls know very well that the most serious penalty is pregnancy, which they alone must face. The real judgment a girl wants to escape is her own. For even if she rejects society's dictum that sexual activity for her is dishonorable, the idea is deeply embedded in her consciousness, so that long after she has changed her ways of thinking, she still has to contend with stubborn feelings, which vary in intensity, of course, depending on family background and past experience. By rationalizing that the boy she is with is responsible for what takes place between them, she is struggling to free herself from feelings of guilt or discomfort, to free herself from the tight, involuntary tensions of her body, to free herself to enjoy her natural, physical response to being touched.

But because this kind of unfolding requires time and experience, being touched does not give a substantial number of young girls, if not the overwhelming majority, the sensual gratification that the boys imagine. What does satisfy the girl is the knowledge that she personally is able to bring pleasure to a boy whose affections she wants. In ways that often seem mysterious to her, she possesses a power and a desirability she had never before experienced. Consequently her excitement arises less from the sensations that a boy's touch evokes within her body than from witnessing his bewilderingly intense reaction to doing the touching. As one young woman explained: "I used to think boys had different kinds of nerves in the palms of their hands, and *that's* why they wanted to touch you."

In these circumstances many girls understandably find confirmation of their traditional role—the female as sexual catalyzer. To please a boy, she simply has to be pretty, passive and permissive. She is not expected to take the initiative, which is how it would seem both to the boy and to herself if she tried to use her hands as he uses his.

Her reluctance to touch is also based on a practical consideration. In early encounters with a boy, she is likely to find that he becomes too excited too soon— and additional stimulation seems not only unnecessary but unwise, if she wishes him to hold onto whatever self-control he can still summon. In fact, the point at which she may finally touch him is very specific and her intention quite clear. If she is determined not to engage in intercourse, she may use her hand in response to the boy's urging, not to prolong the experience but to end it by manually releasing him from physical tension.

Except for occasions when masturbation is the most they can hope for, boys generally have only a moderate interest in being touched—nothing, at any rate, that compares with their drive to do the touching. Two sources fuel that drive, one tactile, the other cerebral. The first is sensual feedback, pleasurable sensations that flow through fingertips moving across flesh that is smooth, soft, warm and curving. The second is a triumphant awareness of doing what is forbidden, of touching those parts of a girl's body that are private and concealed, together with a suspenseful realization that she may be ready to give herself to him.

But he is trapped by ignorance and inexperience. Just as the girl does not understand the intensity with which he reacts to touching her, a touch closer to groping or grabbing than caressing, so he cannot comprehend her failure to respond with an ardor to match his own. He thinks of touching as a sexual starter—once he places his hand on a girl's body, he expects that her sexual motor will automatically shift into high gear. When this doesn't occur, he may be baffled or angry and is likely to try all the harder to overcome the girl's resistance. He interprets her refusal to let his hand go where he wants it to go as proof that she is just afraid of being aroused by his touch, and if he can force his way past her defenses, her resistance will melt.

It might be expected that the futility of such an approach would soon enough correct the idea of touch as a trigger, and for a few fortunate young people, it does. For most, however, it does not; instead there is a boomerang effect. Belief is not evaluated in the light of personal experience; experience is evaluated in the light of prior belief.

When the first, fumbling encounters of a girl and boy produce not the delight they had anticipated but dismay or disappointment for either one or both, they tend not to question their expectations but themselves —or each other. He decides she is uptight because she didn't let him touch her in the right place; she decides he is inept because he didn't know how to touch her in the right way. They remain ignorant of each other's needs and incapable of communicating. They believe that if they just try, try again—with a new partner— before too long they will surely master the trick of sex.

As the search for sexual pleasure continues on a

trial-and-error basis, the misinformed mislead the naive, and almost everyone pretends. They utilize verbal smoke screens: girls do so because they are ashamed of what they are doing and choose to deny doing it; boys, because they are ashamed of doing little or nothing and brag about what they really have not done.

Despite all this confusion, young men and women must try to learn the truth about their own sexual natures and identities, to discover what it means to be male or female, to find new dimensions of their personalities through relationships with the opposite sex, to determine what they can do with comfort and what they cannot. Self-discovery is always a difficult and almost always a painful quest, but never more so than when sex is the unknown dimension—because it takes two persons together to make evident what one of the two wants to know.

In time some young men and women gradually find at least partial answers to their questions. But even for the more fortunate among them success is usually flawed by their continuing inability to grasp the true function of the act of touching. They still think of it exclusively as a means to an end: touching for the purpose of having intercourse.

Once a sexual relationship has been established, most young couples use touch as little more than a wordless way to communicate a willingness, a wish or a demand to make love. It is functional; beyond that, it seems of limited value and is regarded, especially by men, as a waste of time and effort, an unnecessary postponement of intercourse. Highlighting this outlook is the remark of a woman who said she could tell that her young daughter and teenage boyfriend had started sleeping together because, the mother explained, "They stopped touching each other all the time."

Other couples who give up affectionately reaching out to one another once they start sleeping together, provide a variation on the same theme. They too believe that touch is necessary only to initiate sex but they happen to enjoy the means almost as much as the end itself. They have advanced past the adolescent notion of touch-as-trigger to the more sophisticated notion of touch-as-technique.

In essence they have adopted the philosophy of the how-to-do-it sex manuals, where much is made of touch. Sex is removed from the universe of emotions and brought safely into the realm of objects—not something to be experienced but to be used, and not just used but used well. It is a skill that can be taught and learned, like a trade or a sport, and it can be applied wherever desired. All any individual needs to know is how to move a hand, where to place a mouth, when to use a tongue. The sexual union, reduced to its most common denominator, becomes a joining of separate, almost disembodied, anatomical parts. Thus in the name of sexual liberation, men and women are taught not how to touch another human being but how to manipulate another body.

The idea that sexual technique is everything and that practice makes lovemaking perfect is not new. Generations ago it received its classic expression in the words of the French novelist, Honoré de Balzac, who said that for a woman to give herself to a man was like putting a violin in the hands of a gorilla. The sentiment was intended as flattery for the female but the fact is that it describes her as an instrument to be played for pleasure—for someone else's pleasure, obviously, since violins cannot hear themselves sing. What Balzac was decrying was the inability of the gorilla to make beautiful music when he had such a sensitive instrument in his hands.

It may be argued that taking the analogy so literally is merely setting up the customary straw man to be demolished. But there is ample evidence that this conception of the female as a sexual instrument dominates the thinking of contemporary men and women. The clearest substantiation, ironically, comes from women—especially those caught up in the movement for greater equality.

Many of these women echo Balzac perfectly. They too insist that men in bed are like gorillas who do not know how to handle women, and they also think the gorillas should learn to perform more satisfactorily. This is a dead-end approach to the sexual relationship. Preoccupation with manipulative technique turns persons into objects; and touching is turned into the science of stimulation for the purpose of sensual gratification, which in turn is for the purpose of reaching a climax. Instead of sharing of private emotions, sex then comes perilously close to being an exchange of impersonal services, which weakens the bond between a man and woman. Since neither one prizes the uniqueness of the other, all that each partner must do to find a replacement is to choose a person who can perform the necessary functions.

But for the man and woman who value each other as individuals and who want the satisfactions of a sustained relationship, it is important to avoid the fundamental error of believing that touch is a means to an end. It is not. *Touch is an end in itself.* It is a primary form of communication, a silent voice that avoids the pitfall of words while expressing the feelings of the moment. It bridges the physical separateness from which no human being is spared, literally establishing a sense of solidarity between two individuals. Touching is sensual pleasure, exploring the texture of skin, the suppleness of muscle, the contours of the body, with no further goal than enjoyment of tactile perceptions. And yet such is the nature of the sense of touch, which can simultaneously give and receive impressions, that the very pleasure a woman may experience in stroking her husband's face, for example, is relayed back through her fingertips to give him the pleasure of being aware of her pleasure in him.

This constitutes the wellspring of emotion from which sexuality flows. In reaching out spontaneously to communicate by touch as well as with words, a husband and wife reaffirm their trust in each other and renew their commitment. They draw on this emotional reservoir when one turns to the other with physical desire. Because their touching has a continuity, because it is part of an intimate dialogue that does not begin and end in bed, they feel secure. Whoever first makes an overture is secure in the knowledge that the other will understand and respond, and the one who responds is secure in the knowledge that the other partner will accept the response, no matter how limited a degree of erotic arousal may naturally be possible at that particular moment.

Where no such security exists, two individuals in a sexual encounter may touch physically but remain out of touch emotionally. Their feelings may not be entirely unlike those of two acquaintances who find themselves pressed uncomfortably close together in a crowded bus. They accept the situation impassively, perhaps struggling to dissociate themselves from the sensations of their own bodies, until at their destination they can finally separate.

For a husband and wife, of course, the circumstances are far more painful. It is difficult to conceive a situation better calculated to overwhelm a person with feelings of helplessness and outrage, of loneliness, worthlessness and despair, than one in which touching or submitting to being touched, takes place in silence and darkness with an uncaring partner who has made clear that such intimacies are solely for the purpose of intercourse.

Touch can then express neither warmth nor closeness. It is a clue or signal without subtlety, a demand for service or a yielding to such a demand, and it leads to what is required: servicing. And over the years the service deteriorates until finally the sexual relationship ends because one of the partners is no longer able—or willing—to perform. In a sad and ironic reminder of their childhood, a man and woman "do not touch."

Today's young couples have a better chance to avoid living out their later lives in married celibacy. They seem to be more free to talk about sex and, if recent indications are credited, more free to express themselves physically as well. Whether this development is a passing fashion or a lasting change in style remains to be seen as these very young men and women pair off to create a future together.

Perhaps they will succeed in incorporating into their sexual lives a new philosophy of touch. Perhaps they do understand that touching, like seeing, hearing, tasting and smelling, nourishes the pleasure of being alive; that touching another human being satisfies the profound creature need not to feel alone; that being touched by another human being satisfies the need to be desired as a physical presence; and that in touching and being touched by a trusted and trusting person of the opposite sex, one experiences not only the pleasure of being alive but the joy of being a sexual creature—a joy that ultimately and inevitably, as a natural extension of life itself, expresses itself in the sexual embrace.

11

How Pretending Makes Sexual Pleasure Impossible

PAT QUILL: John . . . wouldn't let me get away with any pretending.

VIRGINIA JOHNSON: Pretending?

PAT QUILL: Faking orgasm. He stopped that fast—he said I didn't have to fake anything with him. . . . It was part of [my] old attitude. . . . Call it protectiveness or whatever, it was the old idea of making it nice for the man.

It may seem harmless enough for a woman to pretend that she has had an orgasm. But any form of deception between a man and a woman, even if conceived of as a kind of game, is potentially destructive to their relationship. This is the case when a wife pretends to have an orgasm. The practice is especially unrewarding for a woman—and it is quite unnecessary. It can be avoided by any couple willing to make an effort *as a couple* to communicate openly and truthfully.

The importance of making such an effort can perhaps be more readily accepted once the subject has been looked at in the light of its effect upon a valued relationship.

Pretending orgasm, when it occurs only on occasion, can be intended as a simple, considerate gesture, not unlike the socially acceptable acts with which people try to "make someone happy" or to safeguard thoughts they are not prepared to share. A wife's sole purpose, for example, might be to shield her husband from feelings that would disturb him needlessly or to protect herself from having to disclose emotions which she cannot cope with at that moment.

But regardless of her reasons—and there are any number of generous motives for such behavior—pretending orgasm is potentially dangerous. Though resorted to only rarely, at first, a precedent has been set and the deception can take place more easily on successive occasions. Although it does not reflect a woman's real needs or desires, the practice may become an established part of her sexual response—an invisible wall that separates her from her partner.

Habitual pretense can be linked to the acceptance, by one partner or both, of double-standard values—in particular, the belief that the two sexes are unequal and that they are incapable of understanding each other. These are deeply rooted prejudices and despite changing attitudes today, they remain persistent, widespread and seriously divisive.

They divide the sexes and, as will soon be evident, they tend to divide the individual woman herself. All too often her actions do not correspond to her feelings. Even worse, she may smother her feelings so that she can act as society—that is, the important people in her life, including her husband—expects her to act. She is the victim of distorted, and distorting, cultural values. In an extreme case, a wife may be totally unprepared to give of herself or take for herself sexually, but in pretending to experience orgasm, she attempts to be considerate of her husband. And while the practice cannot be encouraged, it must be viewed with compassion.

To some women, of course, the pretense seems harmless enough. Many a wife defends it by saying that it takes nothing from her and gives something to her husband. She sees her subterfuge as contributing to their relationship and she may even take pride in the fact that her husband never suspects the truth.

There are wives, for example, who maintain that they just want to keep their husbands from prolonging intercourse. The simulated climax is a signal to the man that, as one woman put it, "after that, he's on his own." But the desire to get intercourse over with usually means something specific, with the exception of instances when fatigue or distraction interfere with pleasure. It may mean, for instance, that nothing that she has experienced sexually in the past gives her any reason to hope that this time will be different, that this time she will be spared the frustration of the orgasm that remains just out of reach. Or it may mean, as it often does, that she resents her husband and is rejecting him as a man—but keeping their marriage intact.

Often, in such cases, the wife is sexually submissive because she sees herself as having no choice. She does not consider intercourse to be an opportunity to express herself as a woman but rather a mechanical service she must render. Consequently faking an orgasm becomes a means to an end: getting the business over with as quickly as possible. In such circumstances, the marriage becomes one of appearances—a fake in which both partners knowingly or unknowingly participate.

Following in the footsteps of such couples, although still a long distance behind them, are husbands and wives who do not dream that their marriages may eventually come to the same end. Yet the wives have already started on the path of pretense. Their reason, however, is different; they frequently or consistently fake orgasm because for them it has seemed the simplest solution to a complex problem.

The problem originates in the cultural misconception, shared by husband and wife, that the female is inherently less sexual than the male. Having absorbed this concept as she grew up, a woman tends to adopt the traditionally passive role during intercourse. It is the man's role to initiate, to stimulate, and hers to respond; she accepts and, if she is fortunate, takes pleasure from what he does *to* her. She would never risk taking the initiative and suggesting anything specific that might promise to be sexually more pleasurable, or at least might improve her capacity to respond. To do so would make her seem aggressive and her behavior would not conform to patterns that both she and her husband accept as "normal." Even if she feels she is capable of enjoying sex more than she does, or wishes that she were, she sees her present subdued response as a private problem, even as a personal inadequacy. She certainly does not see it as a concern to be shared with her husband.

Embarrassment, shame or fear keep her silent. Because she misconceives the female sexual role, she is uncertain whether it is "decent" to admit having a desire for greater pleasure than she now experiences. She worries that no matter how tentatively and carefully she approaches the subject of her sexual unfulfillment, it will upset her husband. Will he wonder whether she is comparing him to another man? And can that doubt, once raised, ever be totally erased? Or will he in turn defensively accuse her of being sexually unstimulating and unresponsive? Isn't there a good chance that she will, in fact, gain nothing and risk losing some of the limited satisfaction she sometimes gets from sex?

Such thorny questions abound and they seem a prelude to a confrontation she would prefer to avoid. One way of avoiding such a confrontation is to persuade herself that having an orgasm is comparatively unimportant and not worth making a fuss about. Thus, when she says her failure to have a climax doesn't bother her too much, she may actually mean only that it bothers her less than the thought of having to talk about it with her husband. Faking orgasm, by contrast, is simple. It may even give her self-esteem a boost, because in doing so she is acting out the sexually passive role of trying to please her husband—and isn't that what a wife is supposed to do?

The decision to pretend, however, is not as one-sided as it might seem. In most cases it proves to be a collaboration initiated by an aggressive husband who somehow lets his wife know that that is what he wants of her. He is usually a double-standard male for whom sex must follow the dominant-male, submissive-female pattern, and the simulated orgasm serves to bolster his male pride. This man rarely suspects his wife of faking, not because her deception is so good but because his perception is so poor. Concentrating exclusively on his own sexual pleasure, he usually fails to sense the true level of his wife's sexual response. For such a husband, a fake orgasm is as valued as a real one—perhaps even more so, because the fake can be turned into a dramatic performance, full of sound and fury, while in reality signifying nothing.

A sad and ironic parallel can be found in the case of the woman who, on the face of it, would seem to have no apparent reason to pretend. Since her usual levels of sexual excitement reflect a minimum of physical tension, she is genuinely content with sex that doesn't culminate in a climax. The warmth, intimacy and sensory stimulation that she obtains may be all the satisfaction she wants. If, in addition, her husband is a single-standard male who believes that a woman, no less than a man, has the right to search for sexual gratification to the maximum degree desired, she would certainly seem free of the oppressive problems that troubled the wife of the double-standard male.

There is, however, another "if," and it is critical. This woman will remain free of any need to pretend a level of sexual excitement that she is actually not experiencing *only* if her husband can accept her quiet enjoyment as an authentic expression of her sexual nature and not have this diminish his own desire.

But the stage is set for trouble when, consciously or not, he makes her aware that he is bothered by her failure to be orgasmic. Ironically, his concern may grow out of his acceptance of the principle of sexual equality. He wants to please his wife as much as she wants to please him, and, mistakenly equating his ejaculation with her orgasm, he may feel that she is not getting from intercourse what she should because he is failing to stimulate her adequately.

His motive is commendable; his reasoning, fatally flawed. Instead of granting his wife the same privilege that he unquestionably possesses—the right to respond to sexual stimulation in a spontaneous and natural way, culminating in one's own satisfaction—he decides that her satisfaction should include orgasm. Anything less disappoints *him,* because, in his eyes, a question has been raised as to his sexual effectiveness. Without realizing it, he has stumbled back into the double-standard trap. He is setting goals for his wife to attain. Since he conceives sex as a cause-and-effect situation—his efforts are the "cause," her response the "effect"—he feels responsible for her lack of an orgasmic climax.

Once his wife becomes aware, even if only subliminally, of her husband's concern, her enjoyment of sex is almost certain to be affected. Attention will be diverted from the happy feelings created within her by the physical union with her husband and will turn instead to an attempt to sense her husband's emotional state so that at the right time she can supply the desired effect. Where before she would have been relaxed in his arms, she is now likely to be somewhat tense, if not apprehensive.

In part she is willing to pretend because she does not want her husband to think she is any less female than another woman might be. Conceivably he could reassure her if the communicative bond between them was secure and if he continued to let her know clearly how much he desired her. But his reassurances may not help—they may indeed have the opposite effect—if she worries that her lack of orgasmic release lessens her husband's pleasure in having intercourse. Then his denials, no matter how carefully phrased, may only reinforce her fear for their relationship, particularly if she knows him to be so intent on being supportive that he would unhesitatingly tell a white lie to spare her any unnecessary distress.

But no matter how generous a gesture a wife intends her orgasmic pretense to be, the odds are overwhelming that eventually it will boomerang. One reason—and it is perhaps the most important of all arguments against the practice—is that deception locks a sexual relationship into its existing state. With the orgasm she pretends to have, in effect the wife gives the sexual status quo her stamp of approval. To her husband the message she transmits seems clear: "You satisfy me completely." Who can fault him for being pleased with himself, because he thinks he is pleasing his wife? Consequently he will continue the sexual practices he has presumed to be mutually satisfactory —and his wife will have to perpetuate her deception.

Under such circumstances, there is very little chance for growth and change. The wife who pretends satisfaction may never learn that her failure to achieve orgasm is remediable. How can she hope to eliminate the obstacles to full sexual response if she is ignorant of their existence or chooses to ignore them altogether?

Before she can discover the truth about her lack of responsiveness, she must stop concealing from her husband the truth about their sexual relationship. After all, he may be the primary cause of the problem, the key factor; at the very least, he is deeply involved. But as long as a woman makes believe that she experiences orgasm, she dooms herself *not* to experience it—because her pretense reinforces the attitudes and actions both on her husband's part and on her own that may have created the problem initially.

Obviously, a husband cannot help his wife overcome a deprivation that she successfully conceals. True, he may not be able to help even if she makes him aware of the situation. But once the knowledge of orgasmic dysfunction is shared, there exists a mutual involvement in the problem, and when this is openly acknowledged by both partners, in itself it is a unifying and reassuring experience. This frees the two of them to search together for a solution which, by its nature, requires their cooperation and mutual understanding.

It should be underscored that the mutual search for sexual satisfaction usually requires a substantial period of time. This kind of physical and emotional evolution cannot be speeded up just because, as happens in many cases, a wife discovers that her body seems to have come alive with sharp, insistent desire. It will be difficult enough to express her feelings: to find the right words, gestures and movements that will permit her, gently, to let her husband know that she has new needs and yet not undermine his self-confidence. It will be even more difficult to avoid destroying his confidence in her. She has, after all, been lying.

"Pretending" or "faking" are euphemisms for "lying" and lying divides people. This is especially true in bed. Regardless of motivation, the woman who fakes an orgasm is cutting herself off from the man she is embracing. It is a painful paradox: in the very moment and in the very act in which she and her husband seek to merge themselves in mutual pleasure, she moves her body or utters sounds intended to deceive him—and is instantly aware of how separate she is from him. No act of will can obliterate that awareness. And the greater his delight in what he believes to be their shared happiness, the more sharply is she aware of the distance between them.

Her husband's ignorance of the truth separates them still further. It creates a kind of static between them whenever they talk about sex, even in discussions that have nothing to do with their own relationship, because the unspoken truth interferes with their ability to communicate. If the subject is a movie they have seen together, or the impending divorce of friends, the husband's opinions have a different effect on his wife than he can realize, and her remarks may have overtones that escape him.

Sooner or later any woman who imagines that pretending orgasm is harmless will learn that in reality the practice erodes her confidence in herself and in her marriage. If she cannot bring the subterfuge to an end, it will probably put an end to much of the sexual satisfaction that she—and no doubt her husband—may originally have experienced. Without the stimulation that spontaneous impulses evoke in a man and woman during intercourse, without the challenge to one partner to meet the unpredictable desires of the other, intercourse follows a repetitive pattern and eventually becomes routine and even boring.

The arguments against pretending orgasm are clear and unequivocal. Even so, it must also be acknowledged that every woman has real reasons for fearing to end her deception. There is undeniable risk of injuring the marriage itself, particularly if the revealing of the deception is not handled expertly. When a husband discovers that intercourse with his wife has been a sham, he can hardly help wondering to what extent their entire relationship is also a sham. The truth may be that she pretended orgasm only at certain times and with the best of intentions, and that in so doing she was as self-deceived as he was deceived by her. But this may not be easily understood by a man whose personal pride has been wounded and whose trust has been abused. Moreover, he is not likely to accept freely the possibility that in part he brought the deception on himself—that his eagerness to have his wife be orgasmic may have contributed to her decision to pretend that she was. He is far more likely to react with the usual knee-jerk reflex of anger and disparagement.

What alternatives are there for the wife who values her marriage, cares deeply for her husband, and who no longer wants to continue deceiving him about the intensity of her sexual response? Won't her husband be equally disturbed whether he accidentally discovers the deception or whether his wife finally confesses the deceit?

It would be as irresponsible to give specific advice as it would be to give a prescription for medicine over the phone to an unknown person who has diagnosed himself without the benefit of physical or laboratory examination. At the risk of repeating the obvious, it should be stated that every marriage is a constellation in which two uniquely different individuals have to work out their own particular emotional partnership. Without precise information about the individuals and the partnership, advice is useless at best, poisonous at worst.

However, a general suggestion may offer some insight for a woman who has been faking orgasm as she decides for herself what course of action to follow.

In brief, the husband must be informed. Frequently the disclosure can be handled with the least possible pain by enlisting the help of a third person, particularly if that person is professionally trained and can offer the husband legitimate explanations for his wife's orgasmic deception. A marriage counselor, clinical psychologist, family physician or theologian, to list a few of the more familiar possibilities, may serve as an intermediary in cases where a wife feels that she is unable to cope with the delicate task of divulging her pretense and explaining her reasons.

Whether the approach is direct or with the aid of a third person, the more quickly the problem is dealt with, the better for all concerned. The longer the practice of orgasmic deceit continues, the greater the pain is likely to be when disclosure occurs—and the slower will be the return of both partners to an emotional climate in which the wife can enjoy the opportunity for full sexual response.

Once the truth has been revealed and accepted without recrimination, the future holds considerable hope of a good physical relationship. When emotions are taken into account by husband and wife, when the fears of seeming foolish or inexperienced or clumsy are eased and then banished, astonishing changes in behavior can and do take place. And when the body, which is responsive to pleasurable stimulation of the senses, receives gratification in new and perhaps unexpected ways, it comes to seek the very touch that in the past would have been avoided.

Over and over again, when couples consult a professional therapist, it turns out that both partners have been, figuratively and literally, groping in the dark in their efforts to achieve a good sexual relationship. Their false assumptions, their sexual misinformation and their cultural misconceptions kept them from seeing each other.

To repeat: pretending to have sexual pleasure virtually guarantees never experiencing it. The first step toward orgasmic experience for those who have not enjoyed this birthright is to acknowledge that it is missing.

12

Commitment
The Pleasure Bond

DONNA ROSS: In this marriage I feel that I am a totally free human being. I am me all the way. In my first marriage . . . I didn't really know myself and I couldn't even express my feelings. . . .

BILL MASTERS: How is your second marriage different, sexually, from your first?

DONNA ROSS: [In] my first marriage . . . even though sex wasn't satisfying, I didn't know anything else was possible. Or I just felt that maybe it was me, that I was inadequate. But our marriage [now] is a whole new different kind of thing. . . . I'm much less inhibited than I was because I'm much more trustful. . . .

TONY ROSS: We've gone through terrible emotional crises together, and sometimes—maybe because we felt the need to be close or to reassure each other—it leads to sex.

DONNA ROSS: A comforting, a closeness, an intimacy kind of thing.

A commitment is a pledge to do something. One person tells another, "I promise," and the promise is kept, the obligation fulfilled. Trust has been asked for; trust has been given; and trust has been repaid.

This is the basic meaning of commitment. It is the cement that binds individuals and groups together. Without the ability of one person to rely upon another, the social bond could not exist. Even a legal contract depends, in the final analysis, on the keeping of a pledge. For if a contract is broken, the commitment not kept, the law can penalize the person who failed to perform as he had promised, but penalizing him leaves the obligation unfulfilled, the job undone, the need unmet.

That is all there is to commitment insofar as it relates to associations that exist for practical purposes. When the association is for emotional reasons, however, the meaning of commitment changes. It can still be defined as a pledge to do something, but the pledge possesses a radically different dimension. "I promise," one person tells another, "because I care about you."

Caring—which is defined as paying attention, being concerned, solicitous and protective—flows from two related but different kinds of feelings. One is a feeling of being *responsive to* someone, of *caring for* that person; the other is a feeling of being *responsible for* someone, of wanting to *take care of* him or her. These feelings are generated in entirely different ways. Responsiveness occurs spontaneously, before the mind is consciously aware of what is happening—a sudden surge of interest and attraction, triggered by another person's physical presence. Responsibility is consciously, though often unwillingly, invoked by the mind—an acknowledgment of obligation.

Most human beings experience these elemental feelings when holding an infant. This combination of emotions, this interaction in which each caring impulse reinforces the other—a wish to take care of someone for whom one cares—creates an overpowering sense of involvement and identification, of oneness. Some people call it love, and it is the original source of commitment.

As such, however, it is still a one-sided commitment, one person pledging himself to another, who may not even realize that a commitment has been made. Obviously this is true of the infant and its parents; there is nothing mutual about the bond. The responsiveness and sense of responsibility exist entirely within the parents. They are committed; the baby is dependent.

Before too long, however, emotionally mature parents stop identifying with their child in such a total way. Gradually they accept it as a separate human being whose needs are not only different from their own but often in conflict with their immediate desires. Thus long before parent and child are equals in any sense of the word, each needs something of the other: acceptance, appreciation, affection. And the smallest child soon learns that his parents hope to receive from him precisely what he expects from them—pleasure. *Mutual pleasure sets a seal on emotional commitment.*

This is the foundation on which all future affectionate relationships will be constructed. The search for pleasure—and pleasure is an infinitely deeper and more complex emotional matter than simply sensual gratification—continues throughout life. The quality of marriage is determined by whether the pleasure derived exceeds the inevitable portion of displeasure that human beings must experience in all their associations. When there is more displeasure than pleasure in a marriage, a husband and wife are more aware of the obligations of marriage than they are of its rewards. It may clarify the subject if their bond is characterized as a commitment of obligation.

In contrast, there is the commitment of concern, a bond in which a man and a woman mutually meet their obligations not because they feel *compelled* to but because they feel *impelled* to do so. They do so in response to impulses, desires and convictions that are deeply rooted within themselves, not all of which do they fully understand. When they act in each other's best interests, even though this may at the time be in conflict with their own immediate wishes, they are saying to each other, in effect: "I care very much about your feelings—because your feelings affect mine. Your happiness adds to mine, your unhappiness takes away from my happiness, and I want to be happy."

So obvious does all this seem to most young couples that they believe that they know all that there is to know—or certainly all that they need to know—about how and why being committed to each other is linked to sexual pleasure. They met as two strangers and eventually became lovers, and because this is how life is expected to move, they accept it as a natural sequence of events. They do not reflect on how it actually happened; to them, it seems a matter of elementary logic: love leads to sex, which leads to greater love, which in turn leads to better sex—and so it goes. This, at least, is how they expect it to be, and if it turns out otherwise, they have convenient explanations: insufficient love, inadequate sex. It is as simple as a-b-c. Like the alphabet, however, it does not mean much by itself.

In a more reflective mood, they might say: "Since we enjoy being together, the greater our enjoyment, the more reason we have to stay together." They are describing the circle of commitment. Being together gives them satisfactions, including sex, that reinforce their decision to live together as a couple; these satisfactions, which are highly valued, must be safeguarded. Each partner, to protect his or her own happiness, tries to sustain the other partner's happiness so that their relationship will flourish; and these reciprocal efforts intensify the satisfactions they find in living together—which further strengthen their wish to remain a couple. *They live according to the commitment of mutual concern, and pleasure is the bond between them.*

They expect to be faithful because they want to be. Furthermore they realize that if either or both of them must seek sexual satisfaction with other partners, the circle of commitment will have been broken. The more satisfactions they find with other people, the fewer satisfactions do they need from each other; and the less they need from each other, the easier it is for them to go their separate ways. Beyond all rationalization, extramarital affairs would demonstrate two things: first, that they were incapable of meeting each other's most basic physical and emotional needs, and second, that they did not consider each other unique, and therefore irreplaceable, sources of satisfaction and pleasure.

Just as no one stops to think about what is required for him to breathe until he has trouble breathing, so couples give little thought to what is needed for their happiness to continue—until the day they discover that theirs is no longer a happy marriage. Unaware of what nurtured their relationship in the first place, they have unwittingly deprived it of precisely the emotional rewards that were necessary for it to flourish. Then, to the extent that they never really understood what united them as lovers, they find it difficult to understand what has made them strangers once again. It seems as though the movie of their life has been put in reverse.

If their life together had actually been filmed and could now be reviewed, they might better appreciate some things that, in the beginning of their relationship, greatly contributed to their satisfaction in being in each other's company. There was, for example, the simple fact of acceptance. The need to be recognized and accepted as a unique individual, to have an emotional identity as specific and singular as one's fingerprints, is crucial to an intimate relationship. Its contribution to self-esteem is well established, and it plays a significant part in sexual responsiveness. The more confident a man and woman become that each perceives and values the uniqueness of the other, the more likely they are to be drawn together.

Conversely, the more each believes the other to be judging or evaluating whatever is said or done, the more they pull back from each other. This can be discerned in an incident recounted by a young woman who had been living with a man. One night, while visiting his family, she sat down to dinner feeling happy and secure. During the course of the dinner, she became caught up in the conversation and, without thinking, reached over and took some salad from her friend's plate. He immediately pulled his plate closer to himself and said, in a voice that carried across the table, "That's mine—don't do that."

In itself it was a trivial incident but it had a much greater effect than her friend could have imagined. Apart from the fact that it revealed him as an ungenerous man, and one with rather squeamish tastes, it made her realize that he was evaluating what she did. It became difficult to eat; she became self-conscious about all her motions and any enjoyment of the food that she might have had, disappeared.

Later that night, in bed with him, she found herself unable to behave naturally and spontaneously. She said that she felt "frozen." It would be an exaggeration to claim that this single incident ended their relationship. But she realized that he had told her, without intending to, that he did not accept her as she was. Not long afterward, she broke off with him.

A counterpoint to this episode is contained in the remark of a man who said that he first truly believed that his wife-to-be loved him the evening that she drank from his glass of water. To him, the gesture communicated total acceptance—and this acceptance of one's self as a physical being heralds the acceptance of one's self as a sexual being.

This is particularly important in the beginning of a sexual relationship. What is needed is not simply to be admired or desired, vitally important though that is, but to be confirmed as a sexual person. It is comparatively simple, after all, for anyone to establish the extent to which his personality seems to appeal to other people; there is ample opportunity in the normal course of daily events to observe how people respond. But a person's sexuality, which is just one dimension of personality, is more difficult to assay. It finds its fullest expression in a mutually appreciated physical relationship, which, even among emancipated men and women, doesn't happen often.

In one lifetime, therefore, most men and women will have few reflections of themselves as sexual beings. Consequently, each relationship carries the potentiality of exerting a powerful emotional effect, for better or for worse. In every encounter, no matter how absorbed both partners may be in their own physical and emotional responses, they remain distinctly conscious of the other person's reactions. In part, this reflects concern for the partner: was it good? And in part, it reflects uncertainty about one's self: was I good?

This is one of the satisfactions that all couples seek in their relationships—a validation of their sexual selves. Each hopes to find mirrored in the eyes of the other an image of himself or of herself as a sexually desirable person. This appreciation that they seek—which will free them to appreciate themselves with some security—is paradoxical in nature. On one level, a man wants to be reassured that he is like other men; the woman, that she is like other women. There is a sense of sexual universality that they want to share, and this can come to them only through cross-sex appreciation, a comparatively nonspecific response by which males and females mutually confirm each other's biological nature.

Beyond that, however, lies a need to differentiate themselves from the others of their sex, a wish to be appreciated in an entirely specific way as unique individuals. The lasting satisfaction that comes from having one's individuality recognized and esteemed can hardly be overestimated. It is among the most powerful of all human motivations and it figures significantly in every aspect of life. Such recognition of individuality for most people comes best from a successfully sustained sexual relationship. In the intimacy of a sustained sexual relationship, few things matter more to both partners than to be perceived as the individuals they are. Indeed, it is perception that makes mutual, sustained pleasure possible.

To make an emotional commitment to someone is to be on his or her side, a steadfast ally; it is essentially an expression of loyalty. This is what most people have in mind when they speak of commitments; to some extent, commitments involve obligations and responsibilities but they are obligations that have been voluntarily chosen.

But there is another dimension to commitment.

Becoming committed to someone is, by definition, to entrust one's physical and emotional well-being to that person; it is an act of faith and an acceptance of vulnerability. This is the opposite side of the coin of commitment. If, for example, a woman has had sufficient evidence that a man has made a commitment to her, that she can trust him to be concerned about her welfare and to be there when she needs him, she will then, no matter how slowly, allow herself to become committed to him—that is, to become openly, emotionally vulnerable and sexually responsive.

This vital distinction between *making* a commitment and *becoming* committed is obscured by the English language, which fails to provide words that differentiate one emotional dimension from the other. To say that a man and woman are committed to each other, for instance, in no way indicates the nature of their bond. A woman may be committed to her husband in the sense of being his loyal wife, his co-operative partner in maintaining a family—and yet *not* be committed to him in the sense of trusting him with her deepest feelings, of becoming emotionally vulnerable.

Because this distinction between making a commitment and becoming committed has not been widely appreciated and generally goes unremarked, considerable confusion results among people. They believe that until they have made a mutual commitment, no commitment exists. They tell each other that although they are having an affair, neither one is committed to the other. This is self-deception. Becoming committed happens of itself, as part of an emotional evolution that follows its own course. Not infrequently men and women discover to their astonishment that they have become committed in spite of themselves and without ever openly making a commitment.

A case in point involves a woman in her early thirties who had been married for six years to a professional in the health-care sciences, who was sexually inactive, despite the fact that his wife always welcomed his attention. After having tried unsuccessfully to encourage him to be more responsive, she decided to have an affair. Since her marriage offered her many material and social advantages that she valued, she did not want a divorce. In short, although these two people had made a commitment to their marriage, neither one was committed to the other; they were wasting the opportunities that marriage affords.

Consequently, the wife chose to have an affair with a man who appeared to have little in common with her. He was younger than she was; he worked as a baker; and having recently come to the United States from abroad, he spoke little English. But sex between them was very good and in the warmth and security of the physical relationship, each began to unfold. Without being aware of what was happening, they started to become committed to each other—although they did not think of it in those terms. All they knew was that they chose to be with each other as often as possible and they permitted themselves to reveal more and more of their deepest feelings.

Perhaps because language was an obstacle, they learned to watch each other's faces and to listen to whatever was said with extraordinary intensity. The experience was shattering for the young woman because in comparison her role at home seemed one of catering to her husband's wishes, while he often seemed totally oblivious to her presence. Finding herself truly perceived and appreciated as an individual by her foreign-born friend, she flowered—friends who did not know what was going on commented on her obvious happiness, which was a reflection of the fact that she was discovering aspects of her own personality—a level of sensual awareness—that she had never known existed. This was especially true in sex, where, as she expressed it, she experienced feelings in parts of her body that she hadn't dreamed were there. She was discovering her own sexual identity.

Usually a man and a woman learn to communicate with words first before they communicate sexually; with this woman and her friend, sexual communication became so good that the wish to be able to communicate equally well verbally led her to give him lessons in English. Ultimately, this persuaded her to leave her husband and live with her friend. In doing so, she believed that she was making a new commitment. What she did not realize was that this commitment had been in the making for more than a year, catalyzed by their committed relationship.

When a man and woman marry, they do so believing that as a couple they can improve their chances of increasing the satisfactions that make life worth living. They are confident that the pleasures they have experienced in the past will increase as a consequence of their formal commitment. Unfortunately, what usually happens, through no fault of their own, is that they begin to think of themselves not as two individuals who have the capacity to enhance each other's joy in being alive and who therefore feel committed to each other, but as a couple mutually committed to tasks they must complete. They feel that they must establish a new life pattern, and they find themselves with new needs, facing new problems, and obliged to establish new priorities. They want to make money, to advance in their careers, to set up a home or become socially established and, sooner or later, to have children. These are all reasonable and praiseworthy goals—but secondary in importance to their original commitment: the mutual need to flourish as individuals in the climate of pleasure that each afforded the other.

Of course, it is true that there are people who marry in order to accomplish specific objectives, and for them it is not too important if their personal relationship also becomes businesslike in character. But they are surely in the minority. Generally, when couples discover, after a period of time, that they are acting more as business partners than married lovers, it comes as a bit of a shock and usually with considerable regret. Rarely do they understand what is happening. They have forgotten that before their marriage they were two people who tried to be together as much as they could because they found comfort and security in each other's acceptance, appreciation and understanding. This was the commitment of mutual concern. With marriage, however, they became husbands and wives, individuals who expected to take care of specialized responsibilities and who increasingly followed separate paths if their day's work was to be done. They slowly became emotionally uncommitted—and were left with the commitment of obligation.

Commitment to goals of achievement preempted the commitment to one another. All the forces that brought them together as a man and a woman were now losing intensity. Instead of being joined as a male and a female who could give each other support and pleasure, they now played the roles of husband and wife, or mother and father, who must separately struggle with onerous obligations. And because they were less directly involved in each other's lives, each partner experienced this "disinvolvement" as being less cared for, less valued, less desired.

This is one of the main reasons why sex grows unsatisfactory. In the early years of their relationship, both before marriage and probably for some time afterward, their lovemaking would occur at the end of a day during which, for a few hours at least, they had been closely involved. Intercourse then expressed the feelings that had been accumulating all the while they were enjoying other aspects of their life together. Thus they were prepared to give each other pleasure and to find pleasure in each other's embrace; it was the culmination of all their prior emotional interaction.

But after years of marriage, sex becomes a postscript tacked on at the end of the day. Having had little opportunity to spend time together and little to say beyond discussing their separate obligations, they meet in bed and expect to turn on passion as though with an electric switch. It is hardly surprising, under these circumstances, that sex, which earlier in marriage was one of the strongest forces drawing them together, may later be experienced as an obligation that, at least to one of them, seems close to being an imposition. Instead of uniting them, sex separates them.

Such changes are not always attributable to the

fact that a husband and wife have devoted their energies to other goals that they consider more important than their intimate relationship. Frequently the deterioration of the sexual bond stems from the couple's lack of a secure sense of themselves as sexual beings. The insecurity may stem from negative sexual attitudes and early repressions, from unfortunate sexual experiences, or simply from a lack of sexual information. They remain insecure with their own sexuality.

In the beginning of their relationship, this inadequacy may go unremarked because the earliest sexual encounters generally—although certainly not always—prove stimulating enough to propel them into a sexual union. One naked body touching another is, after all, sufficient to generate a powerful drive that can carry both individuals past inhibitions that might otherwise deprive sex of any real satisfaction.

Even if this were not the case, however, some lack of satisfaction in their early encounters would be what any two inexperienced individuals might anticipate. If they do have problems, they would consider this only natural since either one, or both, may have had little chance to learn what sex is all about. They believe that time alone will overcome their difficulties and allowances are made for their lack of responsiveness. Of course, the concept that time together will increase low levels of sexual response frequently proves correct, particularly for committed couples.

There is no particular reason for a newly committed couple to doubt that in time, and with each of them fully supporting the other in a commitment that is secure enough to allow them to be vulnerable without fear, they will become fully functional sexual beings. They usually will become responsive *if* they have some concept of what it means to be a sexual person. It means more than just the acceptance of male or female identity.

Being a sexual person means being responsive to one's sexual feelings—that is, being conscious of spontaneous sexual impulses generated within the body, accepting them as natural, healthy, and "good," enjoying them without shame or guilt and permitting them to build up into the tensions that then require some sort of release. It means being responsible for the satisfaction of one's sexual feelings—that is, actively reaching out for ways to achieve that release, whether through masturbation, intercourse, or any mutually acceptable caress that couples exchange. And, finally, it means deriving pleasure not only from released tension and from sensual gratification but from the total experience as an affirmation of one's sexual nature. Only with security in these feelings about one's self, is it possible to pursue sexual pleasure as an active goal with one's partner, to be committed to sex as a couple.

One reason why couples become trapped in sexually distressed situations is that they are afraid. This is usually the basis for their lack of commitment to their own sexuality, to their right as human beings to sexual pleasure. For the chief obstacle to sexual pleasure is fear—fear in all its forms: the fear of being hurt, physically or emotionally; the fear of being wrong or making a mistake and being punished or ridiculed; the fear of being considered ugly, clumsy, foolish, incompetent, unresponsive, undesirable . . . an almost endless list that includes every negative thought that human beings have ever had about themselves.

In sex, fear frequently masquerades as acute embarrassment and its effects are so insidious that it can undermine any sense of security a man or woman may have. One recently married young woman, for example, had just finished showering and on impulse decided to walk out of the bathroom naked, feeling quite comfortable in her nakedness. She approached her husband with a smile, anticipating that he would respond with approval at the very least if not with admiration and even desire. He looked at her and he, too, smiled, but his smile was one of embarrassment. Then he reached out and flicked her nipple with his finger in what was intended to be a teasing gesture. It was, in fact, the only way he could think of at the moment to meet a situation for which he was totally unprepared and to which he did not know how to respond. He felt dismayed at the possibility that something was being requested of him that he was too inexperienced to deliver. His crude gesture was enough to humiliate his wife, to make her feel not only rejected but to seem foolish in her own eyes and it filled her with anger as well as mortification. It was a moment she never forgot and, in telling of it years later, long after her divorce, she still found the incident emotionally disturbing.

What her husband had done with his thoughtless and foolish gesture was—once again—to put commitment in reverse. Instead of reaching out, figuratively and literally, to draw his wife closer to him, he was pushing her away. His wife had approached him in total vulnerability, expecting that this would unite them, and he had taught her never to make that mistake again. She approached him in nakedness—but from then on she was always certain to be covered when his eyes were on her. It is concealment personified, one human being protecting herself from another; remaining separate—and separating herself—from the one person with whom she should have been able to reveal herself without fear, in total physical and emotional nakedness.

She could hardly be blamed for not wanting to be vulnerable again, for not wanting to be: "Susceptible to injury, unprotected from danger; unsufficiently defended." The hurt of feeling humiliated and rejected takes a long time healing.

Just as the willingness of a man and a woman to reveal themselves to each other and to become vulnerable brings them closer together, so their unwillingness to be vulnerable leads them *not* to reveal themselves and to become uncommitted. A natural sense of self-protection takes over. In learning not to be vulnerable with each other, a married couple is usually reenacting a scenario that was originally written during childhood years. When these individuals marry, they frequently find it all too easy to react to conflict by what might be described as a conditioned emotional reflex—the deadening of feelings. With their marriage partners, as they probably did with their parents, they hide behind defensive barriers. In time, their partners, too, become guarded, if not equally defensive. In such cases, the husband has not committed himself to his wife and she has not committed herself to him. Neither is willing to be emotionally vulnerable. They may depend on each other but they do not entrust themselves to each other. They are partners, not mates, in a mutual venture in which both are willing to invest time and effort and from which both hope to profit. Thus, for the sake of clarity, their marriage might more appropriately be described as an investment that they share—in truth, a relatively sterile form of mutual commitment.

In successful marriages of this kind, the husband and wife manage to accommodate each other in what amounts to a working partnership, an arrangement that allows them to get the major jobs done without too much emotional stress. Because their commitment is governed by reason and practical considerations rather than by emotion, their feelings are generally low-keyed. The bond between them may be primarily one of toleration, each respecting what the other contributes to their common enterprise rather than exploring and enjoying the nature of their personalities. Or they may even appreciate each other's individuality and share the kind of affection that reflects a sense of comfort with familiar things.

Either way, they relate to each other much as they do to the telephone company. They pay whatever price is required for service to continue—for the house to be cleaned, meals prepared, children cared for, bills paid, possessions purchased, entertainment provided and, when either partner chooses, for sexual relations. They attend to each other's need to the best of their ability but passion is something they must go to the movies to see.

To the extent that each fulfills his or her obligations, their marriage survives. Sexual pleasure, if it ever existed, does not survive for long. Sex becomes perfunctory at best; more often it is either dull, dormant or dead. In many such cases the husband and wife live essentially celibate lives—at least, within the marriage.

Viewed from the outside, such unions seem to fulfill the marriage commitment, and in a sense they do: they fulfill the commitment of obligation. The husband and wife remain faithful to each other but they do so because they are committed to their marriage—not to each other as sexual beings. Their fidelity is not the expression of their sexual commitment; it is the passive acceptance of a way of life which the husband and wife either do not want to change or do not know how to change.

There is a profound difference, however, between being unwilling to change and being unable to change —although not infrequently couples do not discover, until they have sought professional help, that one or the other partner does not want to change the nature of their sexual relationship. This can be illustrated by a comparison of two cases, which at the outset seemed to have much in common. In both cases the husbands were troubled by impotence. Both couples had been married almost thirty years and had children who were young adults. Coincidentally, all four individuals involved in these cases had had an orthodox religious upbringing—and while individual interpretation of this orthodoxy contributed to their sexual problems, it played no part in the outcome of their treatment. As is usually the case, the difference between success and failure in treatment was directly related to the level of interpersonal commitment.

Failure (in the classical sense) is perhaps the wrong word to use because one couple abruptly terminated treatment. It was the wife who refused to continue. Her decision was made the day after she and her husband, following instructions that they had been given by their therapists, had taken turns stroking each other's bodies, trying only to give and get the sensual satisfaction that comes from such caresses. They were not supposed to touch each other's genitals and intercourse had been prohibited. The major purpose of their physical exchange was to experience the kind of sensual gratification that even a child is familiar with.

The next day the wife reported that she had felt nothing at all when her husband touched her—but that was not why she insisted on terminating treatment. What bothered her unendurably was that when she touched her husband, his pleasure was evident and his physiological response was immediate and unmistakable. To him, to be freely touched by his wife was like a miracle and he could hardly contain his joy. This was precisely what the wife could not bear. It was only when she was confronted by her husband's happiness that she realized how unwilling she was to be the source of such satisfaction. From her point of view, he had treated her so wretchedly over the years that she had no reservoir of goodwill to draw from, no incentive to do anything more for him than she absolutely had to do—and no hope that there could be any reward in sex for her. It would not be an exaggeration to say that the only pleasure left for her in her marriage was to deprive her husband of his pleasure.

The other couple offered a striking contrast. Although almost thirty years had gone by, during which intercourse had taken place infrequently and generally unsatisfactorily, the husband and wife had remained affectionate and close. Their faith in one another apparently sustained them in a way that permitted them both to be more sad than angry over their sexual frustration. Most important, the wife never mocked or attacked her husband for his inadequacy in bed—she said that she always knew that he felt miserable enough about it without her saying a word.

In coming for help, this couple, with their high degree of mutual caring, exemplified the meaning of commitment. Thirty years of deprivation had not embittered them, nor had it extinguished for either partner a genuine desire to find sexual happiness together. Their decision to try therapy was a way of telling each other, without saying a word: "Sex matters to me and you matter to me—and I want everything to be as good for both of us as it can possibly be."

In treatment they followed their therapists' directions and almost immediately discovered the pleasure to be derived from the opportunity to touch each other in ways they had never before permitted themselves. The husband was one of myriad men who have grown up believing that there must be something wrong with them if they need any "help" from a woman in order to become physically aroused. Once released from the bondage of ignorance, he reacted to his wife's hands on his body much as an adolescent might have—and both he and his wife eagerly took turns pleasuring each other.

The ability of a man and woman to become sexually committed stands or falls primarily on their willingness to give and receive pleasure in all its forms. But this is not the willingness that reflects an application of will power, which says more of deliberation, discipline and obligation than of desire. It is the willingness that flows from wishing or wanting something, of caring for someone, when the mind serves only as a catalyst and the body asserts itself in ways that the mind may not have anticipated.

Giving and getting pleasure does not mean bartering favors. It involves a mutuality, a flow of excitement and gratification that shuttles back and forth between the partners who frequently find it impossible to draw a line between the pleasure they are receiving and the pleasure they are giving. It is the same as it is with a kiss—only if a man and woman are *not* caught up in the kiss will either one be aware of the physical separateness of their lips.

If a man and woman are committed to the enjoyment of their own sexual natures and to each other as sexual persons, intercourse allows them to express their emotions in whatever ways seem desirable and appropriate at the moment, revealing themselves not only to each other—but to themselves. By responding freely to the urgencies of their own bodies as well as to the urgings of their partner, their actions embody their feelings. Liberated from the domination of reason and discipline, they are able to communicate spontaneous wishes that need no justification.

This does not mean that every sexual embrace is a transcendent experience. On the contrary, precisely because both partners are under no pressure to perform or pretend, any sexual embrace can be as casual as a good-night kiss, if that is what both partners want or if it is what one of them needs and the other is pleased and privileged to provide. Moreover, in such a relaxed atmosphere, each has earned emotional credit in the other's bank. If, as it occasionally must, sex proves unsatisfactory or disappointing or even frustrating to either husband or wife, their security as a committed couple lies in knowing that there is always a tomorrow.

Total commitment, in which all sense of obligation is linked to mutual feelings of loving concern, sustains a couple sexually over the years. In the beginning, it frees them to explore the hidden dimensions of their sexual natures, playing with sex as pastime and passion, seeking the erotic pleasures that give life much of its meaning. Then, when carrying the inescapable burdens that come with a family and maturity, they can turn to each other for the physical comforting and emotional sustenance they need to withstand economic and social pressures that often threaten to drain life of all joy. Finally, in their later years, it is in the enduring satisfactions of their sexual and emotional bond that committed husbands and wives find reason enough to be glad that they still have another day together.

ABOUT THE AUTHORS

WILLIAM H. MASTERS, M.D., and VIRGINIA E. JOHNSON (MASTERS) have been dispelling ignorance and myth for more than twenty years with scientifically verified facts about the physiology and psychology of human sexual behavior. Their medical textbooks, *Human Sexual Response* and *Human Sexual Inadequacy*, though addressed to professionals, met with an overwhelming response from the general reading public, not only in the United States but all over the world. Codirectors of the Reproductive Biology Research Foundation in St. Louis, a public, non-profit organization, they pioneered a new kind of psycho-therapy when, in 1958, they began clinical treatment of sexually dysfunctional men and women. The foundation continues to treat infertility and sexual dysfunction as well as to train therapists and counselors.

ROBERT J. LEVIN has been associated with Masters and Johnson for five years, collaborating with them in pre-senting to the general public reliable information about human sexual nature. A member of the Board of Direc-tors of the Sex Information and Education Council of the United States, he also served on the editorial board of the *Journal of Marriage and the Family*. Mr. Levin, a specialist in sociology and psychology, wrote for many leading magazines before joining the staff of *Redbook* magazine, where he is currently the Articles Editor.

BOOKS AROUND THE WORLD

For your reading pleasure Bantam Books has the following international bestsellers available in your local English language bookstore:

AUGUST 1914 by Alexander Solzhenitsyn	T4931	$1.50
BURR by Gore Vidal	T4939	$1.50
THE EXORCIST by William Blatty	R4921	$1.45
THE FAN CLUB by Irving Wallace	X4945	$1.75
FUTURE SHOCK by Alvin Toffler	T4951	$1.50
THE GOLD OF THE GODS by Erich Von Daniken	T4941	$1.50
JAWS by Peter Benchley	R4942	$1.45
THE LOVE MACHINE by Jacqueline Susann	T5400	$1.50
THE NEW SPANISH-ENGLISH, ENGLISH-SPANISH DICTIONARY by Edwin Williams	S4932	$ .75
THE ODESSA FILE by Frederick Forsyth	Q4924	$1.25
THE OLD MAN AND THE SEA by Ernest Hemingway	S4935	$ .75
ONCE IS NOT ENOUGH by Jacqueline Susann	T4933	$1.50
THE PERSIAN BOY by Mary Renault	Q4930	$1.25
PORTRAIT OF A MARRIAGE by Nigel Nicolson	Q4938	$1.25
POSTERN OF FATE by Agatha Christie	Q4940	$1.25
SLEEPING BEAUTY by Ross Macdonald	Q4936	$1.25

If you are unable to obtain these Bantam Books, fill out the form below and mail it to us with a self-addressed envelope. We will return it to you with the name and address of the nearest place where you can buy, or obtain information about, Bantam Books.

The above books are not available in the British Commonwealth

---

BANTAM BOOKS, INC., INTERNATIONAL DIVISION
666 FIFTH AVENUE, NEW YORK, NEW YORK 10019

The name and address of the nearest place to buy, or obtain information about, Bantam Books is:

Name:_____

Address:_____

City:_____Country:_____

INT—4/75